ASTRONOMY AND EMPIRE IN THE ANCIENT ANDES

ASTRONOMY AND EMPIRE IN THE ANCIENT ANDES:

The Cultural Origins of Inca Sky Watching

Brian S. Bauer and
David S. P. Dearborn

University of Texas Press

Austin

Requests for permission to reproduce material from this work
should be sent to Permissions, University of Texas Press, Box
7819, Austin, TX 78713-7819.

The paper used in this publication meets the minimum require-
ments of American National Standard for Information
Sciences—Permanence of Paper for Printed Library Materials,
ANSI Z39.48-1984.

Library of Congress Cataloging-in-Publication Data

Bauer, Brian S.
    Astronomy and empire in the ancient
Andes : the cultural origins of Inca sky
watching / Brian S. Bauer and David S.P.
Dearborn. — 1st ed.
        p.   cm.
    Includes bibliographical references and
index.
    ISBN 0-292-70829-7 (cloth : alk. paper). —
ISBN 0-292-70837-8 (pbk : alk. paper)
    1. Inca astronomy.   2. Inca calendar.
I. Dearborn, David S. P. (David Simon Paul,
date. II. Title.
F3429.3.C14B38   1995
520'.98'09024—dc20   95-3565

The movements of the heavenly bodies are an admirable thing, well known and manifest to all peoples. There are no people, no matter how barbaric and primitive, that do not raise up their eyes, take note, and observe with some care and admiration the continuous and uniform course of the heavenly bodies.

(BERNABÉ COBO [1653])

Contents

Illustrations

Figures

Tables

.

# **Preface**

THIS BOOK IS A JOINT PROJECT of an astrophysicist, David Dearborn, and an archaeologist, Brian Bauer. It was written for the use of astronomers, archaeologists, and historians, as well as for other individuals interested in the Inca and ancient astronomy. Dearborn's interests in the Inca developed while conducting astronomical research at the Inca site of Machu Picchu in the early 1980s. Bauer's desire to understand astronomy emerged in 1990 as he examined the locations and organization of Inca shrines in the Cuzco Valley. We worked together in Cuzco in 1992, testing various theories of Inca astronomy against Bauer's field data.

The book is divided into seven chapters. The introduction provides background data necessary for understanding the importance of astronomy to the Inca Empire and includes a description of a complex series of shrines and imaginary lines that radiated out from the center of Cuzco, referred to as the "Cuzco ceque system." In addition to containing three sets of pillars used as solar markers, the Cuzco ceque system serves as the foundation for many of R. Tom Zuidema's often-cited interpretations of the Inca calendar. In this chapter, we also discuss the archaeological and astronomical fieldwork we conducted in the Cuzco region.

Chapter 2 provides a chronological compilation of the most important late-sixteenth- and early-seventeenth-century accounts of Inca solar astronomy along with some analysis of the astronomical content. While archaeological and astronomical contexts for these narratives are explored in later chapters, the accounts themselves are presented in this separate chapter to avoid confusing historic data with theoretical interpretations. The sources contain numerous references to horizon pillars used for tracking the motion of the sun. The descriptions are often incomplete and they all differ, but it seems likely that the sunsets on the June and December solstices, as well as on an August planting date, were observed by the Inca and marked with pillars. In addition to the information presented in this chapter, we also examine the practical aspects of making astronomical observations. Certain methods permit public participation, while others do not.

In the third chapter, we examine the Inca year and the people who marked it. There is evidence that the imperial Inca may have used two types of calendars. The first was a twelve-month period defined by lunar phases. The second, less well documented calendar may have involved a fixed solar year composed of twelve thirty-day months.

Efforts to localize the solar pillars of the Cuzco region are discussed in the fourth chapter. The various statements found in different colonial documents concerning these pillars are compared with recent field data. We set constraints and propose possible positions for the best-documented pillars.

Chapter 5 is devoted to the stellar observations of the Inca and is divided into two sections. The first presents a record of the historic accounts of Inca star watching. The second tests various hypotheses concerning the alignment of ceques and shrines with the rising and setting points of specific stars and star groups on the Cuzco horizon. The evidence offers insights into the pre-Inca origins of Andean astronomy.

While celestial cycles provide an orderly tableau that changes little over a human's lifetime, there are striking and dramatic apparitions in the sky that appear and then disappear. Extraordinary events require extraordinary reactions and explanations, and in Chapter 6, we review Inca responses to transient events like eclipses and comets. Finally, the results of this work are reviewed in Chapter 7.

Major funding for the project was provided by a number of generous grants. The archaeological fieldwork and analysis were supported by the National Endowment for the Humanities, The L. J. Skaggs and Mary C. Skaggs Foundation, The Guttman Foundation, The Institute for New World Archaeology, The National Science Foundation, and the University of Chicago Housing System. The astronomical work was largely supported by the Dudley Observatory and a Herbert C. Pollock/Dudley grant. The Instituto Nacional de Cultura in Lima and Cuzco granted permission for the project. We are grateful to all of these organizations.

Peter Bürgi, Terence N. D'Altroy, Mary Glowacki, Martina Munsters, Charles Stanish, as well as Alane Alchorn, Susana Deustua, Sybil Francis, Herald Graboske, Robert M. Sadowski, Thomas

Thomson and Marius S. Ziólkowski, read earlier drafts of this book. We gratefully acknowledge their criticisms and suggestions. Special thanks to Patricia Lyon for her careful editorial assistance as well as to Susan A. Niles and Jeffrey R. Parsons for their readings of the manuscript. Evan Franke, Roland Hamilton, and Martín Giesso helped us prepare the translations. Additional assistance was provided by Anthony Aveni, Steve McCluskey, John H. Rowe, Gary Urton, P. Wiktor Gramatowski, and Tom Zuidema, as well as by Fernando Astete Victoria, Luis Barreda Murillo, Manuel Chávez Ballón, José Gonzales Corrales, Wilbert San Román Luna, Wendy Weeks, and Alfredo Valencia Zegarra.

Field assistance was provided by Wilton Barrionuevo Orosco, Luis Guevara Carazas, Silvia Flores Delgado, and Xander Dearborn. We would like to extend our special thanks to Peter Frost, who let us live in his house during our 1992 stay in Cuzco and who first showed us the Inca pillars that stand above the town of Urubamba.

ASTRONOMY
AND EMPIRE
IN THE
ANCIENT
ANDES

1. The Inca and the Sky

Oh Sun Inca, our father . . . We beg that your children, the Inca . . .
may be conquerors always, for this you have created them.

—MOLINA (1989 [CA. 1575])

SO ENDED A PRAYER FOR THE INCA and their ruler. They were children of the sun, and he was the master of an empire that spanned their known world. All of the subject peoples of this empire were taught that through the ruling Inca's intercession, the synchronization of celestial motions with the seasons was maintained.

Half a millennium ago in the central highlands of Peru, the sun, moon, and stars were watched and interpreted by the Inca. The astronomical observations made in and near the former Inca capital, Cuzco, formed the nuclei of the most important public rituals of the empire. As the regulator of time, the ruling Inca scheduled the rituals that bound this society together. Orchestration of these rituals centralized power and authority in the hands of the ruling elite. It also conferred legitimation to the state and its rulers as they became associated with the passage of time itself.

The integration of astronomical knowledge into the Inca system of governance raises questions pertinent to the foundation of imperial social systems: Is there a connection between the development of the state and the rise of complex astronomical systems? Why should astronomy, of all human endeavors, serve as a focus for organizing social activity? What institutions are supported by astronomical knowledge, and how do they promote the development of astronomy? We explore these questions in the context of the Inca society and the astronomical practices conducted in their capital.

To approach these questions, we have two independent sets of primary data for investigation. The first set is composed of historical accounts dating to the late sixteenth and early seventeenth centuries. These accounts were not written by the Inca themselves, as no South American culture developed a system of writing. Instead, they are the outgrowth of the European conquest and colonization.

Some of the documents were written by Spaniards like Cristóbal de Molina, a parish priest and Quechua scholar, who recorded the prayer quoted at the beginning of this chapter. Others were produced by indigenous people trained by the Spanish. Some accounts were written only a few years after the Spaniards arrived on the shores of the Inca Empire, while others were composed more than a hundred years later. None of these documents were intended to be texts of Inca astronomical knowledge; rather, they are conquest and early-colonial-period attempts to record the history, organization, language, and religion of the Inca Empire. Elements of Inca astronomy were preserved in these records, because they were of central importance to Inca society.

The second set of primary data used in this investigation consists of archaeological research results from the Cuzco region. Archaeological survey and excavation findings from the Inca heartland are incorporated in the study to enhance our understanding of ancient Andean sky watching beyond the limited Spanish accounts. Unlike some studies of ancient astronomy, astronomical measurements were not simply taken within and between monuments in hopes of finding unspecified astronomical alignments. Such haphazard work rarely provides supportable insights into the social organization of ancient cultures and their astronomical knowledge. Instead, the information provided in the historical accounts of the Inca was used to develop specific hypotheses that were then investigated in the field. Models of Inca astronomy developed in earlier studies were also tested with archaeological evidence from the Cuzco region. This combination of systematic fieldwork with historic documentation provides perspective on the role that Inca astronomy played in state organization.

The Empire of the Inca: An Overview

The Inca Empire, Tahuantinsuyu, was one of the greatest states to develop in the Americas. Last in a series of complex Andean societies, it emerged from the Cuzco region, expanded across the western highlands and coast of South America, and ultimately encompassed a territory that stretched from modern-day Colombia to Chile (Map 1). By the time of European contact in 1532, the ruling Inca led a population of at least six million. As a result of regional and ethnic conflict, conquest by the Spaniards, and the spread of deadly European diseases, the empire collapsed even more quickly than it began. By 1572, thousands of Spaniards occupied the

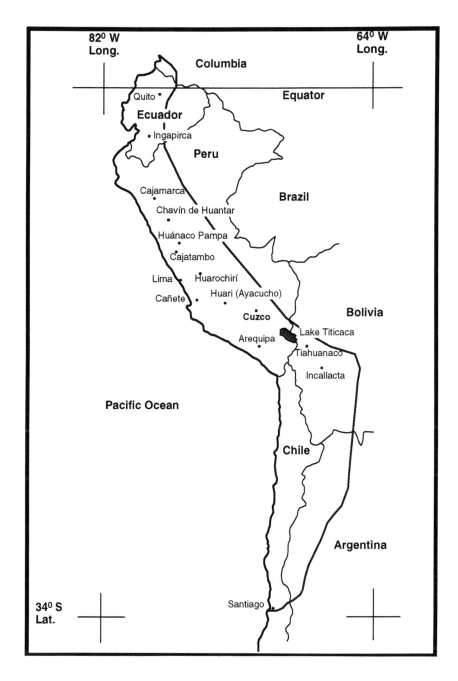

Map 1. The Empire of the Inca, 1531 (after Hyslop 1990).

important cities of the former empire, and the last direct heir to the
Inca crown, Topa Amaru, had been executed. In 1653, the date of
the latest document used in this study, the Spaniards had been in
Peru for more than four generations, and Andean culture had been
forever altered. As the history and social organization of Tahuantinsuyu may be new to many readers, we offer introductory material on the cosmology of the Inca, the important features of their capital, and the dynastic order of Cuzco.[1]

The Cosmology of the Inca

Inca cosmology developed from a broader Andean system that associates powerful "animas" with individual mountains, caves, springs,
rivers, and rocks. These sacred objects and locations are known in
Quechua, the language of the Inca, as *huacas*.[2] The Inca worshiped
many such huacas. Their cosmology, however, placed paramount
importance on the sun and the moon. Conquered peoples were not
required to abandon their own huacas, but they were compelled to
acknowledge the superiority of the sun and its Inca descendants.

The Inca were not the first Andean people to watch the sky and
certainly not the first to worship the sun. Historic accounts provide
evidence of an agrarian basis for Andean astronomical interests that
predates the Inca. How far into the past interest in the sun, the
state, and astronomy extends is, however, speculative. Huari and
Tiahuanaco were two of the earliest states to develop in the Andes.
These polities controlled the central and south central Andean
highlands respectively. The Huari state expanded from the Ayacucho region of Peru between A.D. 550 and 900. Less is known concerning the development of the Tiahuanaco polity, which was centered in the Lake Titicaca region of Bolivia. It seems, however, that
the Tiahuanaco expansion began around A.D. 450 and that it waned,
like Huari, near the end of the millennium.

Cuzco lies between the highland centers of Huari and Tiahuanaco. The region was occupied by the Huari from around A.D. 600 to
the collapse of the empire. The fall of Huari and the concomitant
abandonment of its administrative center in the Cuzco Valley, perhaps as late as A.D. 900 or 1000, marked the beginning of autochtho-
nous state development in the Cuzco region (McEwan 1987:80;
1991). By about A.D. 1400 the Inca had united the Cuzco region under their rule, and the city of Cuzco had emerged as their capital. It
is currently unclear which elements of Huari or Tiahuanaco statecraft were adopted by the Inca in the development of their own ex-

pansionistic state, but it seems likely that the association of the ruling elite with the sun was one such element. Attempts have been made to understand the calendrical systems of Huari (Zuidema 1977a; Anders 1986a, 1986b) and Tiahuanaco (Posnansky 1942; Anders 1986a), based substantially on models developed for the Inca. Extrapolations between Inca astronomy and those of earlier states can be no firmer than the information on which they are based. Accordingly, it is our hope that this reevaluation of Inca astronomy will also aid in understanding the astronomical, ritual, and social organization of these and other early Andean states.

Origin of the Sun and the Moon

Despite a long period of Huari presence in the Cuzco region, Inca mythology suggests that the Inca associated themselves more closely with Tiahuanaco than with Huari. The ruined city of Tiahuanaco is mentioned specifically as a location of primeval importance in Inca myths. Furthermore, numerous chroniclers indicate that the Inca and other peoples of the Andes believed that the sun and the moon emerged from two islands in Lake Titicaca (see Bandelier 1910 and Urbano 1981). The sun is said to have risen from an outcrop on the island of Titicaca (today called the Island of the Sun), while the moon rose from the nearby island of Coati (now called the Island of the Moon). Elaborate offerings were left on the islands in pre-Inca times. The Inca built large temples on them after they conquered the Titicaca region. Several chroniclers also speak of the first Inca and his sister/wife as emerging from Lake Titicaca, emphasizing the link between these rulers and the sun. To understand why this great lake became associated with the beginnings of the Andean cosmos and with one of the Inca origin myths, we must examine how Andean peoples traditionally viewed their own origins.

Many Andean kin groups, or *ayllus*, traced their lineage back to mythical ancestors who emerged from a sacred place on the landscape. The location from which ancestral kin were believed to have emerged were a special class of huacas called *paqarina*. While paqarinas could take various forms, they were most commonly caves, lakes, and springs. Members of an ayllu would visit their mythical origin place on special occasions to make sacrifices for the continuation of their lineage. The largest and most powerful kin groups built elaborate temples at their origin place, such as the one built by the Inca near the cave from which Manco Capac, the first mythical Inca, was said to have emerged (Urton 1990; Bauer 1991, 1992b).

The concept of "paqarina," the primordial emergence of mythical ancestral kin from unique locations on the Andean landscape, is embedded within the Inca understanding of the origin of the cosmos. Lake Titicaca is the largest lake in South America, providing a paqarina of suitable importance for the origin point of the cosmos. The recovery of pre-Inca and Inca sacrificial materials on both the Island of the Sun and the Island of the Moon suggests that offerings were made there to the sun and the moon for millennia.

By the time the Inca expanded their empire into the Lake Titicaca region, the royal Inca and his queen were believed by many to be the human descendants of the sun and the moon. Accordingly, the origin myths regarding the sacred islands of Lake Titicaca may have begun to change. It is possible that during this later period, rather than simply explaining the origin of the cosmos, the Lake Titicaca myth was transformed, with the Inca (analogous to the sun) and his sister/wife (analogous to the moon) emerging from these sacred islands. This association was used to compel a recognition of the Cuzco elites' right to rule.

Inca Cuzco

Cuzco was the empire's sacred center (Map 2), the royal seat of the dynastic order that ruled Tahuantinsuyu, and the site of the most important temples of the realm. It lies at an altitude of 3,300 meters above sea level, near the northwest end of a long valley. While the northern, southern, and western horizons are less than three kilometers from the city center, the southeastern horizon is much farther away. In this direction one can see well beyond the east end of the valley (about fifteen kilometers from the city) to the mountain of Ocongate some fifty kilometers away. As will be discussed in later chapters, the nearness of the western horizon to the city center and the remoteness of the eastern horizon have practical implications for astronomical observations made in Cuzco.

Of primary importance for the maintenance of the cosmos was the Coricancha, which the Spaniards called the "Templo del Sol" (Temple of the Sun). This was a complex of temples dedicated to various deities: the Sun, the Moon, the Stars, the Thunder, the Rainbow, and the Creator god Viracocha. It was located on a natural rise near the confluence of two small rivers in the heart of Cuzco. The central icon of the Coricancha was a highly venerated gold image of the sun called Punchao (sunlight), which by the end of the empire had become almost synonymous with Inca rule.

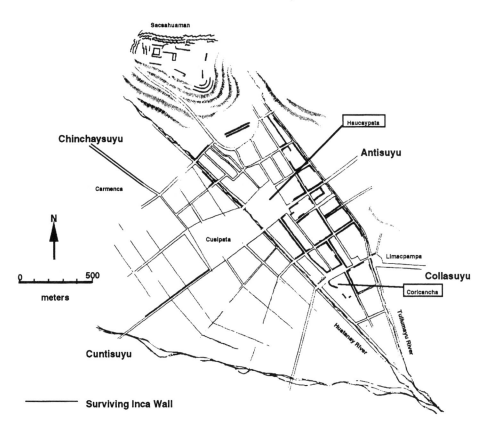

Map 2. Inca Cuzco. The imperial capital of Cuzco grew between the Rivers Huatanay and Tullumayu. Many historical accounts describe ceremonies and festivals held in its environs. Among the most important locations were the Coricancha, Haucaypata, Limacpampa, and Sacsahuaman.

Because the Coricancha contained the finest gold and silver works of the empire, it was sacked by the Spaniards even before they established a secure rule over the Andes. After the conquest, the church and monastery of Santo Domingo were built on the site. Nevertheless, many of the former structures, and the superb Inca stonework of the temple complex, can still be seen (Photos 1 and 2). Because the Coricancha was the central shrine of the solar cult, scholars have long speculated that solar observations were made from there.

The central plaza of Cuzco, called Haucaypata by the Inca, was

Photo 1. Exterior of the Coricancha. After the conquest, the church and monastery of Santo Domingo were built on the site of the Coricancha.

the second most important ceremonial area in the city (Photo 3). Hundreds, if not thousands, of people gathered in this plaza during major rituals. The mummies of the dead Inca rulers were set in the plaza on ceremonial occasions and ritual battles took place there between the young men of the city. Near the center of the plaza stood a large stone called the *usnu*. Early documents indicate that this usnu served as a dais from which the ruling Inca watched elaborate rituals in the plaza and observed the sunset on specific days of the year.

Another important feature of Inca Cuzco was the monumental structure of Sacsahuaman (Photo 4). Situated on a hill immediately north of the city, Sacsahuaman provides a clear view of the entire valley. World famous for the massive stones that form parts of its walls, Sacsahuaman is frequently referred to as a "fortress." Some early accounts of Cuzco (Cieza de León 1976:154 [1554: Pt. 2, Ch. 51]) indicate that Sacsahuaman included a sun temple, which suggests that it was the focus of ritual activities. The flat open area at its base, capable of holding thousands of people, is well designed

Photo 2. The interior buildings of the Coricancha. The interior of the Coricancha was the site for a series of buildings dedicated to different gods.

Photo 3. The central plaza of Cuzco. Major rituals were held by the Inca in this central plaza, which they called Haucaypata. The boundaries of today's plaza are much reduced from those of Inca times.

Photo 4. Sacsahuaman stands on a hill just outside the city of Cuzco. It includes a large plaza area, zigzagging walls, and a set of fine Inca buildings at its summit. (Photograph courtesy of Servicio Aerofotográfico Nacional: Peru)

for ceremonial practices, and several large structures on Sacsahuaman's summit may also have been used during rituals.

A number of other important ceremonial locations existed in or near Cuzco. On the edge of the ancient city, just east of the Coricancha, was Limacpampa. This plaza contained its own usnu and was the focus of several rituals, including those dedicated to the harvesting of maize and those conducted during Capac Raymi, the month associated with the December solstice. Although certainly reduced in size, the plaza of Limacpampa still exists in the urban core of the modern city (Photo 5). There was also a sun temple on a hill named Puquín just outside the city on the southwestern slope of the Cuzco Valley. The Inca spent part of Capac Raymi at this temple. On the other side of the valley was a hill called Mantocalla, where the Inca stayed in another sun temple during part of Inti Raymi, the month associated with the June solstice.

Cuzco and its environs were also endowed with a host of smaller sacred locations. In the words of one early writer, "Cuzco was house and dwelling place of gods, and thus there was not a fountain or a wall in it that they did not say contained a mystery" (Polo de Onde-gardo 1916c:55 [1571]). There were three hundred to four hundred huacas surrounding the city. Many of these sacred places were orga-nized into forty-one or forty-two lines that originated at the Cori-cancha. This complex of shrines, now known as the "Cuzco ceque system," has been the subject of recent investigations and is be-lieved by some to be intimately related to Inca astronomy.

Dynastic Order of the Inca

At the time of the European invasion, the royal Incas traced their ancestry back eleven generations from the last undisputed ruler of the empire, Huayna Capac, to the mythical founder of Cuzco, Manco Capac (Table 1). Since much of Inca astronomy is related to

Photo 5. The Plaza of Limacpampa was the focus of the maize planting and harvesting rituals.

Table 1. *The Traditional List of Inca Succession*

Manco Capac	
Sinchi Roca	
Lloque Yupanqui	
Mayta Capac	
Capac Yupanqui	
Inca Roca	
Yahuar Huacac	
Virachocha Inca	
Pachacuti Inca Yupanqui	
Topa Inca Yupanqui	
Huayna Capac	
Huascar	A.D. 1532
Atahualpa	
Manco	
Sayri Topa	
Titu Cusi Yupanqui	
Topa Amaru	A.D. 1572

the imperial works of these leaders, we outline the lineage of the last generations of Inca kingship. Traditionally, the Inca are thought to have expanded their state beyond the limits of the Cuzco region under Pachacuti Inca Yupanqui, the ninth ruling Inca. A warrior king of legendary proportions, Pachacuti Inca Yupanqui is frequently credited with reorganizing the economic, social, and calendric systems of the empire. According to oral tradition recorded by colonial writers, Pachacuti Inca Yupanqui's eldest son, Amaru Topa, was passed over as heir to the throne and the rule was given to a younger son, Topa Inca Yupanqui. Decades later, Huayna Capac, the eldest son of Topa Inca Yupanqui, inherited the rule from his father and continued expanding the empire until his sudden death in an epidemic that swept the empire in the 1520s, shortly before European contact. Following the death of Huayna Capac, the rule of Tahuantinsuyu was disputed between two half brothers, Atahualpa and Huascar. The Spanish forces of Francisco Pizarro arrived in Peru in 1532 just as Atahualpa defeated Huascar. Pizarro captured Atahualpa in the highland city of Cajamarca, and after holding the ruling Inca hostage for most of a year, executed him.

For some forty years after the execution of Atahualpa, the Spaniards established and supported a series of puppet Inca kings in Cuzco. During this period, the Spaniards fought a protracted war against Manco (a half brother of Atahualpa) and his descendants, who attempted to maintain an independent Inca state with a capital at Vilcabamba. The end of indigenous rule came in 1572 with the capture and execution by the Spaniards of Topa Amaru, the last surviving son of Manco Inca.

At the hour of his execution, Topa Amaru professed his conversion to Christianity and renounced the worship of the sun (and other huacas). Although the speech was made under duress, it reveals the intimate relationship believed to exist between the ruling Incas and the solar deity. Topa Amaru proclaimed:

> Everything that so far I and the Incas my ancestors have told you, that you should adore the Sun, Punchao, and the huacas, idols, rocks, rivers, mountains, and vilcas [sacred objects], is false and a lie. And when we said that we were going to go in to speak to the Sun, and that he commanded that you should do as we ordered you to do, and that he spoke to us, it was a lie. For it was not the Sun but we who spoke, for the Sun is a lump of gold and cannot speak. My brother Titu Cusi informed me that when I planned to say anything to the Indians, I should arrange to enter alone before the idol Punchao, and no one should come with me; and that the idol Punchao would not speak with me, because it is a lump of gold; and that afterwards I should come forth and tell the Indians that Punchao had spoken to me and had said what I wanted to tell them, because in this way the Indians would comply better with what I was ordering them to do. And that what should be revered was what was inside the Sun Punchao, which is the hearts of my ancestors the Incas.
> (Salazar 1867:280 [1596]; translation by S. MacCormack 1991:249–250)[3]

The denial of Andean religion and the "conversion" to Christianity of Topa Amaru at the time of execution is understandable. Atahualpa had made a similar conversion four decades earlier and was thus spared execution by burning.[4] What is, however, of central importance to this study is the statement that during their rule, the kings of Tahuantinsuyu frequently consulted with the major icon of the Coricancha, an image of the sun called Punchao, and that these consultations sanctioned their rights to power and authority. The close relationship between the ruling Inca and the sun was made undeniable by the fact that the Punchao contained a dough in its center made from the dried hearts of previous Inca kings (Toledo 1924:344–345 [1572]).

The Cuzco Ceque System

Since our research on Inca astronomy uses the Cuzco ceque system as a primary information source, it is important to detail the physical form of this system and to explain its intrinsic connection with Inca astronomy.

The Inca divided the Cuzco Valley (and by extension their empire) into four regions, or *suyus*. The city of Cuzco was at the junction of these four parts and was for the Inca the center of the Andean cosmological order. The physical partitioning of the city and the surrounding valley was reflective of a societal division into moieties (or halves). The upper half of Cuzco, Hanansaya, was occupied by two quarters. The northwest quarter was referred to as Chinchaysuyu and the northeast was named Antisuyu. The lower half of Cuzco, Hurinsaya, also contained two quarters, with Collasuyu lying to the southeast and Cuntisuyu to the southwest (Map 3). From these four quarters the empire was given the name Tahuantinsuyu, or "the four parts."

The suyu divisions of Cuzco may be found in most of the chronicles. Bernabé Cobo's 1653 work also describes a related, but vastly more complex, partitioning system of the Cuzco Valley by the Inca (Cobo 1980 [1653: Bk. 13, Chs. 13–16]). The Cuzco region was, according to Cobo, further partitioned by forty-one or forty-two *ceques* (lines) that radiated from the Coricancha in the center of the city. The orientations of these lines were determined by the locations of at least 328 shrines that surrounded Cuzco. In the introduction to his ceque system description Cobo writes:

> From the Temple of the Sun as from the center there went out certain lines which the Indians call ceques: they formed four parts corresponding to the four royal roads which went out from Cuzco. On each one of those ceques were arranged in order the guacas and shrines which there were in Cuzco and its district, like stations of holy places, the veneration of which was common to all. (Cobo 1980:15 [1653: Bk. 13, Ch. 13])[5]

Cobo described the ceques contained in each of the four suyus, as well as 328 individual shrines, or huacas, that formed the ceques. His account indicates that the first three suyus, Chinchaysuyu, Antisuyu, and Collasuyu, contained nine ceques each, while the last, Cuntisuyu, contained fourteen or fifteen. The number of shrines in an individual ceque varied from three to fifteen.

We used a modified version of Rowe's (1980) numbering method

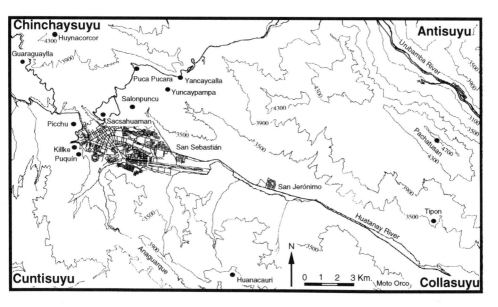

Map 3. The Cuzco Valley and the surrounding area were divided into four regions, or *suyus*.

of the ceques and huacas to describe their locations in the ceque system.[6] In this method, the ceques and huacas are identified according to the number that Cobo gives them in his description of the ceque system. For example, Co. 1:1 signifies the first shrine of the first ceque of Collasuyu, while Co. 9:13 designates the thirteenth shrine of the ninth ceque of Collasuyu.

The Huacas

The huacas of the Cuzco region included natural features of the landscape, such as caves, boulders, springs, mountain tops, and artificial features, like houses, fountains, and canals. Besides giving the name of each shrine and a short description of its physical form, Cobo provides fragments of oral traditions concerning the origins of the huacas, and information on what offerings were made at them. Many of the shrines gained status as holy places through their association with events in Inca mythic history. Other shrines marked land boundaries between social groups or were related to the local irrigation systems (Sherbondy 1982, 1986; Zuidema 1986b). Certain huacas marked symbolically important locations, such as mountain passes or summits where the city was lost from sight. Especially significant to this study of Inca astronomy are sets of twin pillars located on the hills of Quiancalla, Picchu, and Chinchincalla, which marked specific sunsets. Several other early writers mention these pillars and their importance to the Inca calendar.

The Cuzco Ceque System and Inca Astronomy

The first major study of the ceque system, and its relation to the social and political organization of Cuzco, was published by anthropologist R. Tom Zuidema in 1964, and the first map of the system appeared in his introductory investigation of the Inca calendar (Zuidema 1977a). Working with him on many aspects of this research has been Anthony F. Aveni, a specialist in native American astronomy who has provided important insights into Inca sky watching. Zuidema (1977a, 1977b, 1981a–c, 1982a–c, 1983a–b, 1988a, 1988b, 1990) and Aveni (1981, 1987) have developed a complex argument suggesting that a central function of the Cuzco ceque system was as a counting device for the Inca calendar. They propose that the ceque system had astronomical functions beyond those specifically mentioned in Cobo's chronicle. In Zuidema's (1977a:220) elaborate hypothesis, each shrine of the ceque system represents one day of the year. He also argues that some of the ceques were aligned for observing astronomical events on the horizon. Zuidema (1981b, 1982b, 1983b) has proposed that, besides containing markers for the December and June solstices, various ceques, huacas, and parts of the Temple of the Sun were used to sight the rise or set of the Pleiades, the Southern Cross, Alpha and Beta Centauri, as well as the solar zenith. The basic evidence for this detailed hypothesis has been questioned (Dearborn 1987; Dearborn and Schreiber 1986, 1989).

For his work with the ceque system and Andean astronomy, Zuidema (1981b) has also developed the concept of an "antizenith passage" of the sun. As this term is not used by other scholars of ancient astronomy, it needs some explanation. In the tropics, the sun passes through the zenith (i.e., directly overhead) on a pair of days. The term "antizenith passage" is used by Zuidema to refer to a solar observation that is in "opposition" to the zenith passage. Since the passage of the sun through the nadir (i.e., directly below your feet) is not visible, Zuidema dubs the dates—when the sun sets 180 degrees from the position that it rises on a zenith passage day—the "antizenith passage dates." He suggests that several ceques of the Cuzco system, and at least one pillar on the Cuzco horizon, were aligned with the passage of the sun on the "antizenith passage date."

The archaeological and astronomical research that we conducted in the Cuzco region contributes directly to an understanding of the ceque system and its relation to Inca astronomy. The identification of huaca locations, and the determination of ceque projections across the landscape, test current models of Inca calendrics. Our studies challenge earlier models in which ceques were thought to be physically aligned to the rises and sets of stars or to the sun on dates when it passes through the zenith/antizenith. The results of our tests are presented in the appropriate chapters of this book.

Research on Inca Astronomy

One of the earliest postcolonial attempts to study Inca astronomy was made by William Bollaert (1860, 1861, 1865). Building on observations made by Sir Clements Markham (1856), Bollaert believed that he had found symbols for the twelve lunar months of the Inca calendar on a small gold disk found in Cuzco.[7] As noted by Gary Urton (1981a: 5–6), other late-nineteenth- and early-twentieth-century scholars also made attempts to reconstruct the Inca constellations within the confines of classic Greek and Roman constellation systems (DuGourcq 1893; Hagar 1902, 1904, 1905; Callegari 1914). More sophisticated approaches to understanding Inca astronomy were made by Horacio H. Urteaga (1913), who reviewed various accounts concerning Inca solar markers, and by Rolf Müller (1972), who surveyed the city of Cuzco in the 1920s for possible astronomical alignments. During this period Erland Nordenskiöld (1925) examined a series of Inca *quipus* (knotted strings on which the Inca recorded information) for possible calendrical information, and Robert Lehmann-Nitsche (1928) conducted an extensive study of historic references to the Coricancha.

Authors of the mid-twentieth century concentrated on reviewing the classic chronicles from Peru for information on Inca astronomy. John H. Rowe (1946) and Luis E. Valcárcel Vizquerra (1946) provide two of the earliest, yet most complete, syntheses. The 1970s and 1980s witnessed a worldwide increase in studies concerning the astronomy of ancient peoples. Zuidema (1977a, 1977b, 1981a–c, 1982a–c, 1983b, 1988a, 1988b) and Aveni (1981, 1987), who have proffered a number of original theories and a complex model of Inca astronomy, have been on the forefront of research on Inca astronomy. Theories proposed by Zuidema and Aveni have been used to interpret Inca sites outside the Cuzco region, such as Incahuasi (Hyslop 1985; 1990:232–234) in the Cañete Valley and Ingapirca in Ecuador (Ziólkowski and Sadowski 1985), as well as pre-Inca sites like the Huari center of Azángaro in the region of Ayacucho (Anders 1986a, 1986b). They have also influenced surveys of archaeoastronomical alignments on the coast (Urton 1982). Other astronomical work has been conducted at Machu Picchu in the Urubamba River Valley near Cuzco (Dearborn and White 1983; Dearborn and Schreiber 1986, 1989; Dearborn, Schreiber, and White 1987), on the shores of Lake Titicaca (Trimborn 1959; Rivera Sundt 1984), at Incallacta in Bolivia (Hyslop 1990:226–228), and in Cuzco itself (Williams León 1992:101–113).

Other prominent researchers of the ancient Andean sky have been Robert M. Sadowski and Marius S. Ziólkowski. Individual studies by these researchers (Sadowski 1989a, 1989b; Ziólkowski 1985, 1989a, 1989b) and their co-authored studies (Ziólkowski and Sadowski 1980, 1985) have explored a wide range of issues including comets, the Inca calendar, and the astronomical alignment at Inca sites. They have also edited a volume on time and calendars in the Inca Empire, and written a book on the archaeoastronomy of the Andes (Ziólkowski and Sadowski 1989, 1992)

A watershed in the study of the astronomy of Andean peoples was Urton's ethnographic work in contemporary Andean villages in the Cuzco region. He explored various issues concerning modern Andean cosmology in a monograph and a series of articles (Urton 1980, 1981a, 1981b, 1982). While we use data and theories presented in Urton's studies (especially in our discussions of Inca star watching), we have refrained from including a large amount of modern ethnographic information on Andean astronomy. Instead, we describe Inca astronomy as preserved in the early documents from Peru, and we compare that information with recent archaeological findings from Cuzco.

Archaeological Research Methods

Historic accounts describe Inca astronomical observations made to and from various huacas of the Cuzco ceque system. Understanding these accounts required an archaeological survey of the Cuzco region to locate as many of the shrines of the ceque system as possible. The archaeological sites that were thought to be shrines were then tested for their utility as astronomical observing stations.

Bauer's archaeological research began by gathering historic data (from archives in Cuzco and Lima, as well as from chronicles) on the locations of former Inca shrines. Survey crews composed of students from the Universidad Nacional San Antonio Abad del Cuzco then conducted fieldwork in areas of the Cuzco Valley believed to have contained particular huacas. Members of the crews also interviewed local inhabitants in Quechua to locate shrines that had retained their original names. A toponym was considered to be confirmed when three independent informants provided similar answers. The identification of a huaca was accepted when the description provided by Cobo matched the physical features of a specific object (e.g., a cave, spring, or outcrop) that had also retained a shrine name. These well-identified huacas provided a firm physical framework of the ceque system, and, working systematically from these points, teams surveyed the surrounding area to identify other possible shrines that had not retained their toponyms. The shrines and shrine candidates thus located were photographed and plotted on a map.

The huaca identifications were assigned in this fashion with varying degrees of confidence. Unique sites that maintain their toponyms, and fit available descriptions, can be identified with little ambiguity. In other cases, the exact location of a shrine could not be determined, yet the general area was identified. In still other cases, a number of possible candidates for the same shrine were found. In such instances the full range of options is presented.

Astronomical Research Methods

Like the archaeology research, the astronomical inquiries were guided by references to solar and stellar observations contained in historical accounts as well as by archaeological fieldwork conducted in the Cuzco region. Understanding the colonial references to Inca astronomy requires a working knowledge of the appearance of the sky as well as some perspective on the astronomical beliefs common in sixteenth-century Europe. This perspective may be glimpsed through the numerous books, pamphlets, and reports in circulation that provided calendrical, astronomical, and astrological information to sixteenth-century priests and explorers. Following the model developed by Claudius Ptolemy a millennium earlier, Europeans of this period generally thought that the earth was at the center of the universe. An almanac by the Spanish cosmographer Rodrigo Zamorano (1585:1–14) pictured and described the earth surrounded by spheres carrying the sun, moon, planets, and stars. Prepared at the direction of the president of the Royal Council of the Indies, this document included information on several calendar

systems and, of particular importance, proscribed ways to determine the dates of movable feasts in the newly adopted Gregorian
calendar (Zamorano 1585:149). In addition, it contained a list of the
solar and lunar eclipses that would occur between 1584 and 1606
(Zamorano 1585:225), along with the locations of Cuzco, Quito,
Nasca, Guamanga (Ayacucho), and a dozen other towns in the area
that had been Tahuantinsuyu. Using this information, Spanish
priests could predict the times at which their congregations would
see eclipses begin. The almanac also contained astrological interpretations of various signs, and used a vocabulary that included the
words *astrologers, houses,* and *seats.*

Of particular importance to the task of identifying Inca constellations is information on European designations for stellar groups.
While Zamorano (1585:14–21) used classical constellation designations common to astronomers across Europe, few of the accounts of
Inca activities were authored by men trained in astronomy. Most
chroniclers use the folk names, calling the Pleiades (a group of stars
in Taurus) Las Cabrillas (the Little Goats), and referring to the Tres
Marías (Three Marys) for Orion's belt instead of to Orion itself.
Crosses also seem to have been a popular motif in Christian Europe,
as Cygnus was commonly called the Cross, and Delphinus referred
to as the Lesser Cross.

One chronicler, Bernabé Cobo (1956:27–31 [1653: Bk. 1, Ch. 8]),
provides a description of the southern sky in which he relates the
positions of particular stars to the constellations of the zodiac. For
example, he locates the (Southern) Cross and the Guards of the
Cross (Alpha and Beta Centauri) in the sign of Scorpio. The stars of
Triangulum Australe are placed in the sign of Sagittarius and are described as forming another figure of a cross when combined with
the brightest of the Guardians (Alpha Centauri).

With guidance from historical references, we began collecting and
examining archaeological evidence for Inca astronomical activities.
During the summer of 1992, Dearborn and Bauer spent several
weeks in Cuzco testing various hypotheses concerning Inca astronomical activities and the calendrical functions of the Cuzco ceque
system. Astronomical data were collected in the following manner.
Upon selecting a site, its latitude was determined on an accurate
map of the Cuzco area. A solar sight was performed to determine
the direction of true north. Measurements of altitude and azimuth
were then taken with an optical theodolite, and calculations were
made on a portable computer.[8]

We located the solstice and equinox positions from each test site
and measured the azimuths of prominent horizon features and other

sites. These measurements were then used to calibrate photographs taken from the sites, which were subsequently employed to test the consistency of measurements and, if necessary, to provide a means for extracting additional azimuths and altitudes without returning to the sites.

The positions at which celestial objects rise and set change slowly with time. Since the days of the Inca, changes in the "obliquity of the ecliptic" have shifted the position at which the sun rises and sets on the solstices by nearly 0.1 degrees. Precession changes the orientation of the earth's rotational axis, and has moved the positions at which some stars rise and set by several degrees. Furthermore, in 1584 the Spaniards in Peru shifted from the Gregorian to the Julian calendar. The effects of these shifts are easily calculated and are included in our analysis.

Summary of Goals

The rapid expansion of the Inca Empire, from a small polity in the Cuzco region to an empire running the length of the Andes, created tremendous pressure on Inca social and political institutions. The empire's growth required an increasingly complex, hierarchical structure and the organization of an extensive ruling elite. This book provides a summary of Inca astronomy and how it developed during state expansion. Specifically, it focuses on how Inca elites asserted their right to rule through control of ritual and by their dominant position within the state cosmology.

Tom Dillehay (1990) has recently discussed the important role that public ceremonies held in the growth and confirmation of dynastic chiefdoms among the Mapuche of central Chile. He suggests that elite kin groups extended their influence over other groups beyond their immediate territory by controlling time and the scheduling of public events: "By scheduling and regulating . . . ceremonies the chiefs of one lineage controlled both local and regional opportunities for alliance-making, ancestral worship, trade, and exchange, and appealed to the deities for productive harvests. Such control placed his lineage at a competitive advantage, for it was in a better position to negotiate more potentially productive and secure trade and marriage alliances with desirable non-local groups" (Dillehay 1990:237). Similar processes of centralization occurred among other complex societies, including the Inca, and we present evidence that astronomy played a critical role in the definition and demonstration of state powers.

As Cuzco grew to be the capital of an empire, local astronomical practices developed with it. The sun became the preeminent source of power and the primary deity worshipped by the Inca and those they subjugated. Cobo (1979:134 [1653: Bk. 12, Ch. 12]) tells us that Pachacuti Inca Yupanqui "ordered that solemn temples dedicated to the sun be built throughout all of the lands that he subjugated under his empire, and he endowed them with great incomes, ordering that all his subjects worship and revere the Sun." The development and spread of this solar cult by the Inca state complemented and extended local belief systems of celestial objects as deities. In particular, the recognition of the importance of the sun for agriculture, as well as its general acceptance as a deity, was probably widespread in the Andes well before the Inca.

The principal ceremonies of the Inca, as described by Cristóbal de Molina (1989 [ca. 1575]), were related to celestial objects (primarily the sun) and to agriculture. The festivals of Inti Raymi and Capac Raymi occurred near the June and December solstices respectively, astronomically significant times when the sun's motion on the horizon seems to stop and then change direction. The Coya Raymi celebration fell near the September equinox, further dividing the year. In Cuzco, the time to begin planting maize, August, and the time of its harvest, April, were also marked by major festivals during which the sun was observed. Bartolomé de Segovia (1943:51–52 [1553]), an early Spanish visitor to Cuzco, observed a Cuzco harvest ceremony in April of 1535 and described a large celebration in which the ruling Inca and his nobles participated in public observations of the sun.[9] It is a telling account of how intimately related agriculture, the sun, and the ruling Inca were in Inca ideology. This rare eyewitness account describes the people of Cuzco going out of the city to a place in the direction that the sun would rise. There, over six hundred Inca nobles stood in two parallel rows:

They were all orejones, very richly dressed in cloaks and tunics woven with silver. They wore bracelets, and the disks on their heads were of fine gold and very resplendent. They stood in two rows, each of which was made up of over three hundred lords. It was like a procession, some on one side and the others on the other, and they stood very silent, waiting for sunrise. When the sun had not yet fully risen, they began slowly and in great order and harmony to intone a chant; and as they sang, they each moved forward . . . and as the sun went on rising, so their song intensified. The Inca had his awning in an enclosure with a very fine seat, at a little distance from the line of the others. And when the singing began, he rose to his feet with great authority and stood at the head of all, and he was the first to begin the chant; and when he began, so did all the others, . . . And so they sang from the time when the sun rose until it had completely set. And since until noon the sun was rising, they heightened their voices, and after noon they slowly softened them, always in step with the movement of the sun. (Segovia 1943:51–52 [1553]; translation by S. MacCormack 1991:75–76)[10]

The ruling Inca was both the head of state and the central figure in all public ceremonies involving sun worship. Direct participation in these ceremonies by the rulers of Cuzco confirmed their position as descendants of the sun and as the primary authorities of the empire.

The Inca elite usurped direct access to the generally acknowledged powers of the sun, taking it as both ancestor and patron. The inseparable relation that existed between the sun and the Inca elite was clearly portrayed in the Punchao, the central sun idol of the Coricancha. As the central figure in all public ceremonies for sun worship, the ruling Inca stood as the sole mediator between the populations of the Andes and the cosmogonic forces of the heavens. This position gave him control over the ritual celebrations of Cuzco. Accordingly, the study of Inca astronomy is not simply an investigation of indigenous interpretations of celestial movements and of the native calendar, but a study of the social and ritual organization of Cuzco and the processes by which elite kinship groups centralized authority in themselves.

2. Historical Accounts Concerning Inca Solar Astronomy and the Year

A VARIETY OF EARLY DOCUMENTS provide information on Inca astronomy in and near the ancient city of Cuzco. The classic chronicles, as well as a number of clerical and governmental reports, present detailed descriptions of Inca rituals, calendrics, and sky observations. Other important information sources for Inca astronomy are the early dictionaries produced by Spaniards working in areas of the former Inca Empire. We present in chronological order the major references to Inca solar astronomy that have survived from the early colonial period. This compilation serves as a reference base for our interpretations of the Inca calendar and solar observations presented in following chapters.[1]

We begin with the early chronicle of Betanzos (1551) and conclude with the later works of Calancha (1638) and Cobo (1653). Many of the accounts are difficult to read, so we provide English translations in the text and the original Spanish passages in the endnotes. Additionally, we note that caution must be used in reading some of the later writers, such as Acosta (1590), Murúa (ca. 1615), Calancha (1638), and Cobo (1653), since they acquired much of their information secondhand from earlier writers. Furthermore, we do not know the author or the exact date for several important sources (e.g., Anonymous Chronicler ca. 1570; Molina ca. 1575).

The Julian and Gregorian Calendars

The period spanned by the historical documents used in this study includes the Julian–Gregorian calendar reform. Throughout most of the sixteenth century, the Spanish followed the Julian calendar established by Julius Caesar in 46 B.C. and refined to its final form in A.D. 8 under Augustus. This calendar inserted a leap day in every fourth year, which resulted in a three-day shift (with respect to the solar year) over the course of four hundred years. By the time of Pope Gregory XIII (A.D. 1502–1585), this shift amounted to ten days and was considered serious enough to require correcting. In 1582, the ten days were simply omitted from the calendar year by requiring 15 October to immediately follow 4 October, and a revised counting system was introduced to stabilize calendrical time. The new Gregorian calendar corrected the frequency at which leap years were inserted by eliminating those years evenly divisible by one hundred, unless they were also evenly divisible by four hundred. As a result, A.D. 1600 and A.D. 2000 are leap years in both the Gregorian and the Julian calendar, while A.D. 1900 is a leap year in the Julian but not in the Gregorian calendar.

As a Roman Catholic nation, Spain and her territories adopted the Gregorian calendar. The orders to convert to the new calendar arrived in Cuzco on 10 July 1584 and are recorded in the archives of the ecclesiastical council. The calendar adjustment occurred in October 1584 with the 4th day of that month followed by the 15th (Esquivel y Navia 1980:248–249 [1749]).

Dates given in the accounts written before 1584 must be increased by ten days for comparison to the modern calendar. For example, a "mid-March" feast that Polo de Ondegardo describes in a 1571 document needs to be shifted ten days, and thus becomes a late-March celebration. On the other hand, Cobo writing in 1653 used the Gregorian calendar and placed the December solstice on the 23d day of that month. In this work, we will present the pre-1584 dates as originally stated, and then convert them to the Gregorian equivalent.

Solar Astronomy in Cuzco

The most tangible historical evidence for Inca astronomical observations concerns the use of pillars to mark solar motion along the Cuzco horizon. The existence of these pillars was noted by a variety of people who lived in or visited Cuzco between 1541 and 1630. Prominent among them were Betanzos, Cieza de León, Polo de Ondegardo, Cobo, Sarmiento de Gamboa, Garcilaso de la Vega, Guaman Poma de Ayala, Montesinos, and an anonymous writer. Their accounts provide useful but often conflicting information on the number of pillars, their locations on the hills surrounding Cuzco, the positions from which they were observed, and the solar events that they marked. These accounts will be reviewed below and compared in Chapter 3 with archaeological findings from the Cuzco region.

One of the earliest detailed reports on Inca society was written by Juan de Betanzos for the second viceroy of Peru, Antonio de Mendoza, the Marqués de Cañete. Betanzos was an early Spanish settler of Cuzco who married an Inca princess. His mastery of Quechua and his close contacts with members of the former ruling class demand that special attention be paid to Betanzos' writings. In 1551 Betanzos completed the first major chronicle of Peru, which he entitled *Suma y narración de los Incas* (Account and narration of the Incas). In this monumental work, he provides the following information on the Inca calendar and solar observations:

This lord [Pachacuti Inca Yupanqui] named the month of November Cantaraiquis. In this month they start to make the *chicha* that they will drink in the month of December and January when the year begins and hold the celebration of the *orejones* as you have learned in this account. Inca Yupanqui gave the months the names that you now have heard . . . Each of these months had thirty days and the year had three hundred and sixty and so as time passed they would not lose the count of these months and the times in which they had to plant and perform the celebrations, . . . he made those *Pacha Unan Chac*[2] which means clocks. He had these clocks made during the ten days that he waited not wanting to tell what you have heard. The clocks were made so that: every morning and afternoon of each month of the year he also observed the sun watching for the time to plant and to harvest and also when the sun set, and he watched the moon when it was new and full and waning. Those clocks were made of cut stone on top of the highest hills at the place where the sun rose and where it set. . . . in the highest place in the hills [were] made four pyramids or columns of worked stone. The two in the middle were smaller than the other two on the sides. [They were] square, each two *estados* high and separated one from the other by one *braza* except he made the two smaller ones in the middle closer together, about a half a *braza* between them. When the sun rose, Inca Yupanqui stood in a place to watch and estimate, the sun comes straight up and goes right in the middle of the two pillars, and it did the same thing when it went down to the place where it sets. In this way the common people understood when it was time to plant and harvest. . . . there were four clocks where the sun rose and another four where it set, that mark the courses and movements which in this way the sun made in the year.[3]

Betanzos describes how Pachacuti Inca Yupanqui organized the year, designating the months and the annual celebrations. He claims that this was done in a ten-day period during which "clocks" for maintaining the year were also built. With the most direct access of any of the chroniclers to imperial Inca practices, Betanzos describes a 360-day year composed of 12 months of 30 days each. The resulting 360 days is more than 5 days short of an actual year. Betanzos indicates that to maintain the phase, the solar year was begun by observing the sunrise and sunset on the December solstice, and he states that solar observations were made during the mornings and evenings of each month.

Betanzos continues with a description of what we presume to be the "clocks." There were at least eight pillars (pyramids) arranged in two groups of four on the hills around Cuzco. One group marked sunrise positions, and the other sunsets. The pillars were square, and each group consisted of two large outer pillars framing two smaller inner ones. Betanzos separates the outer pillars from the inner ones by a fathom (braza), or approximately two meters. As viewed from central Cuzco, this narrow spacing permits the pillars to mark an individual pair of days.[4] Betanzos, however, links them to a range of tasks (and dates) including marking the months of a solar year, which he begins near the December solstice, and recording the local planting and harvest periods for the common people.

Another early Spanish chronicler, Pedro de Cieza de León, visited Cuzco in 1550. Three years later, after his return to Spain, Cieza de León published the first part of his Crónica del Perú (Chronicle of Peru). He was a careful writer, describing what he saw with little embellishment. Cieza de León provides an early description of a set of pillars near Carmenca, a sector of ancient Cuzco, used for monitoring the sun:

> In another section stands Karmenka [Carmenca] hill, where at intervals there are small towers which they used to study the movement of the sun, to which they attached great importance. (Cieza de León 1976:143, 144 [1553: Pt. 1, Ch. 92])[5]

Carmenca was situated on the lower slopes of Picchu hill in an area now called Santa Ana. Since this hill stands to the northwest of Cuzco, the pillars may have been used to mark sunsets on important days in the Inca calendar. Unfortunately, Cieza de León does not record the number of pillars present on Carmenca, nor does he provide information on their size, beyond the comment that they were small, or the location from which they were observed.

Cieza de León does, however, mention these pillars a second time in the context of the Inca calendar:

The world in its totality they call *Pacha[c]*, and they know the revolutions the sun makes, and the waxing and waning of the moon. They counted the year, by this, and it consists of twelve months, by their calculations. They had a number of small towers, of which there are many on the hills of Cuzco, now in a state of neglect, so that they could tell by the shadow the sun made on them when to plant, and other things they gathered from this. (Cieza de León 1976:172 [1554: Pt. 2, Ch. 26]; translation modified)[6]

Cieza de León indicates that the pillars around Cuzco may have been used for shadow casting. Although other authors also suggest that the Inca practiced shadow casting, the evidence for the Inca's use of the horizon pillars in Cuzco to mark solar positions is overwhelming. Furthermore, a single column designed for shadow casting can be used all year long, and it would be unnecessary to construct a series of such pillars along the horizon. Cieza de León states that the solar pillars were still visible on the Cuzco horizon in 1550, but that they were in ruins. Despite their abandonment and deterioration, these pillars continued to be seen and discussed for nearly a century after Cieza de León's description.

Juan Polo de Ondegardo arrived in Peru around 1546 and lived there for more than thirty years. He served twice as Corregidor of Cuzco (1558–1560 and 1571–1572), and while holding this office, he interviewed numerous native elders. He wrote a number of reports concerning various aspects of Inca society (Polo de Ondegardo 1872, 1916a–e, 1917, 1940, 1965a–e) that provided useful information for the Provincial Councils of Lima and for later writers.

There are several references to the Cuzco solar pillars in works known to have been written by Polo de Ondegardo. One is found in an extract of a lost document originally called *De los errores y supersticiones de los indios* (On the errors and superstitions of the Indians). The extract was published in 1585, though the original manuscript was based on data collected during Polo de Ondegardo's first term as Corregidor of Cuzco in 1559. In this work, Polo de Ondegardo describes the Inca year:

The year was divided into twelve months by the moons; and they spent the days which are left over each year with these moons.[7] Each moon or month had its monument or pillar around Cuzco, where the Sun reached that month. And those pillars were important shrines, to which various sacrifices were offered, and everything that was left over from sacrifices to the Huacas was taken to these spots, which were called Sucanca; and that which is the beginning of winter, pucuy sucanca, and the beginning of summer, Chirao sucanca. The year is called Huata in Quechua, and Mara in the Aymará of the Collas. The moon and month is called Quilla, and Pacsi in Aymará.

Each month of the year they had different celebrations and sacrifices in order, as decreed by Pachacuti Inca. He had the year begin in December, which is when the sun reaches the end of its course from here to the Antarctic Pole. (Polo de Ondegardo 1965b:20–22 [1585: Ch. 7]; translation modified)[8]

The chronicles of José de Acosta (1954 [1590: Bk. 6, Ch. 3]), Martín de Murúa (1946 [ca. 1615: Bk. 7, Ch. 70]), and Antonio de la Calancha (1981 [1638: Bk. 2, Ch. 12]) present information similar to that provided by Polo de Ondegardo in the above passage. Since each of these authors copied much of their information on the Inca from Polo de Ondegardo's reports, their writings should not be considered independent data sources.

In the above passage, Polo de Ondegardo relates the pillars of Pucuy Sucanca to the winter solstice and those of Chirao Sucanca to the beginning of summer. While many Spaniards knew that the June solstice was technically the beginning of winter in Peru, they were not consistent in this usage. June is also the beginning of the sunny, dry season, and the June solstice was frequently called the beginning of summer. Polo de Ondegardo's predilection for the term "summer" can be inferred from the early Quechua dictionary of Gonçález Holguín (M. Ziólkowski pers. com. 1994). Gonçález Holguín (1989:292 [1608]) includes Poccuy as the time of the rain, and Chirau as the dry season (1989:113 [1608]). The word *Pucuy* also appears in the names reported for the months of February and March (see Table 2), two of the rainiest months of the year in the Peruvian highlands. Pucuy Sucanca almost certainly refers to the pillars that mark the December solstice, the beginning of the rainy season, and Chirao Sucanca refers to the June solstice, and the dry season.

A second reference by Polo de Ondegardo to the sun pillars of the Inca comes from his *Relación de los fundamentos acerca del notable daño que resulta de no guardar a los Indios sus fueros* (A report on the basic principles explaining the serious harm that follows when the traditional rights of the Indians are not respected), written in 1571. In this work, Polo de Ondegardo mentions the Cuzco solar pillars in a description of a feast occurring near the equinox (11 March in the Julian calendar):

In the middle of March, according to the moons which they count by observing the course of the sun through those columns or posts which

Table 2. *The Names of Inca Months from Selected Sources*

	Betanzos [1551]	Anonymous Chronicler [ca. 1570]	Fernández [1571]
January[a] (23 December)[b]	Hatumpo Coiquis	Hatumpocoy	Pura Opiaiquiz
February (22 January)	Allapo Coiquis	Pachapocoy	Cac Maiquiz
March (21 February)	Pacha Pocoiquis	Ayriuaquilla	Pauca Ruaraiquiz
April (23 March)[c]	Ayriguaquis	Haocaycusqui	Ariquaquiz
May (22 April)	Haucai Quos Quiquilla	Aymorayquilla	Aimuraiquiz
June (23 May)	Hatun Quosquiquilla	Hatuncusqui	Aucay Cuxqui
July (23 June)[d]	Caguaquis	Chauaruay	Chaguar Vayques
August (23 July)	Carpaiquis	Tarpuyquilla	Cituaquiz
September[e] (23 August)	Satuaiquis	Cituaquilla	Puzcuaiquiz
October (22 September)[f]	Omarime Quis	Chaupicusqui (Cantarayquilla)	Cantaraiquiz
November (22 October)	Cantaraiquis	Raymiquilla	Laimequiz
December (22 November)	Pucoy Quillaraimequis	Camayquilla	Camaiquiz

[a]In this table we present the approximate beginning and ending dates for twelve months of (near) equal length as they would be determined by a set of appropriately spaced horizon pillars. Following Betanzos, Polo de Ondegardo, and Guaman Poma de Ayala, we begin the year on the December solstice. In the names of the months, it should be noted that "quis" and "quilla" are both Quechua words for *moon* or *month*.

[b]The day following the solstice in the Gregorian calendar.

Molina [ca. 1575]	Polo de Ondegardo [1585]	Gonçález Holguín [1608]	Guaman Poma de Ayala [1615]
Camayquilla	Camay	Kollappocoy	Capac Raymi, Camay Quilla
Atunpucuy	Hatun Pucuy	not named	Paucar Uaray Hatun Pocoy Quilla
Pachapucu	Pacha Pucuy	not named	Pacha Pocuy Quilla
Paucarguara	Antihuaquiz	Ayri huaquilla	Ynca Raymi Mamay Quilla
Ayriguay	Hatun Cuzqu Raymoray	Hatun Cuzqui Aymorayquilla	Atun Cusqui Aymoray Quilla
Hacicay Llusque	Aucay Cuzqui	Yntiraymi	Haucay Cusqui Quilla
Cauay (Chahuarhuay)	Chahua Huarquis	Antta cittua	Chacra Conacuy Quilla
Moronpassa Tarpuiquilla	Yapaquis	Kapak cithua	Chacra Yapuy Quilla Quilla
Coyaraymi	Coya Raymi	Umaraymi	Coya Raymi Quilla
Omacrayma	Homa Raimi Puchayquis	Ayar maca	Uma Raymi Quilla
Ayarmaca raymi	Ayamarca	Kapakraymi (Aya marca)	Aya Marcay Quilla
Capac Raymi	Capacraymi	Raymi	Capac Ynti Raymi

ᶜ Approximately two days after the equinox.
ᵈ The day following the solstice.
ᵉ Molina (1989:73 [ca. 1575]) claims that Citua is the name of a festival that occurs in the month of Coya Raymi. The month names of Betanzos and the Anonymous Chronicler may result from this difference.
ᶠ Two days before the equinox.

they call *Saybas* [sayhuas] and which surround the City of Cuzco, the
Inca divided them [young women], or his lieutenants did, a solemn ceremony for this purpose having been held in this form, so that women
were taken from there for the Sun. (Polo de Ondegardo 1965c:101
[1571])[9]

These passages indicate that the Cuzco solar pillars were called both
sucancas (i.e., Pucuy Sucanca and Chirao Sucanca) and *sayhuas*.[10]
The word *sucanca* is no longer in use in Cuzco Quechua, nor is its
meaning recorded in the early Quechua-Spanish dictionaries. The
word *sayhua* was, and continues to be, commonly used for *mojón*,
or "marker" (Gonçález Holguín 1989:325, 591 [1608]).

Bernabé Cobo's much later 1653 chronicle includes an account
of the same pillars and their use for defining the year. Sections of
Cobo's account are believed to have been derived from a complete
version of the now-lost *De los errores y supersticiones de los indios*,
researched and written by Polo de Ondegardo around 1559 (Bauer
n.d.a). Indeed, Cobo states that he had the original version of this report with Polo de Ondegardo's own signature on it.[11] Since Cobo's
synthesis of Polo de Ondegardo's work contains details that have
not been preserved in the summary published in 1585, it is reproduced here:

> They identified our solar year by observing the solstices and starting the
> year by the summer solstice of this Antarctic Hemisphere, which falls
> on the twenty-third day of December and ends at the same point where
> it started. Therefore, their year turned out to have the same number of
> days as our year, with the exception of the bissextiles or leap years,
> which they did not understand. For this reason, it is impossible to ascer-
> tain how accurate their year was; but I really do not think that their ob-
> servations were so accurate that they avoided making many errors, in
> spite of the fact that they utilized the best means that they knew in or-
> der to fix their year and keep an accurate record of the passage of time.
>
> So that their record would be correct and accurate, they used the fol-
> lowing method. On the crest of the hills that surround Cuzco, two
> markers or pillars were placed on the eastern side and two more such
> pillars were placed on the western side of that city, on the spot where
> the sun rises and sets when the tropics of Cancer and Capricorn come;
> and at the time when the sun rose and set exactly along the pillars of
> the south side, as observations were taken from the city of Cuzco, it
> was considered to be the beginning of the year. Since that city is located
> at twelve to fifteen degrees south, that was the time when the sun
> reached the farthest point on that southern side. From there, returning

to the equinoctial line, it passed its zenith, and when it moved to the farthest point away on the northern side, as the sun rose and set it was aligned over those other pillars that marked the farthermost point on that side; and on returning from there to the point where it left, the Tropic of Cancer, which the first pillars marked, the year was concluded. The word for year was *huata* in Quechua and *mara* in Aymara.

Their year was composed of twelve months, and these months were counted by moons, and thus they use the same word for "month" and "moon," which is in Quechua, the language of Cuzco, *quilla*, and in Aymara, *pacsi*. The days that were left over each year were incorporated into the moons themselves. Thus, on the eastern as well as the western sides, where they had their markers placed at the point where the sun rose and set when it reached the tropics between these two posts or markers, they had others placed, each one at the point where the sun reached that month; all of these pillars together were called Sucanca, and they were important objects of worship, and sacrifices were offered to them at the same time as the rest of the sacred objects. The two pillars that marked the beginning of winter were called Pucuy Sucanca, and the other two that marked the beginning of summer were called Chirao Sucanca. All the months had an equal number of days and each had its own name. (Cobo 1979:251–252 [1653: Bk. 12, Ch. 37])[12]

In agreement with Betanzos' record, this account begins the year with the December solstice. Cobo also states that their year had the same number of days as our year, except for an ambiguity with leap years. This suggests the use of a solar year of 365 days instead of a year of 12 lunar months totaling 354 days. Cobo uses the Gregorian calendar, and correctly begins summer with the arrival of the sun at the December solstice, on about the twenty-third of that month. He then simply copies Polo de Ondegardo's statement that summer was marked by the pillars Chirao Sucanca. As discussed above, Chirao Sucanca probably marked the beginning of the dry season in June, not the beginning of summer in December.

Elsewhere in his chronicle, still using information obtained from Polo de Ondegardo, Cobo notes that the pillars were called sucancas.

Fourteen universally worshiped shrines came about as a consequence of their Sun worship. These were the markers or pillars called Sucanca that indicated the months of the year. These pillars were considered very important, and sacrifices were offered to them at the same time as they were made for the other *guacas* and in places designated for this purpose. These sacrifices were made in the following way. After the sacrifices were taken to the other *guacas* in the order in which they were located along the *ceques*, as will be explained in the proper place, what was left over was offered to these markers. This was because the markers were not located in the same order as the other shrines but were distributed according to the course of the Sun, and each one came with a sacrifice to the marker-shrine located nearest to his *ceque*. (Cobo 1990:27–28 [1653: Bk. 13, Ch. 5])[13]

Here Cobo states that there was a total of fourteen solar pillars in the area around Cuzco. He also indicates that the sacrifices offered to these sucanca were related to those made to a much larger system of shrines (huacas) and ritual lines (ceques) in the region.

These descriptions by Cobo support much of the information provided by Betanzos. Cobo and Betanzos each state that pillars marked the rise and set positions of the sun on the solstices. Betanzos claims, however, that four pillars were used for each solstice, while Cobo describes twin markers. Both correlate the beginning of the Inca solar year with the December solstice. Cobo specifically states that the beginning of each of the months was marked by a single solar pillar. His total count of fourteen pillars is consistent with this statement. A year evenly divided and beginning on a solstice requires seven positions to be marked along the horizon, or fourteen if sunrises and sunsets are marked.

While Betanzos mentions that the Inca watched the waxing and waning of the moon, he claims that they used fixed months of 30 days. A 30-day period has no intrinsic meaning in the solar year. It is a convenient approximation to the 29.5-day lunar (synodic) period that, with the occasional addition of a day, can be used to divide the solar year. A fixed 30-day period cannot, however, be used with a lunar calendar. After only two months of 30 days, the phase of the moon at the beginning of the month has changed visibly.

Cobo states that there were twelve months in a year, and follows Polo de Ondegardo in claiming that the months were marked by the motion of the sun past horizon pillars. He also states, "The days that were left over each year were incorporated into the moons themselves." The time between new moons is fixed, and it is impossible to insert days into this period without ignoring the moon itself. Since Cobo noted that in Quechua the words for *moon* and *month* were the same (*quilla*), he could be referring to fixed months of approximately 30 days like those of Betanzos. Alternatively, Cobo's words might suggest that the days left over in each year were accumulated and incorporated into an extra moon every few years (see Chapter 3).

Two additional works containing references to the Cuzco solar pillars were written in the early 1570s. The first, recorded by an anonymous chronicler, includes one of the best available accounts of the pillars. The second, written by Pedro Sarmiento de Gamboa, an official crown historian, is perhaps less useful. The Anonymous Chronicler wrote a report in Cuzco in about 1570 titled Discourse of the Succession and Government of the Incas (*Discurso de la sucesión y gobierno de los Yngas*) (Rowe 1980:74). In this report, the Anonymous Chronicler (1906:151 [ca. 1570]) describes the use of horizon pillars to officially begin the time to plant in the Cuzco region:

> . . . in the highest hills in view of the city of Cuzco, to the west, they built four pillars in the form of small towers, that could [be seen] from two or three leagues, The first placed two hundred paces from the last and the two in the middle were fifty paces from one another, and the separation of the two extremes was suitable for their intended use; with the result that when the sun reached the first pillar they prepared for the general planting and began to plant vegetables in the heights, as slower [to mature], and when the sun reached the two pillars in the middle, was the point and the general time of the planting in Cuzco, and it was always in the month of August. It is in this way that, to take the point of the sun between the central two pillars they had another pillar in the middle of the plaza, [a] pillar of well worked stone one *estado* in height, in a suitable indicated place, that they called *usnu*, and from there they watched the sun between the two pillars, and when it was exactly there, it was the time for sowing in the Cuzco Valley and its region.[14]

Both the Anonymous Chronicler and Betanzos write that there were four pillars on the western horizon of Cuzco marking solar movements. The size given for the pillars is reasonably consistent. Betanzos states that the outer two pillars were two *estados* (approximately three meters) high and the inner two were smaller. The Anonymous Chronicler notes that the pillars could be seen at a distance of two to three leagues, suggesting that they were slightly taller.[15] Their estimates of the spacing, however, are significantly different. Betanzos indicates that the two inner pillars were separated from each other by half a braza (approximately one meter) and from the two outer ones by a braza (approximately two meters). This description conflicts with that of the Anonymous Chronicler, who records a larger separation of two hundred paces between the first and last pillars. Finally, the Anonymous Chronicler states that the pillars marked a time during the month of August that indicated the ritual beginning of the planting season. While the separation

that he gives is so wide that the sun would have been seen to set between the pillars for a broad range of dates, this use agrees with Betanzos' comment that the pillars gave the common people a means
of determining when to plant. However, Betanzos specifically states
that the pillars were also used to mark solar movements on or near
a solstice.

The Anonymous Chronicler is the only writer to identify the
location from which the pillars were observed. He states that the
sun was watched moving between the horizon markers from a stone
called usnu in the central plaza of Cuzco. The Anonymous Chronicler (1906:158 [ca. 1570]) again refers to this usnu, and the four horizon pillars, in a discussion of the months of August and September:

> The moon of the month of August they called Tarpuyquilla. This
> month the only thing they did was plant, generally everyone, the poor
> and the rich, helping one another. And in this month of August the sun
> entered between the two small towers of the four that the Incas fixed, as
> has been spoken of before.
>
> The moon of the month of September they called Cituaquilla. This
> month all the Indians of the entire region gathered in Cuzco, and all to-
> gether in the principal plaza, called Haucaypata, that they made their
> sacrifices to the sun with many ceremonies, on a pillar of stone that
> they had in the middle of the plaza, . . . called usnu.[16]

The usnu of the central plaza of Cuzco must have been a prominent
feature since it is mentioned by Betanzos (1987:52 [1551: Pt. 1, Ch.
11]), Albornoz (1984:205 [ca. 1582]), Cieza de León (1985:109 [1554:
Pt. 2, Ch. 36]), and Segovia (1943:22 [1553]) as a stone of monumental importance.[17] It should also be noted that the Anonymous
Chronicler speaks of "the moon of the month of August" and "the
moon of the month of September," suggesting the use of a lunar calendar. He correlates the solar observation made during the planting
ceremony with the month of August, but does not mention any observation associated with a solstice.

The Anonymous Chronicler wrote his work about the time that
Sarmiento de Gamboa was gathering information on Inca history
for Francisco de Toledo, the fifth viceroy of Peru. Sarmiento de
Gamboa's history of the Inca, written in Cuzco in 1572, contains
some of the finest recorded descriptions of Inca mythology. His formal training, however, was not in literature or historiography but in
navigation, and he was a well-known captain and navigator. As
such, Sarmiento de Gamboa (1906:67–68 [1572: Ch. 30]) must have

been well versed in European astronomy, and his prior training may have distracted him in his function as a historian:

> And so that the time of planting and of harvesting would be known precisely and never lost he [Pachacuti Inca Yupanqui] ordered there be placed on a high hill to the east of Cuzco four posts, separated from one another by about two *varas* and through their tops [were] some holes, through which the sun entered like a clock or an astrolabe. And considering where the sunlight fell through those holes at the time of fallowing and planting, he made marks on the ground, and put other posts in the corresponding part to the west of Cuzco for the time of the grain harvest. And as he had adjusted these posts precisely, he put for permanence in their place some stone columns with the [same] measurement and holes as the posts, and all around he ordered the ground paved, and on the stones made certain leveled lines conforming to the movements of the sun which entered through the holes in the column in such a way that everything was a clever annual clock, by which planting and harvesting were controlled. And he delegated people to take charge of these clocks and notify the community of the times and their changes, which those clocks indicated.[18]

Sarmiento de Gamboa describes two sets of four poles, later replaced by permanent stone pillars, that were used to make astronomical observations on the hills around Cuzco. The number of poles and their positions on the eastern and western horizons is reminiscent of the solar horizon pillars described by other writers. Sarmiento de Gamboa, however, makes no mention of their use for defining sunrise or -set positions. In his account, they are much shorter (two *varas* is about 1.5 meters), and he suggests that they were used for light casting. One possible explanation for this discrepancy is that the remains of horizon pillars were still visible on the hills surrounding Cuzco in 1572, though the Inca practice of using a solar year regulated with horizon observations had long since ceased. Having been told that they were part of a "clock," Sarmiento de Gamboa may have relied on his own knowledge of light casting to speculate on their use.

At the same time that the Anonymous Chronicler and Sarmiento de Gamboa were recording their observations of Inca society, a third Spaniard, Cristóbal de Molina (el Cusqueño), also was writing his impressions. He was a Quechua scholar and the author of a number of important documents on the Inca. In contrast to many other chroniclers, Molina focuses on Inca ceremonies that took place dur-

ing the year, rather than on how the Inca measured the year's
length. While his contemporaries, the Anonymous Chronicler and
Sarmiento de Gamboa, provide descriptions of the solar pillars, Molina fails even to mention their existence. One of Molina's works,
Relación de las fábulas i ritos de los Ingas (An account of the fables
and rites of the Inca), was recorded around 1575, and contains a detailed account of the use of a lunar calendar for the ceremonial organization of Cuzco.[19] This account began the Inca year in mid-May
(Julian calendar), on the first day of the new moon, with the festival of Inti Raymi. His starting date requires the June solstice to
occur during this month and his account places the ruling Inca and
his nobles on a hill, Mantocalla, at the time of the solstice. Molina
(1989:67–68 [ca. 1575]) states that during this festival offerings were
made in the morning on the mountain of Huanacauri, at noon in the
court of the Coricancha, and in the evening at a sunset point on a
hill called Aepiran (or Aepitan):

> And then in the morning they sent a sheep[20] to Huanacauri, which is
> the principal huaca that they have as is told in the *History of the Incas*,
> where the Tarpuntaes killed and burnt it, who were those that had the
> charge of giving food to the huacas. While they burnt it, at sunrise,
> many Incas and caciques came and pulling out the wool of the said
> sheep, before they burnt it, walking around the sacrifice with the wool
> in their hands, saying in a loud voice "Oh Creator, the Sun and Thun-
> der, be always young and multiply the people, and be always in peace."
> And at noon, in the same way, they burnt another sheep in Coricancha
> in the patio of the House of the Sun; that is now the cloister of the Friars
> of Santo Domingo, and at sunset they took another sheep to the hill
> called Aepiran, because above it the sun sets.[21]

Unfortunately, a hill west of Cuzco called Aepiran is not mentioned
by any other chronicler, and its location remains unknown. A place
called Atpitan is mentioned by Cobo (1980:41 [1653: Bk. 13, Ch.
15]) as a huaca in the ceque system. Murúa (1946:51 [ca. 1615: Pt. 1,
Ch. 2]) also refers to this place, calling it Apitay. Both of these authors suggest, however, that this location was near Huanacauri
Mountain, which is situated southeast of Cuzco. It could be suggested that the name Aepiran is another name for Picchu, since the
June solstice sun sets on the lower slopes of Picchu as seen from the
Coricancha. It must be noted, however, that the sunset data from
Molina's document is ambiguous since he does not specifically state
from where the set sun observation was made. Furthermore, many
of the activities described by Molina were suppressed at the time

of his account, so his description of the Inca year may have been pieced together from material provided by informants, rather than from events that he actually witnessed.

Perhaps the best-known chronicler to mention the sun pillars of Cuzco is Inca Garcilaso de la Vega, son of a Spanish captain and an Inca princess. Garcilaso de la Vega was born in Cuzco in 1539 and lived there until he departed for Spain in 1560. Because he left Peru as a young man of twenty and did not write his commentary until after he had lived in Spain for many years (1609), Garcilaso de la Vega's information is not reliable. He drew many of his "facts" from other sources and romanticized certain aspects of Inca society. However, Garcilaso de la Vega's physical descriptions of early colonial Cuzco are usually accurate. What is important to this study is that Garcilaso de la Vega, like Betanzos, the Anonymous Chronicler, and Sarmiento de Gamboa, describes sets of pillars that existed on the hills of Cuzco. He states that there were a total of sixteen pillars, arranged in four sets of four, on the Cuzco horizon (two sets to the east and two to the west):

> They also understood the summer and winter solstices; these were marked by large and visible signs consisting of eight towers built to the east and eight built to the west of the city of Cuzco. They were arranged in sets of four: two small [towers] about three times the height of a man were between two larger ones. The smaller [inner] towers were separated by about eighteen to twenty feet, and at the same distance from them stood the larger, which were higher than those used as watch towers in Spain. These large towers served to guard and to give the smaller towers better visibility. The space between the small towers was where the sun rose and set on the solstices. One set of towers to the east corresponded to another in the west for the summer solstice.
>
> In order to confirm the time of the solstice an Inca stood in a certain place to watch the sun rise and set between the small towers. With this observation they established the time of the solstices in their astrology. (Garcilaso de la Vega 1966:116 [1609: Vol. 1, Bk. 2, Ch. 22]; translation modified)[22]

Elsewhere Garcilaso de la Vega mentions that both Cieza de León (1984:258 [1553: Pt. 1, Ch. 92]) and Acosta (1954 [1590: Bk. 6, Ch. 3]) described solar pillars. The dimensions that Garcilaso de la Vega provides, however, seem to be his own, as neither of these writers gives dimensions. He states that the smaller pillars stood about three times the height of a man and that the pillars were separated by about twenty feet (six to seven meters).

This Cuzco-born chronicler implies that the two outer pillars aided the eye in finding the inner ones against the glare of Cuzco sunsets. This statement shows a practical understanding of the difficulty of observing the sun against a high horizon from a mountain site like Cuzco. The horizon, as viewed from the central portions of the city, is high, typically 5 to 10 degrees. This feature, combined with the altitude of the city (3,300 masl), results in searingly bright sunsets. Unlike a low-altitude, low-horizon, red sunset that occurs in coastal areas, the bright glare of the sunset in Cuzco makes it difficult to observe except for the last few seconds when the sun has almost entirely set. The sixty feet (eighteen meters) between the two large outer pillars result in an apparent separation of approximately half a degree as seen from central Cuzco. These pillars would frame the setting (or rising) sun. By occulting the disk of the sun itself, one could see if it was entirely between the markers. Such a relatively large separation would not permit a precise determination of the solstice date. This precision, however, could be achieved with the inner pillars.

Garcilaso de la Vega provides several other interesting comments on Inca astronomy and the sun pillars of Cuzco. For example, he states that the horizon markers were still above the city in 1560 when he left for Spain:

> I saw these towers standing in 1560, and unless they have since been pulled down, the point from which the Incas observed the solstices can be verified: I cannot say whether it was a tower in the house of the Sun or another place. (Garcilaso de la Vega 1966:117 [1609: Vol. 1, Bk. 2, Ch. 22])[23]

It seems that less than thirty years after the Spanish invasion, the horizon markers of Cuzco were in complete disuse, and that the location from which they were once observed was lost from common knowledge.

Garcilaso de la Vega is very specific in linking the solar pillars with the solstices as a means of maintaining the phase between a solar and a lunar year:

> The Incas could establish the solstices only roughly because they did not know how to fix them by the days of the months in which the solstices occur. They counted the months by moons, as we shall see, and not by days; and although they divided the year into twelve moons, they did not know how to allow for the difference of eleven days by which the solar year exceeds the normal lunar year. They therefore relied en-

tirely on the movement of the sun by the solstices to calculate their year, and not on the moons. They thus divided one year from another and ordered the sowing of their crops by the solar and not the lunar year. (Garcilaso de la Vega 1966:116 [1609: Vol. 1, Bk. 2, Ch. 22])[24]

In this statement, Garcilaso de la Vega describes separate solar and lunar calendars that were kept in phase with solstice observations. In this respect, he corroborates independent information provided by two of the most reliable earlier writers of Cuzco, Betanzos and Polo de Ondegardo. However, he does not mention the use of fixed solar months marked by solar motion, which is suggested by these other authors.

Felipe Guaman Poma de Ayala, an indigenous chronicler who wrote in the early seventeenth century, traveled widely while working with various Spanish officials as a translator. He is known to have visited Cuzco, Lima, and many other cities, and to have written extensively about them. Additionally, his description of an indigenous astrologer from the Lucana Province, near modern Ayacucho, suggests that some of his information on Andean astronomy originates with a knowledgeable source. Unfortunately, the Spanish of this native writer is hard to decipher, and at times his insights on Inca society are obscured by his difficult writing style. According to Guaman Poma de Ayala (1980:830 [1615:884 (898)]), the sun was understood by the Inca to move along the horizon just as a journeyman alternately travels and rests:

And thus is the sun's summer and winter cycle, from the month that begins with January. The philosopher says that one day he [the sun] seats himself in his seat and the sun rules from that principal degree and grants power from there.

And in the same way in the month of August, the day of St. John the Baptist, he seats himself in another seat; in the first seat of his arrival, in the second seat he does not move from there. In this his principal day he rests and rules and reigns from that degree. On the third day he begins to move and makes himself ready for his travel but only very little; for this it is said that he makes himself ready.

And from that degree he begins moving every day, without resting, about half an hour, towards the left, facing the sea to the north of the forest [Atlantic], the six months from the first month of January, *Capac Raymi, Camay Quilla;* February, *Paucar Uaray, Hatun Pocoy Quilla;* March, *Pacha Pocuy Quilla;* April, *Ynga Raymi, Camay Quilla;* May, *Atun Cusqui, Aymoray Quilla;* June, *Haucay Cusqui Quilla;* July, *Chacra Conacuy Quilla.*

After this month of August he begins again, from the principal seat to the second principal seat, that these two seats and houses he holds greatly empowered that each month has its seat in each degree of heaven; the sun and the moon who follows as wife and queen of the stars. She follows the man as he continues indicating the clocks of the months [and] of the year: August, *Chacra Yapuy Quilla*; September, *Coya Raymi Quilla*; October, *Uma Raymi Quilla*; November, *Aya Marcay Quilla*; December, *Capac Ynti Raymi Quilla*. All the months end the sun's cycle beginning once again in January. In this month he sits in his chair as said, thus goes each year.[25]

One may interpret Guaman Poma de Ayala's description to be that of solar and lunar observations using horizon markers. In the first two sections of this passage, he states that the year begins with the sun at rest on one seat. Guaman Poma de Ayala writes that the sun rules from that seat for one day and then starts a journey, which begins very slowly, across the horizon to a second seat. In the third and fourth sections, he discusses the names of the months of the year and indicates that each month had its own seat.

If the seats mentioned by this indigenous chronicler were horizon markers, then the first and second sections of the passage eloquently describe the movement of the sun from solstice to solstice. The sun starts at the December solstice pillar, where the year was thought to begin, and then moves across the sky to the June solstice marker. The sun would appear to rest for a few days on the solstice markers (i.e., rise in the same place on the horizon several days in a row, rather than moving farther north or south), since the lateral movement of the sun is difficult to detect with the human eye on the day before and on the day after a solstice. Near a solstice, the sun's movement across the horizon is minute compared to the distance it covers between days near the equinox. This feature of the solar cycle is reflected in the statement that the sun, after leaving a seat (i.e., solstice marker) "begins to move and makes himself ready for his travel but only very little."

In the third and fourth sections of this passage, Guaman Poma de Ayala comments that "each month has its own seat in each degree of heaven," which suggests that each month had an identifiable location on the horizon and that the Inca calendar used both solar and lunar observations. Moreover, it supports the writings of early chroniclers like Betanzos and Polo de Ondegardo, who noted that the Inca year was divided into twelve months and that the beginning of each month was marked by a solar pillar.

On the other hand, Guaman Poma de Ayala offers some information in this passage that may be in error. While indicating that the year began and ended with the sun above a December solstice marker (seat), he seems to suggest that a second marker was correlated with the sun's movement in August: "And in the same way in the month of August, the day of St. John the Baptist he seats himself in the other seat. . . ." Zuidema (1988b:148) proposes that Guaman Poma de Ayala's reference to the day of St. John the Baptist refers to the traditional date of the latter's death, 29 August. Building on this proposition, Zuidema speculates that the pillar described by Guaman Poma de Ayala as the sun's August seat was one of the four principal pillars on Picchu hill near Cuzco, described by the Anonymous Chronicler and others. Zuidema further suggests that another of these four pillars marked the sunset on 18 August, on what he has termed the "antizenith passage" for the sun.

While this is a possible explanation, there are several points that need to be examined before this particular reading of Guaman Poma de Ayala is accepted. Since neither Cuzco nor Picchu is mentioned, Guaman Poma de Ayala could be providing a generalized description of how the Inca perceived the movements of the sun, rather than a detailed account of specific pillars that stood above the city of Cuzco. Furthermore, our reading of this passage suggests that Guaman Poma de Ayala was describing the movement of the sun between two major locations, not four as inferred by Zuidema. In addition, Guaman Poma de Ayala states that the journey of the sun between its two principal seats takes six months: "He [the sun] begins moving every day, without resting, about half an hour, towards the left, facing the sea to the north of the forest [Atlantic], the six months from the first month of January." Since a period of six months correlates with the time it takes for the sun to cross the horizon from December to June, it is reasonable to argue that the two principal seats described by Guaman Poma de Ayala marked the December and June solstices. Finally, as noted by Zuidema (1988b:148), in the traditional European ritual calendar, the birthday of John the Baptist—24 June—is correlated with the June solstice. Thus, Guaman Poma de Ayala's reference to the "day of St. John the Baptist" may be a direct reference to the June solstice. Accordingly, it seems more appropriate to posit that the mention of August as the month in which the sun reached its second seat represents an error in Guaman Poma de Ayala's work, rather than to interpret it as evidence of antizenith solar markers on Picchu hill above Cuzco.

In 1628, the Carmelite monk Antonio Vázquez de Espinosa completed a lengthy description of the Spanish occupation in the New

World titled *Compendio y descripción de las Indias Occidentales* (Summary and description of the West Indies). Although Vázquez de Espinosa lived in Peru for a number of years (1615–1619) and traveled to various locations including Chavín, Huánuco Pampa, Cajamarca, and Arequipa, he extracted much of his information on the history of the Inca from earlier writers such as Acosta and Garcilaso de la Vega. Important to this study is that Vázquez de Espinosa (1948:515 [1628: Pt. 2, Bk. 4, Ch. 76]) states at the end of his Cuzco description that there were a series of solar pillars above the Carmenca area:

> Next is the great neighborhood of Carmenca, from which leaves the road, called Chinchaysuyu, to all the area below, to Lima, Quito, and all the other provinces to the north. On the mountain ridge of Carmenca were many small towers, which were spaced to measure the movement of the sun and its declination, which were very well made and very curious.[26]

The first half of this quote has been copied directly from Garcilaso de la Vega's (1966:421 [1609: Pt. 1, Bk. 7, Ch. 8]) narrative of Cuzco. Since Garcilaso de la Vega never specifically states that the solar pillars of Cuzco were located above Carmenca, it can be concluded that the second half of this passage was added by Vázquez de Espinosa. Whether Vázquez de Espinosa actually saw the pillars, or extracted this information from other writers, is unclear.

One of the latest accounts to record the presence of solar pillars on the hills near Cuzco was written by Fernando de Montesinos (1920 [1630]) in *Memorias antiguas historiales del Perú* (Ancient historical memories of Peru). The credibility of Montesinos' writing, especially his description of the Inca dynastic succession, is in question because it varies radically from that of other early colonial writers. Nevertheless, he provides an interesting account of the Cuzco solar pillars, which he claims to have seen himself.

> This king called a great assembly of wise men and astrologers, and with the king himself (who was deeply learned), they all studied the solstices with care. There was a sort of shadow-clock by which they knew which days were long and which were short, and when the sun went to and returned from the tropics. They showed me four very ancient walls upon a hill, and a creole, a true and skilled translator, assured me that this edifice served the ancient Indians as a clock. As this prince was so learned in the movements of the stars, they called the month of Decem-

ber, in which he was born, *Capac Raymi* after his own name. They called the month of June *Citoc Raymi*, or, as we should say, greater and lesser solstice. (Montesinos 1920:52 [1630: Ch. 12]; translation modified)[27]

It is apparent from this statement that the Cuzco solar pillars were still visible in the early seventeenth century, one hundred years after the Spanish invasion, although their function as sunrise and -set markers, rather than gnomons, was misunderstood.

In 1653, a Jesuit priest and formidable naturalist named Bernabé Cobo finished one of the last and most important chronicles of Peru, *Historia del Nuevo Mundo* (History of the New World). The book took more than eleven years to write and was based on Cobo's own well-founded knowledge of Peru and the Inca, as well as on earlier writers. As discussed above, Cobo's best source of information was a series of reports written approximately eighty years earlier by Polo de Ondegardo. It has been suggested (Bauer n.d.a) that one of these reports—now lost—contained an extensive description of some 328 huacas that surrounded Cuzco (Cobo 1956:169–186; 1980:14–61; 1981:209–261; 1990:51–84 [1653: Bk. 13, Chs. 13–16]). Cobo's description of the Cuzco ceque system records the location of several solar pillars in Chinchaysuyu and Cuntisuyu, the northwest and southwest quadrants of Cuzco. Nine ceques crossed through Chinchaysuyu and fourteen or fifteen passed through Cuntisuyu; Cobo provided descriptions of each of the many shrines along these lines. Through these descriptions we know that three pairs of solar pillars were among the shrines of the ceque system.

The first description of solar pillars given by Cobo is that for the ninth shrine of the sixth ceque of Chinchaysuyu (Ch. 6:9). These two pillars marked the summer (June) solstice sunset on a hill called Quiancalla (Quiangalla):

> The ninth guaca was a hill named Quiangalla which is on the Yucay road. On it were two markers or pillars which they regarded as indication that, when the sun reached there, it was the beginning of the summer. (Cobo 1980:25 [1653: Bk. 13, Ch. 13])[28]

If Cobo's account of the huacas of the ceque system indeed originated with Polo de Ondegardo, these pillars marked the beginning of the dry season in June, and were probably called Chirao Sucanca.

The second reference by Cobo to solar markers may be found in his depiction of the seventh shrine of the eighth ceque of Chinchaysuyu (Ch. 8:7). These pillars marked a ritual planting date for maize:

> The seventh was called Sucanca. It was a hill by way of which the wa-
> ter channel from Chinchero comes. On it there were two markers as an
> indication that when the sun arrived there, they had to begin to plant
> the maize. The sacrifice which was made there was directed to the Sun,
> asking him to arrive there at the time which would be appropriate for
> planting, and they sacrificed to him sheep, clothing, and small minia-
> ture lambs of gold and silver. (Cobo 1980:27 [1653: Bk. 13, Ch. 13])[29]

Cobo's placement of these pillars on the hill with the Chinchero canal is important since this irrigation canal crossed the hill of Picchu above Carmenca. These pillars are probably the same markers described by Cieza de León, the Anonymous Chronicler, and Vázquez de Espinosa. Cobo also notes in this passage that elaborate offerings were made to the pillars. The presence of offerings may be what led the Spaniards, in their search for gold and silver, to destroy these and other solar markers in the Cuzco environs.

The third reference by Cobo to a set of solar pillars near Cuzco is found in his listing of the third shrine along the thirteenth ceque of Cuntisuyu (Cu. 13:3):

> The third, Chinchincalla, is a large hill where there were two mark-
> ers; when the sun reached them, it was time to plant. (Cobo 1980:59
> [1653: Bk. 13, Ch. 16])[30]

This passage suggests that the arrival of the sun at Chinchincalla hill correlated with the ritual commencement of the planting season, which duplicates the use that Cobo had noted previously for the arrival of the sun at the hill that contained the Chinchero channel. Aveni (1981:308) addresses this inconsistency by proposing that there is an error in Cobo's document. His field research indicates that the thirteenth ceque of Cuntisuyu, which contained the Chinchincalla pillars, ran southwest of Cuzco. Aveni suggests that the Chinchincalla pillars may have marked the December solstice and the end, rather than the beginning, of the planting season.

The Equinox Passages

The Inca solar year began with a solstice and contained twelve months. There is also some tenuous evidence indicating that the Inca held ritual celebrations to mark the arrival of the sun at the equinoxes near 21 March and 21 September (11th or 12th in the Julian calendar). Polo de Ondegardo (1965c:101 [1571]) mentions that a mid-March (Julian calendar) ritual occurred in Cuzco and was timed "according to the moons which they count by observing the course of the sun through those columns or posts which they call *Saybas* [sayhuas] and that surround the City of Cuzco." Garcilaso de la Vega specifically states that the Inca witnessed and celebrated the equinox:

> They were also acquainted with the equinoxes, which they observed with great solemnity. At the March equinox they reaped the maize in the fields of Cuzco with great rejoicing and celebrations, especially on the terrace of Collcampata, which was like the garden of the sun. At the September equinox they held one of the four principal festivals of the Sun, called Citua Raimi. . . .
>
> To ascertain the time of the equinox they had splendidly carved stone columns erected in the squares or courtyards before the temples of the Sun. When the priests felt that the equinox was approaching, they took careful daily observations of the shadows cast by the columns. The columns stood in the middle of a very large circular enclosure filling the whole extent of the squares or spaces. Across the middle of the enclosure a line was drawn from east to west by a cord, the two ends being established by long experience. They could follow the approach of the equinox by the shadow the column cast on this line, and when the shadow fell exactly along the line from sunrise to sunset and at midday the sun bathed all sides of the column and cast no shadow at all, they knew that that day was the equinox. They then decked the columns with all the flowers and aromatic herbs they could find, and placed the throne of the Sun on them, saying that on that day the Sun was seated on the column in all his full light. (Garcilaso de la Vega 1966:117 [1609: Vol. 1, Bk. 2, Ch. 22]; translation modified)[31]

In this passage, Garcilaso de la Vega accurately describes the straight east-west motion of a gnomon's shadow on the equinox (Figure 1a).[32] He then provides a cultural context for these events by linking the March equinox with the maize harvest celebration, and the September equinox with the Citua Raymi festival.[33] It is commonly noted, however, that sections of Garcilaso de la Vega's chronicle are inaccurate and that his writings should be used with caution. Furthermore, he could not have seen the columns in question himself, since the church of Santo Domingo was already constructed over part of the Coricancha by the time he was born.

Garcilaso de la Vega continues his description of Inca astronomy

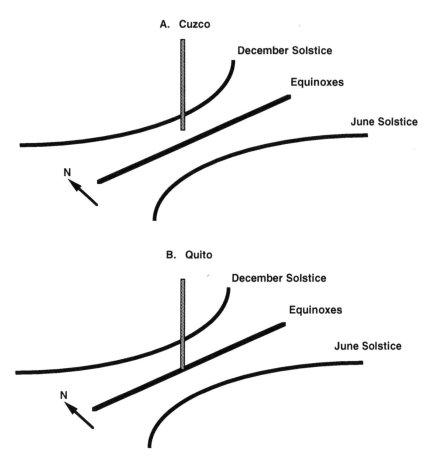

Figure 1. The shadows cast by a vertical gnomon on the solstices and equinoxes. As the sun moves across the sky, the shadow of a gnomon traces a path across the ground. Garcilaso de la Vega claimed that the Inca in Cuzco "knew that the day was the equinox" when the shadow cast by a column traversed a straight east-west line. The Inca also knew that on the equinox in Quito the sun passed directly overhead, casting no shadow at noon. Garcilaso de la Vega further claimed that for this reason the columns in Quito "were held in the greatest veneration."

by saying that when the Inca traveled toward Quito, the form of the shadow cast by the gnomon changed:

> It is worthy of remark that the Inca kings and their *amautas,* or philosophers, discovered as they extended their provinces that the nearer they approached the equator, the smaller was the shadow cast by the column

at midday. They therefore venerated more highly the columns that were nearer to the city of Quito, and were especially devoted to those of that city itself and in its neighborhood as far as the sea, where the sun is plumb, as bricklayers say, and shows no shadow at all at midday. For this reason they were held in greater veneration, it being thought that they afforded the Sun the seat he liked best, since there he sat straight up and elsewhere on one side. (Garcilaso de la Vega 1966:117 [1609: Vol. 1, Bk. 2, Ch. 22]; translation modified)[34]

Garcilaso de la Vega noted that governor Sebastián de Belaloázar had probably destroyed those columns in the Quito region in an effort to prevent idolatry. Although Garcilaso de la Vega never visited Quito, he notes correctly that the date when the sun passes through the zenith approaches the equinox as one journeys from Cuzco toward Quito (Figure 1b), and that on the equator a vertical object will cast no shadow at noon of the day of an equinox. Though Zamorano's almanac of 1585 includes nothing on shadow casting, the use of sundials was common practice in Europe, and it is possible that parts or all of this account were influenced by Western perceptions. Yet, it should be mentioned that while a sixteenth-century European astronomer would have understood the link between latitude and the dates of the zenith passage (when a column would cast no shadow at noon), this information would not have been part of any Western knowledge that Garcilaso de la Vega could have casually acquired.

Montesinos also provides information on Inca observations of the equinox. In the following description he suggests, as does Garcilaso de la Vega, that the Inca observed the equinoxes, and that the equinoxes and the solstices were used to divide the year into four equal parts:

This king was very wise and a great astrologer. He found the equinoxes, which the Indians call *illaris*, and, for this reason, they call the month of May *Quilla Toca Corca*, or, as we should say, vernal equinox. And they call September *Camay Tupac Corca*, which is the autumnal equinox. Thus he divided the ordinary year into four parts and seasons, in conformity with the four points of the solstices and equinoxes. (Montesinos 1920:53 [1630: Ch. 12])[35]

Since much of the information presented in Montesinos' chronicle differs radically from that of his contemporaries, it is difficult to evaluate the reliability of his writings. In addition, this particular passage is perplexing because Montesinos errs in stating that the vernal equinox occurs in May, rather than in March.

Finally, the relatively late work of the Augustinian Antonio de la Calancha (1981:850 [1638: Bk. 2, Ch. 12]), *Corónica moralizada del Orden de San Augustín en el Perú* (Moralized chronicle of the Order of Saint Augustine in Peru), mentions that the Inca observed the equinoxes with the shadow cast by two pillars placed in the Temple of the Sun. However, Calancha, who drew data from a number of sources, provides no further details, suggesting that this information was based on his own reading of Garcilaso de la Vega.

Summary and Discussion

In the time of the Inca, farmers took note of the annual motion of the sun along the horizon, as they do today. However, the historical materials on the solar astronomy of the Inca describe a more developed system for marking solar motion in open and elaborate public ceremonies. It is evident that some pillars were built on the hills surrounding the city of Cuzco to record the movement of the sun from solstice to solstice. To envision such a system the annual movement of the sun must be understood, both in time and on the horizon. Constructing it requires an understanding that could only have been attained by someone who systematically monitored the sun.

The Cuzco solar pillars must have been of considerable size, since they were visible from a distance of two to three leagues. They also must have been well constructed, as they remained standing for at least one hundred years after the conquest. The number, locations, and spacing of these pillars are neither consistently nor systematically presented in the surviving accounts. Furthermore, the range of solar events that the pillars recorded has not been clearly established. Some documents suggest that besides marking the December and June solstices, pillars were used to divide the solar year into twelve months, and that they marked the beginning, and perhaps the end, of the planting season.

Within the diverse descriptions provided by the early documents from Peru concerning the Cuzco solar pillars, some conclusions can be reached. At least one set of pillars stood northwest of Cuzco on Picchu. The exact number of pillars on this hill, however, is open to interpretation. Cobo, in his description of the eighth ceque of Chinchaysuyu, lists two pillars on Picchu. It seems more likely that a total of four existed, since Betanzos, the Anonymous Chronicler, and Garcilaso de la Vega describe four pillars. The function of the Picchu pillars also remains open to debate. Betanzos and Garcilaso de la Vega imply that their primary function was recording the solstices, while Cobo and the Anonymous Chronicler indicate that they marked a maize planting ritual in August.

Many of the Cuzco chroniclers mention that the Inca used pillars to define the December and June solstices, yet few precisely locate these pillars. A section of Cobo's chronicle, probably based on information collected by Polo de Ondegardo nearly a century earlier, provides some information on the positions of the Cuzco pillars by placing them within a system of shrines. Besides confirming that there was a set of pillars on Picchu, Cobo indicates that there were two pillars on the hill of Quiancalla used to mark the beginning of summer. Furthermore, he states that there were two additional pillars on the hill of Chinchincalla. His claim that these pillars marked the time to plant may have been a transcription error, as suggested by Aveni, or could simply indicate that he received erroneous information. From these various accounts it can be proposed that there were at least eight pillars on the western horizon of Cuzco: two marking a "summer" solstice on Quiancalla, four on Picchu (two of which marked the time to plant), and two on Chinchincalla. Yet, information contained in Betanzos, Polo de Ondegardo, and Cobo indicate that there may have been fourteen pillars on the horizon of Cuzco, and Garcilaso de la Vega mentions a total of sixteen.

From where in Cuzco were the solar pillars observed? This is difficult to answer since the documents provide little information on the point or points from which the Inca witnessed these solar phenomena. The Anonymous Chronicler is unique in specifically mentioning that the sun was watched in August from the central plaza of Cuzco, as it set between the central pillars on Picchu. It should not, however, be assumed that all solar observations were made from the same point, and locations other than the central plaza must be considered possible observation sites.

Additional information indicates that the Inca may have watched and recorded the arrival of the sun at the equinox. References to equinoctial observations are found in Garcilaso de la Vega, Montesinos, and perhaps in Calancha and Polo de Ondegardo. Since the reliability of the first three of these authors is frequently questioned, the actual occurrence of equinoctial observations by the Inca is open to debate, though the importance of Citua Raymi, the September festival mentioned by Garcilaso de la Vega, is not.

While the overwhelming preponderance of the data describes solar observations using pillars to mark the horizon positions of specific sunrises and sunsets, several accounts suggest that shadow (or light) casting was also practiced. Nevertheless, Cieza de León's claim that the pillars on the hills were used for shadow casting may simply have been an assumption incautiously stated by this normally careful chronicler. Sarmiento de Gamboa describes the possible remains of gnomons near Cuzco, Garcilaso de la Vega records Inca observations made using shadows to define the day of the equinox and the zenith, and Guaman Poma de Ayala indicates in a number of different passages that the Inca cast light through windows or openings.[36] Furthermore, evidence that light and shadow casting activities may have been conducted by the Inca has been found at the sites of Machu Picchu and Pisac in the Urubamba River Valley near Cuzco (Dearborn and White 1983; Dearborn, Schreiber, and White 1987), as well as at Copacabana on the shore of Lake Titicaca (Trimborn 1959; Rivera Sundt 1984; Hyslop 1990). It is hardly surprising that there are fewer references to Inca shadow (or light) casting activities than to the use of horizon pillars. Because only a few people can participate in a firsthand experience of shadow (or light) casting, the number of possible sources of information on this practice is limited.

Why would a society incorporate a combination of horizon pillars and shadow (or light) casting techniques into their ritual practices? The physical limitations of each observation method suggest a resolution to this question. The use of columns or windows for monitoring the sun provides a highly accurate means of obtaining calendric information, but the size of useful gnomons is limited. The angular size of the sun reduces the sharpness of a shadow. Extending a gnomon in height results in a longer shadow, but one that becomes less distinct and fainter. Widening the gnomon will darken the center of the shadow, but the "edge" of the shadow is difficult to distinguish with precision. The limits on the useful size of gnomons restrict the number of people able to witness any particular event. In other words, it is difficult to build large gnomons that can be watched by numerous people and still give accurate calendric information. Because of their relatively small size, gnomons are not suitable for ceremonies which involve large-scale public participation; in fact, their use can, in certain cases, promote sacred or restricted components of astronomical knowledge (i.e., quite the reverse of public ritual).

The use of natural horizon features, or the construction of artificial horizon markers, allows temporal observations to be made. Depending on the distance and size of the markers, the sunrise or sunset on a specific date may be accurately witnessed by many people. With a distant horizon (e.g., 20 km), it is possible for a very large group to observe a precisely marked sunrise or -set. However, a structure to mark the horizon at such a distance must be extremely large (at least eight meters high for ideal observing conditions, and three to four times larger to be clearly visible against the sun). For such distant locations on the horizon, it is simplest to select a prominent horizon feature, and then locate a position from which the sunrise or -set can be seen against it on the chosen day.

From central Cuzco, most of the horizon is at a distance of two or three kilometers. Such a close horizon is necessary if the sun's rises or sets are to be marked by structures of modest size (four or five meters high). Structures of this size provide a prominent display, accurately marking a particular date, and are visible to a large number of people. The hierarchical grouping of pillars described by Betanzos and Garcilaso de la Vega, in which two large pillars flank two small ones, permits an even larger group to participate in the observations, while maintaining the temporal accuracy for the smaller group of centrally located observers.

In sum, horizon markers and gnomons form the basis for two different kinds of observatory experiences, and both may have been used by the Inca. Horizon markers are most logically used in conjunction with large public ceremonies, whereas light and shadow casting are best employed in smaller, more private activities. The construction of markers on the horizons of Cuzco indicates that the shared act of observing the sunrise and -set was of significant importance to the ruling Inca and his people during their various rituals in Cuzco. The entire population (including non-Inca residents) would have had some knowledge of their use, and hundreds, if not thousands, of people could have witnessed the arrival of the sun at the pillars on the Cuzco horizon.

3. The Year

IT IS NO COINCIDENCE THAT astronomical observations are used by many cultures to organize the year. The seasonal cycles that drive the rhythm of human subsistence and social activities are themselves driven by the apparent motion of the sun. While observations of flora and fauna may adequately define when a season has arrived, the ability to prepare for agricultural activities increases the available growing season and extends people's range into otherwise marginal areas. In the Andes, irrigation is used to begin planting well before the commencement of the rainy season. However, planting too early leads to a risk of crop failure from frost. Determining the time to plant requires knowing the length of the year and one's position in it. Astronomical observations also provide a fixed temporal structure for social activities essential to all societies. The major festivals of many cultures are correlated with the solstices, and other celebrations are frequently linked to the phases of the moon.[1] The appearance or disappearance of specific stars from the night sky has also been used to mark important ritual celebrations in the calendar. Within state societies, the coordination of the calendar by elites cedes them control over time and the major rituals of the society.

In the first section of this chapter we explore the question, Who watched the sky? The current evidence indicates that many Andean villages had specific individuals who watched the movements of the sun, moon, and stars for the benefit of the community. In the rest of the chapter, we discuss how the Inca calculated their year.[2] Historical sources suggest that the Inca used two separate methods for partitioning the year. The accounts originating nearer to the time of the conquest, such as those of Betanzos and Polo de Ondegardo, describe a sophisticated system based on fixed months—each approximately thirty days long—that were coordinated with regular solar observations. Later writers describe a calendar based on twelve consecutive lunar months, requiring the insertion of an intercalation month approximately every third year. Without this extra month, the calendar would rapidly lose phase with the seasons, shifting the planting festival into the heart of winter. As we will discuss, the simultaneous use of these calendar methods necessarily results in dates marked by particular sunsets shifting between lunar months.

Who Watched the Sky?

The Inca held large and elaborate ritual celebrations in and around Cuzco that included public observations of the sun. Coordinating the considerable preparation for these large ceremonies with the solar motion required precise timing, which suggests that the Inca may have supported a class of specialists who oversaw the scheduling and carried out the technical and ceremonial aspects of astronomical observations.

Various early colonial documents support the notion that the Inca, as well as other indigenous peoples of Peru, trained individuals to carefully observe the movements of the sun and the moon. The anonymous author of the Huarochirí manuscript, who wrote around 1608, provides a description and margin notes about officials that he calls *yanca*, who watched shadows cast by gnomons:[3]

> From early times these officiates were only one or two people, and, as for their title, it was *yanca*. The same title is used in all the villages. This man observes the course of the sun from a wall constructed with perfect alignment.
>
> When the rays of the sun touch this calibrated wall, he <crossed out:> [proclaimed] to the people, "Now we must go"; or if they don't, he'd say, "Tomorrow is the time." (*Huarochirí Manuscript* 1991:72 [ca. 1608])

Francisco Avila, the priest who collected this manuscript, made notes in its margin. He amplifies the term *yanca*, saying, "The master is called *yanca*." He also provides his understanding of how the wall was used to mark the course of the sun: "That is, the shadow that the wall casts in the sun."

An alternative description of how such a wall was used in the region of Huarochirí is contained in the Carta Annua for 1609 in the Jesuit archives of the Vatican (Taylor 1987:93):

And though the month is known, the precise day is not. To know when
it is (the date), the Yañac sits in a particular place, and waits for the sun
to rise. He sees if it appears over a certain part of a hill that they have
marked. When the sun arrives at this marker, it gives notice to these
officials.⁴

This 1609 report describes the Yañac (or yanca?) choosing a location
from which, on the date of interest, the sun could be seen to rise behind a prominent horizon feature. This suggests the use of horizon
markers similar to those of Cuzco. Whether shadows were used, as
suggested by the Huarochirí manuscript, or horizon markers, as described in the Carta Annua for 1609, these two sources confirm that
even in village settings, observations were carried out by specialists.

Evidence suggesting that there was a class of Andean specialists
whose responsibility was to interpret the movements of the heavens
is also provided by Guaman Poma de Ayala (1980:829 [1615:883
(897)]), who includes a drawing of a so-called Inca astrologer in his
1615 chronicle (Figure 2). The man is shown walking along on a
trail with the sun and moon above him.⁵ Additional information
provided by Guaman Poma de Ayala (1980:210, 830 [1615:235 (237),
884 (898)]) indicates that windows may have been used for light
casting in calculating time. Again, the limited access to such activities suggests use by a small group of skilled observers.

There is also evidence to suggest that quipus were used to record
years and months. Guaman Poma de Ayala's astrologer is shown
carrying a quipu (Figure 2). Elsewhere in his chronicle Guaman
Poma de Ayala (1980:331 [1615:358 (361)]) describes what he calls a
"secretary" and states that during Inca times they were called *quilla
uata quipoc,* or "quipu readers [for] months [and] years" (Figure 3).
Other studies (Nordenskiöld 1925; Zuidema 1977a, 1988a) have
noted the fact that these devices would have provided an excellent
means to record calendrical information.

An examination of Andean traditions in stellar astronomy presented in Chapter 5 shows a popular belief in the power of astronomical objects over the health and propagation of llamas and other
animals. There is also a documentary link between the Pleiades and
the cultivation of corn. These beliefs, and the importance of successful agricultural activity, may have led to the development of local experts or folk astronomers like those described by Guaman
Poma de Ayala, the Huarochirí manuscript, and the Carta Annua
for 1609. With the development of an Inca state religion dedicated
to the sun, such experts would have evolved into a true class of
specialists.

Figure 2. An Inca astrologer. Guaman Poma de Ayala (1980:829 [1615: 883 (897)]) depicts an Inca astrologer carrying a quipu.

Figure 3. An Inca secretary. Guaman Poma de Ayala (1980:331 [1615: 358 (361)]) indicates that specialists in the Inca Empire may have kept track of years and months on quipus.

A Lunar Calendar

Dividing the year according to phases of the moon (i.e., a synodic or lunar calendar) was a common, if not universal, practice in the ancient world. Andean peoples are no exception, and there is rich linguistic evidence of their interest in lunar phases (Ziólkowski and Sadowski 1992:65, 111, 293–368). Gonçález Holguín's early dictionary provides numerous Quechua phrases describing the waxing and waning of the moon (1989:179, 268, 296 [1608]) and Urton's study of modern Andean astronomy (1981a:77–85) shows continued interest in lunar phases.

Accounts from Peru testify to the Inca's use of a twelve-month calendar based on the waxing and waning of the moon (Table 2).[6] A late document (ca. 1608) commissioned by the descendants of Paullu Inca incorporates an account purported to be from a 1542 inquiry (Duviols 1979; Urton 1990:43–46), in which four indigenous informants, said to be *quipucamayocs* (quipu keepers) for the Inca, were questioned (Callapiña, Supno, y otros Quipucamayos 1974 [1542/1608]). The informants describe the use of a calendar with twelve lunar months:

> The years and months that make the count, are lunar months and years, making every month from the new moon, and there are twelve of these months to a year, giving every month its name.[7]

This 1542 account seems consistent with Cieza de León's statement that "they know the revolutions the sun makes and the waxing and waning of the moon," as well as his notation that "they counted the year by this and the year consists of twelve months by their calculations." It is also consistent with the much later description by Molina, who also began months on new moons. The 1542 account contrasts, however, with the chronicles of Betanzos and Polo de Ondegardo that describe the use of a purely solar calendar in the imperial capital. If accurate, the 1542 account suggests that a lunar calendar was used by the people during the imperial period, and that its use survived the collapse of the empire, continuing into the colonial era.

Molina (1989:66 [ca. 1575]) describes a year that begins with a new moon within a few days of mid-May (near the 25th of May in the Gregorian calendar). His description (Molina 1989:112 [ca. 1575]) of the eighth month, Camayquilla (December/January), indicates that the fifteenth day of this month was a full moon, requiring the month to have begun with a new moon. This account is inconsistent with the use of fixed thirty-day months as mentioned by Be-

tanzos, and it requires a purely lunar calendar in which each month
starts with a new moon.[8] As the lunar phase on any particular date
varies, Molina's account can be correct only for a particular year,
possibly not even one that he witnessed personally.[9]

While Molina (1989:66 [ca. 1575]) and Diego Fernández (1963:
86–87 [1571: Pt. 2, Bk. 3, Ch. 10]) begin the year with the month
that includes the June solstice, this date cannot be accepted without reservation.[10] The Anonymous Chronicler (1906:156–160 [ca.
1570]) begins the year with Ayriuaquilla, or what he calls March,
the month of the equinox. Betanzos (1987:73–74 [1551: Ch. 15]),
Polo de Ondegardo (1965a:20–22 [1585: Ch. 7]), and Guaman Poma
de Ayala (1980:830 [1615:884 (898)]) indicate that the year started
around the December solstice.[11] Betanzos is specific in stating that
the months were not aligned with those of the Spanish but were
shifted because of this starting date. Cobo (1979:251–252 [1653:
Bk. 12, Ch. 37]) provides what is perhaps the clearest description of
the start of the year. He states that the Inca "identified our solar
year by observing the solstices and starting the year by the summer
solstice of this Antarctic Hemisphere, which falls on the twenty-
third day of December and ends at the same point where it started."
This confusion on the starting date of the year may be the result of
attempts to impose a European concept on an Andean activity. The
year is an astronomical cycle, for which a beginning and end point
is an ad hoc choice. Arbitrarily defining one point in this cycle as
the beginning is useful in counting years, but on this topic Cobo
(1956:142–143 [1653: Bk. 12, Ch. 37]) writes:

> Because they neither counted the years of their lives nor the length of
> their achievements, nor had they any fixed point in time from which to
> measure events, like we count ours from the birth of Our Lord Jesus
> Christ, nor was there ever an Indian, nor is there hardly any one today,
> who knows how old he is, nor much less how much (time) has passed
> since some memorable event occurred here. What they are used to re-
> spond when some one asks about past things, like what happened more
> than four or six years (ago), is that happened ñaupapacha, which means
> in past times; and they give the same response to events of twenty years
> past and to those of one hundred and a thousand, except when the thing
> is very ancient, they make it understood with a certain tone and weight-
> ing of the words.[12]

If counting the years was not a significant activity to Andean peoples, the confusion over when the year began may be related to the
problem that the period defined by twelve lunar months is not com-
mensurate with the length of the solar year.

A Calendar of Solar Years and Lunar Months

The year and seasons are demarcated by the return of the sun to a specific solstice point every 365.25 days. A full lunar month, defined by the changing phases of the moon, is equal to 29.5 days. Twelve lunar months equal 354 days, eleven days short of a solar year. The following section examines how the Inca may have addressed this asynchronization of lunar months within a solar year.

The Spaniards as well as the Inca recognized that a year of twelve lunar months falls short of a solar year. Garcilaso de la Vega (1966: 116 [1609: Vol. 1, Bk. 2, Ch. 22]) wrote that "although they [the Inca] divided the year into twelve moons, they did not know how to allow for the difference of eleven days by which the solar year exceeds the normal lunar year." Garcilaso de la Vega then claims that the Inca relied entirely on the movement of the sun for dividing one year from another, describing the observation of the solstices using four towers on a hill. After three years, the annual eleven-day excess between twelve lunar months and a solar year accumulates to about thirty days. This results in the periodic need to add an intercalation month to maintain the alignment between the lunar calendar and the solar year. Among those many ancient societies that used intercalation months to synchronize the solar and lunar calendars, this extra month was most frequently added immediately before a solstice. There is tantalizing evidence that such an intercalation period was used by the Inca; Gonçález Holguín (1989:48 [1608]), for example, provides an appropriate term—*Dias interpolados. Allca allca punchaucuna*—in his dictionary. Unfortunately, as noted by Ziólkowski and Sadowski (1992:95), Gonçález Holguín does not mention the exact number of days which made up this period, or when it was applied. As an example of this type of calendar, Ziólkowski and Sadowski (1992:167–196) have developed and presented a possible reconstruction of the Inca calendar between A.D. 1500 and 1572, and give an excellent discussion of the uncertainties. In their reconstruction, there are twelve consecutive lunar months, each beginning on a new moon. Following Molina's account in which the first month of the year includes the June solstice, they insert an extra (thirteenth) month in May/June when necessary to maintain the phase of the solar year.

Even with an intercalation month, the use of twelve consecutive lunar months within a solar year causes further complications. Solstices, and festivals linked with the passage of the sun between pillars, for example, in mid-March or August, will shift between lunar months. An illustration of this calendrical shift can be shown using information provided in Molina's account. In the fifteenth century, there were 182.4 days between the June and December solstices. This is more than five days longer than the 177 days in six lunar months (composed of 29.5 days each). Accordingly, if the year began with a new moon on 25 May, as suggested by Molina, then the month of Capac Raymi ended four days before the solstice. This is inconsistent with the traditional association of the December solstice with the month of Capac Raymi. The relationship between the phases of the moon and the earth's rotation around the sun dictates that a shift by as much as five days will occur approximately every six years. A five-day difference between the sunrise and sunset positions and the horizon locations marked by solar pillars for the December solstice would be small, but observable. The asynchronization between festivals associated with lunar months and the solar motion cannot be avoided simply by aligning the lunar and solar years at the December solstice, following the more common claim in the chronicles of Betanzos, Polo de Ondegardo, and Guaman Poma de Ayala. In these cases, it is the June solstice and the lunar month containing Inti Raymi that lose synchronization.

This asynchronization also complicated the Inca solar observation that marked the beginning of the planting season. According to the Anonymous Chronicler, a sunset observation was made from a stone (the usnu) in the central plaza of Cuzco, and this event occurred in the lunar month of Tarpuyquilla (which he associates with August). If the lunar count started with the first new moon following the December solstice, then the eighth month, Tarpuyquilla, began sometime between 17 July and 16 August and ended twenty-nine or thirty days later. Regardless of where the pillars were located on Picchu, the sun would not always have arrived there during the eighth lunar month, but depending on the year and the exact pillar location, the sun could have set behind these markers in the seventh or ninth month.[13] The problem of being unable to observe a marked sunset in a particular lunar month was intrinsic once the Inca began formally marking more than one sunset/sunrise position. One means of resolving this dilemma is the insertion of an intercalation month whenever necessary to maintain alignment with the solar observations, instead of at only one time of year.

A Calendar of Fixed Solar Months

Both Betanzos and Polo de Ondegardo suggest that the Inca developed a more evolved calendar system than one based on twelve lunar months. These writers imply that the Inca used a calendar that

included months which were fixed and determined by solar observations. As Betanzos and Polo de Ondegardo are among the earliest
chroniclers with direct experience of imperial Inca practices, it is
important to examine their statements concerning the year.

Betanzos (1987:73–74 [1551: Ch. 15]) states that the Inca established a year in which the months have fixed lengths of thirty days.
In twelve months, such a calendar shifts phase with the moon by
six days, or nearly a quarter moon. Betanzos indicates that the Inca
established four pillars marking sunrises and four more marking
sunsets on the horizons of Cuzco in order to resolve the difference
between the length of months and the solar year. Furthermore, this
long-time resident of Cuzco suggests that sunrises and sunsets were
observed for each solar month of the year, stating that ". . . every
morning and afternoon of each month of the year he also observed
the sun watching for the time to plant and to harvest and also when
the sun set, and he watched the moon when it was new and full and
waning" (Betanzos 1987:73–74 [1551: Ch. 15]).

More direct evidence that a fixed solar calendar was used in
Cuzco is offered by Polo de Ondegardo: "Each moon or month had
its monument or pillar around Cuzco, where the Sun reached that
month" (1965b:20–22 [1585: Ch. 7]). In another passage, Polo de
Ondegardo (1965c:101 [1571]) reports that "in the middle of March,
according to the moons which they count by observing the course of
the sun through those columns or posts which they call Saybas
[sayhuas] and which surround the City of Cuzco, the Inca divided
them [young women]." Cobo (1990:27–28 [1653: Bk. 13, Ch. 5])
specifically states that there were fourteen markers called Sucanca
near Cuzco that were used to calculate the months of the year. He
refers to these pillars again in a section of his chronicle that discusses offerings made to the huacas of Cuzco:

> Apart from these daily sacrifices, other general sacrifices, including
> prayers and fasting, were made to the Sun at specified times. In particu-
> lar, each month when the Sun reached the markers or posts that desig-
> nated the months sacrifices were made to him. (Cobo 1990:114 [1653:
> Bk. 13, Ch. 21]).[14]

Guaman Poma de Ayala (1980:830 [1615:884 (898)]) also alludes to
monthly solar positions, writing that "each month has its own seat
in each degree of heaven."

Defining twelve individual "months" by sunset (or sunrise) locations on a single horizon requires marking seven locations: two for
the solstice positions and five others to calibrate the monthly sun-

sets between them.[15] If twin pillars were used, then the fourteen pillars described by Cobo would be required. The position of these pillars could easily be established to divide the year evenly into twelve months of thirty or thirty-one days. If such a solar-based calendar existed during imperial times, it would have eliminated the occasional "shift" between the observable solar motion and the festivals tied to specific lunar months that is inherent in a calendar system incorporating twelve lunar months into a solar year. Furthermore, in such a solar-based calendar, a lunar month could be unambiguously associated with each fixed solar month by observing the first new moon after the sun passed its marker. In such a system, a new moon takes on the name of the solar month in which it occurs. Every three years, on average, a second new moon would rise while the sun was moving between the horizon markers of a thirty-day solar month. The appearance of this second new moon would then begin an intercalation month, maintaining the alignment of the solar and lunar calendars.

The Sidereal Lunar Calendar Hypothesis

All historical accounts of Inca lunar months are consistent with synodic months (i.e., months based on the phases of the moon), and there are numerous references that explicitly indicate that the Inca paid close attention to the waxing and waning of the moon. This lunar calendar was phased with the solar year—at least with a solstice—and during imperial times there may have been a calendar based fully on the motion of the sun. In addition to these two calendrical systems, Zuidema (1982c) has proposed a third type of calendar that was linked with the sidereal period of the moon and that was used in conjunction with the ceque system. If true, the popular use of a sidereal calendar would make the Inca extremely unusual, if not unique, in human history, as there are no other known cases of its use in this manner. Zuidema's sidereal calendar model has been accepted by some researchers and used in interpreting pre-Inca remains (Anders 1986a, 1986b), although it has been sharply criticized by others (Sadowski 1989a; Ziólkowski 1989b).

The "sidereal period" is the time required for a celestial body to move once around the sky with respect to the fixed stars. It is useful for calculating the stellar background that an object will have (the appearance or disappearance of the moon or planets depends on the synodic, not the sidereal, periods). Over a thousand years before the Inca, astronomers in Europe and the Middle East interested in predicting lunar and planetary motions against the background of stars had identified these periods for the moon and visible planets. The sidereal period of the moon—27 1/3 days—is easily observed. If the moon was seen to pass through the Pleiades early one evening, it would next be seen near these stars late at night twenty-seven days later, but it will not have the same phase (new, full, etc.).[16] It must travel over two more days to reach the phase with which it started at the beginning of the observation period. Passage of twelve sidereal lunar months requires 328 days, a figure coincident with the number of huacas presented in one part of Cobo's account of the Cuzco ceque system.

Combining this numerical coincidence with a large body of circumstantial ethnohistoric information, Zuidema hypothesizes that the Inca used a 328-day calendar, organizing the year into twelve sidereal lunar months. This is followed by a 37-day intercalation period to maintain the phase with the solar year. He associates this 37-day period with the time when the sun is too close to the Pleiades for the latter to be visible.[17] In imperial Inca times, this "disappearance" of the Pleiades occurred around 13 May. The exact duration depends on horizon altitude, the phase of the moon at that time, and local atmospheric conditions; thus, it changes from year to year. While it is certainly possible for an observer to detect the reappearance of the Pleiades after a period short of 37 days, the choice of a specific number of days is arbitrary, and must be consensual.

The hypothesis that the Inca used a calendar composed of sidereal lunar months is built on a complex synthesis of indirect information gathered from diverse chroniclers. Ziólkowski (1989a) summarizes the historic material used to support the sidereal-lunar-month-calendar hypothesis and, with Sadowski (1989a), considers its numerous difficulties and inconsistencies. We simply point out that all historic references to months found in the early colonial sources of Peru are consistent with, or require, the use of a twelve-synodic-month calendar that is synchronized to the year through solar observations. In the absence of a single clear historic reference to the sidereal period of the moon, or relating the observation of the moon to a specific stellar group, the use of a sidereal calendar by the Inca remains highly speculative.

Summary and Discussion

Undoubtedly the range of skills attributed to Andean sky watchers varied considerably. As suggested by the Huarochirí manuscript, the Carta Annua for 1609, and Guaman Poma de Ayala, each village held individuals who watched the rising and setting positions of celestial objects, and possibly the shadow or light cast by different objects. From these observations they chronicled the passing of the year and provided a temporal matrix for the village rituals. Andean villages also used a twelve-month calendar based on the waxing and waning of the moon. The asynchronization of lunar months within a solar year resulted, however, in the need to observe the sun in order to add an intercalation month for maintaining alignment with the solar year.

During the period of imperial Inca rule in the Andes, it is likely that the commoners used a simple lunar calendar, along with a few independent stellar and solar observations, to organize their year. In the capital of an empire, however, rituals and the means through which they are scheduled were given greater significance. The ability to mark and measure the year lends authority to the state and its ruling elite. Through astronomy the ruling class can define and regulate the ritual calendar of the capital and the empire as a whole. In the latter period of the Inca Empire, there may have been a movement away from the use of the traditional lunar calendar and an attempt by the ruling Inca to establish a new calendar system based on calendar months fixed and determined by solar observations. The development of such a system would have led to a further centralization of ritual authority in the hands of the elite. It would also have strengthened the perception that the elite maintained special relations with the sun. As only the earliest chroniclers describe the existence of a fixed solar calendar, we speculate that this was a Cuzco-based imperial practice that fell quickly into disuse as the Spaniards exerted control over the indigenous Andean populations. Once the practice of regular solar observation ended and the established markers were abandoned, Andean populations would have regressed to the lunar calendar that had been the basis of their year for millennia.

4. Seats of the Sun:
The Solar Pillars of Cuzco

THE SOLAR PILLARS OF CUZCO were monuments tying social activities on earth to celestial activities in the sky. These pillars, and the locations from which they were observed, provide students of Inca society with a foundation for understanding the Inca calendar and its uses. As early as 1609, Garcilaso de la Vega (1966:117 [1609: Vol. 1, Bk. 2, Ch. 22]) suggested that the Inca observation points in Cuzco could be rediscovered by observing sunrises and sunsets against the ruined remains of the solar pillars. Rowe (1946:327 n. 38) made a similar suggestion centuries later: "It should not be difficult to locate the ruins of the 'calendar towers' on the skyline of Cuzco, and to make observations as a check on the chroniclers." Locations in central Cuzco where large gatherings were held, and from which the pillars might have been observed, include Haucaypata (now the Plaza de Armas), as well as the flat areas inside and just in front of the Coricancha and Limacpampa. Other areas of important gatherings around the city of Cuzco include Sacsahuaman, Puquín Cancha, and the region of Mantocalla. We tested each of these locations in this study of Inca sky watching.

From any fixed location, the place on the horizon at which the sun rises or sets shifts in a cyclic manner as the sun follows its annual path around the sky. Accordingly, multiple dates can be determined from the same location by observing the progress of the setting (or rising) sun as it moves along the horizon. Alternatively, on different dates, the sun can be observed to rise or set behind a particular horizon position by changing the location from which the observation is made. Take, for example, the pillars that existed on Picchu. The Anonymous Chronicler indicates that the two inner pillars of a set of four marked a specific sunset in August as viewed from Haucaypata. However, other authors suggest that the pillars on

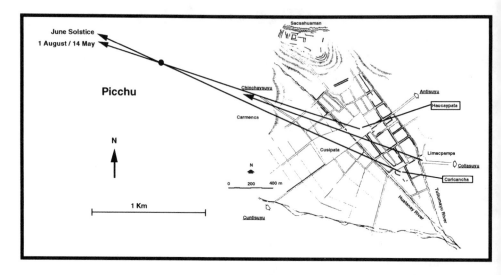

Map 4. A point on Picchu as observed from the Plaza de Armas, Limacpampa, and the Coricancha. The date on which the sun sets behind a spot on Picchu depends on the location from which the observation is made. A pillar that marks the June solstice when viewed from the Coricancha identifies a day in August (or May) when observed from the center of the Plaza de Armas (Haucaypata). Viewing the same pillar from Limacpampa marks dates near 23 May and 23 July.

Picchu defined the sunset on the June solstice. These are not necessarily contradictory statements, since by changing observation locations in Cuzco both could be true. To illustrate this point, we have marked the position of a small foundation on Picchu on Map 4. The location of this foundation marks the dates of the 14 May and 1 August sunsets as viewed from the center of the Plaza de Armas.[1] From one end of Limacpampa, the location of an important Inca maize harvest ceremony and a part of the Capac Raymi ceremony, this foundation records the sunset on 23 May and 23 July. Moving the observation point to within the courtyard of the Coricancha, however, converts this marker into a fiducial for the June solstice sunset. The fact that a single horizon fiducial could have marked a number of different solar events may explain certain apparently contradictory statements in the chronicles. Although it may be speculative, we encourage additional historical and archaeological research on this topic. Furthermore, it is possible that pillars were constructed around Inca centers other than Cuzco. Additional archaeological investigations could test whether markers were constructed in areas where the ruling Inca resided when absent from Cuzco for extended periods. Such a dynamic system would have allowed the ruling Inca to perform his public ritual duties while on campaign.

Recent archaeological and astronomical research in Cuzco has yielded new data on the solar pillars and their observation points. These recent data will be examined in this chapter in conjunction with information from the Spanish chronicles, and their importance in assessing current models of Inca astronomy will be explored.

What Did Inca Pillars Look Like?

Determining what the pillars of the Cuzco might have looked like is a difficult task, since the chroniclers provide differing descriptions of them and their foundations have yet to be found. Nevertheless, some insight into their form and dimension may be provided by a set of surviving Inca markers on a ridge above the town of Urubamba, approximately thirty-five aerial kilometers from Cuzco.[2] These twin markers can easily be viewed three to four kilometers away as small protuberances against the skyline. The towers are 36 meters apart and have been built on a terraced section of the ridge (Photo 6). One of the towers has been repaired in modern times, while the other is well preserved and displays good Inca stonework. The well-preserved tower is rectangular and measures 3.3 meters long, 1.5 meters wide, and 4.5 meters tall. While the function of these markers is not known, aspects of their size, shape, and separation are similar to those of the solar pillars of Cuzco as described by Betanzos, Garcilaso de la Vega, and Cobo. We present them as useful examples of what Inca solar pillars might have looked like.

The Pillars of Picchu

Spanish accounts consistently refer to a set of solar pillars on Picchu, the hill that forms the northwest horizon from the central sector of the imperial city, yet there is considerable discrepancy in the recounting of the organization and location of these solar markers (Figure 4). In some chronicles, the pillars are said to have recorded the beginning of individual months. This would require marking three to four positions on Picchu, depending on the locations from which observations were made. In other accounts, the Picchu pillars are presented as marking a solstice, and in still others, they are described as recording an August planting date.

Betanzos specifically describes four markers on what seems to be

Photo 6. The Twin Pillars of Urubamba. A set of Inca pillars stands on the shoulder of a high ridge above the town of Urubamba. The pillar on the left is well preserved, the one on the right has been reconstructed in modern times.

Picchu. He states that the outer pillars were larger than the inner ones and that they stood approximately five meters apart (two and a half brazas). The smaller inner pillars were separated by only one meter (half a braza). Depending on the observation location in Cuzco, which is not specified by Betanzos, the sun sets over Picchu from late March through late September. If pillars marked a sunset for each month of the year as Betanzos and Polo de Ondegardo suggest, there could have been four pillars on Picchu.[3] Their positions, however, would need to be spread along seven hundred meters of ridge, not the five meters described by Betanzos.

Picchu is approximately 1.9 km from the Plaza de Armas (Haucaypata) and 2.4 km from the Coricancha. The five-meter spacing of the outer pillars given by Betanzos results in an angular separation of 0.15 degrees as seen from the plaza and 0.12 degrees from the Coricancha. The separation of the inner pillars would appear to be 0.02 to 0.03 degrees, again depending on the location from which they

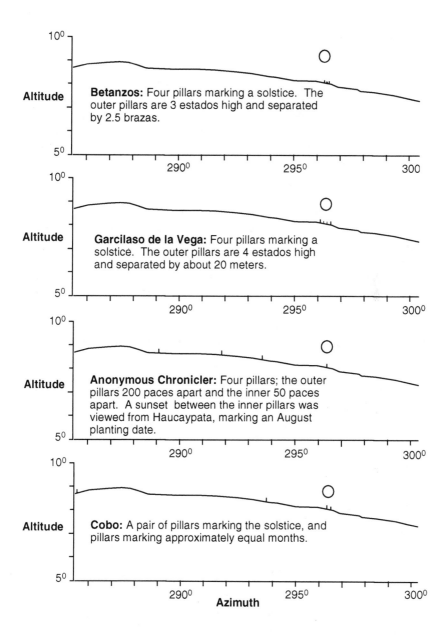

Figure 4. The pillars of Picchu. The sun is shown next to the pillars on Picchu, as seen from the region of the Coricancha. These hypothetical reconstructions are based on the accounts of Betanzos (1551), Garcilaso de la Vega (1609), the Anonymous Chronicler (ca. 1570), and Cobo (1653).

were viewed. The pillar distance furnished by Betanzos is extremely narrow, given that the diameter of the sun is 0.5 degrees.

At the high horizon of Picchu, the strong glare of the sun makes it difficult to look at until it is nearly set. The 0.02-to-0.03-degree separation of Betanzos' inner pillars would have been difficult to observe, even against the last gleam of the sun. Nevertheless, an observer situated in just the right spot in central Cuzco would be able to see the sun set behind the inner pillars for approximately two days before and two days after the June solstice, during which time there is no perceptible motion of the sun to a naked-eye observer. An observer would also see the sun pass one of the outer pillars four days before and four days after the solstice.

The measurements given by Betanzos render these monuments impractical for marking a series of monthly sunsets even if there were several groups of pillars. Only from about 31 May until 14 July is the motion of the sun slow enough that it would set between the pillars every year. Outside this range of dates, either the sun does not set over Picchu or its daily movement is so great (the sun moves 0.4 degrees per day along the horizon near the equinox) that there would be years when the sun would miss setting between the outer pillars entirely. In sum, although Betanzos provides information about and measurements of the horizon markers near Cuzco, there are practical reasons to question some of his details. On the basis of Betanzos' description, the pillars were too closely spaced to record the passage of months, even as observed from different positions. Furthermore, their separation was so narrow as to make them difficult for even an individual observer to use.

The spacing of six to seven meters between each pillar (or approximately twenty meters between the outer pillars) claimed by Garcilaso de la Vega is more practical than that proposed by Betanzos. The resulting angular separation of 0.6 degrees of the larger outer pillars nicely frames a setting sun. The inner towers would have been separated by 0.18 degrees, readily visible to an observer with good eyesight watching the last gleam of the sun. In this case, the sun would cross the outer pillar approximately eight days before and after the solstice. The separation of the inner pillars is sufficiently wide to permit their usage on a specific date, while also allowing a considerable number of people to simultaneously witness the sunset between the outer pillars. The separation distance given by Garcilaso de la Vega permits the outer pillars to be used to monitor solar motion anytime the sun sets behind Picchu. The spacing of the pillars, however, is too narrow for them to be used in marking a series of sunsets in consecutive months from a single location.

A substantially different view of these solar towers comes from the Anonymous Chronicler. He places the outer pillars two hundred paces apart and the inner ones at fifty-pace intervals. The Anonymous Chronicler also identified the location from which an August planting sunset was watched on Picchu: a stone called the "usnu" in Haucaypata, which he states was about the height of a man. According to Zuidema (1982b:205), who employed Roman, or two-step, paces to calculate the distance, the outer markers were approximately 350 meters apart and were separated from the inner pillars by approximately 70 meters.[4] The angular separation, as viewed from the plaza, would be about 10.5 degrees for the outer pillars and approximately 2.1 degrees for the inner ones. These separations are too close together for the pillars to mark the individual months when the sun sets over Picchu, and vastly too far apart for the determination of a precise date.

The spacing between the Picchu pillars, as described by the Anonymous Chronicler, is great enough to permit a large group of people to observe the sunset between them. For a small range of dates, the separation of the outer pillars is sufficient for everyone gathered in the plaza to see the sun set between these markers, while a slightly smaller group of people located within thirty meters of the usnu could see it set between the inner two markers. Since the relatively wide separation of the inner pillars would permit individuals at the usnu to see the sun set between them for a period of six to ten days, such observations would have been more ceremonial than useful in determining a specific date in the calendar year. But then, like a farmer's almanac, the pillars would have furnished a useful set of dates on which to begin planting.[5]

The Anonymous Chronicler wrote that the sun entered the inner pillars in August and that it marked the time to begin planting; but what did this writer mean by "August"? In a separate section of his document that reports on the months of the year, the Anonymous Chronicler (1906:158 [ca. 1570]) repeats his claim that the sun entered the pillars in August, and he notes that offerings were made to the usnu in September. However, the Anonymous Chronicler states that these events took place during the Inca lunar months that were most closely associated with the European months of August and September. In other words, when the Anonymous Chronicler noted that the sun set between the inner pillars of Picchu in August, he was referring to the eighth lunar month of the Inca calendar that most closely corresponded to a month beginning on 11 August (Gregorian calendar). If the lunar calendar began with the first new moon after the December solstice, the eighth Inca lunar month was

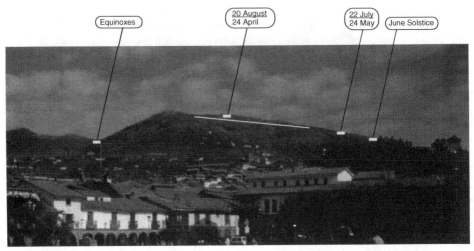

Figure 5. Picchu as viewed from the Plaza de Armas. By most accounts, four pillars were located on Picchu. They are said to mark a solstice, the beginning of individual months, or a date in August. The Anonymous Chronicler described the outer pillars as separated by two hundred paces and claimed that from the plaza, the sun was observed to set between the inner two pillars in the month of August.

not a fixed date but began between 17 July and 16 August and ended between 15 August and 25 September, depending on the lunar phases of any particular year. If the Anonymous Chronicler was claiming that the passage of the sun between the pillars always occurs in his month of August, then this event must have taken place between 10 August and 10 September. While the date referred to by the Anonymous Chronicler is quite uncertain, a day between 10 and 15 August will fall in the "correct" lunar month in most years (five out of six).

In Figure 5 we summarize the accounts of the pillars on Picchu. We show the approximate locations where horizon pillars would mark "solar" months—as seen from the Plaza de Armas—beginning at the June solstice sunset. While the Anonymous Chronicler claims the usnu was near the middle of the plaza, there is uncertainty concerning the exact size of the original plaza and, hence, the specific position of the usnu. To give an idea of how this uncertainty affects pillar positioning, we have indicated the result of moving plus or minus ten meters (or a total of twenty meters) from our observation position near the center of the modern plaza. This is approximately the distance offered in Garcilaso de la Vega's description of the pillars and about four times the separation of Betanzos' solar markers. In addition, we have shown the range of the horizon spanned by the two hundred paces (350 m) that the Anonymous Chronicler claimed separated the outer pillars.

Archaeologists, historians, and anthropologists have walked the slopes of Picchu looking for physical evidence of the Inca pillars. This search is quickly ending, not because of positive research results, but due to the increased construction activities on the hill. The lower third of the hill, including the important area of the June solstice sunset as seen from the Plaza de Armas, has been destroyed in recent years by the growing population of Cuzco. Furthermore, in the early 1990s several radio antennas were built near the summit of Picchu, obliterating much of the upper slope. On the summit of Picchu are several small stone foundations for crosses, and a thin scatter of Inca pottery (Photo 7). Since crosses and Inca ceramics can

Photo 7. The summit of Picchu (foreground), which rises above the city of Cuzco, holds several small stone foundations for crosses and a thin scatter of Inca pottery.

be found on the summits of many of the hills surrounding Cuzco, these remains alone are not evidence of the solar markers. Accordingly, we are pessimistic that physical remains of the Inca pillars on Picchu will be found. Their exact locations and the days that they marked will thus remain subject to speculation.

Chinchincalla and the December Solstice Sunset

Cobo's account of the ceque system indicates that a hill near Cuzco called Chinchincalla contained two markers used in solar observations. These pillars were the third huaca of the thirteenth ceque of Cuntisuyu (Cu. 13:3), and their general area can be deduced from the courses of other ceques in the system.[6] The fourteenth ceque of Cuntisuyu ended at a well-known shrine called Pantanaya (Cu. 14:4), which is a cleft hill where the roads of Chinchaysuyu and Cuntisuyu divide. Following the general systematics of Cobo's ceque account, the huacas of the thirteenth ceque of Cuntisuyu must be located to the southeast of the fourteenth. While little is known concerning the courses of the eleventh and twelfth ceques of Cuntisuyu, that of the tenth ceque, which traveled though Puquín Cancha (Cu. 10:2), a temple of the sun on Puquín Hill, and terminated at the summit of a hill called Viracochaurco (Cu. 10:4), has been documented (Bauer n.d.b). The huacas of the thirteenth ceque are to the northwest of this ceque. The tenth and the fourteenth ceques of Cuntisuyu demarcate an area southwest of Cuzco, which includes the hill of Killke and a ridge above a hamlet called Llamacancha, in which the huacas of the thirteenth ceque must be located (Map 5).

Further information concerning the location and function of the Chinchincalla pillars is provided by Cobo, who writes that when the sun reached them it was time to begin planting. By comparing the courses of Cu. 14 and Cu. 10, Aveni (1981:308–309) has determined that the thirteenth ceque of Cuntisuyu ran southwest of the city, and he proposes that the Chinchincalla pillars marked the December solstice sunset. A difficulty with this interpretation is Cobo's claim that the Chinchincalla pillars were linked to planting, an activity that begins in the Cuzco region in August and ends in December. Aveni addresses this inconsistency by implying that Cobo, or the original author of the material that Cobo copied, made an error and that Chinchincalla actually marked the time to conclude planting rather than the time to start it.[7] This proposition is supported by Guaman Poma de Ayala (1980:225 [1615:251 (253)]), who writes that "they [the Inca] begin to sow the maize up to the

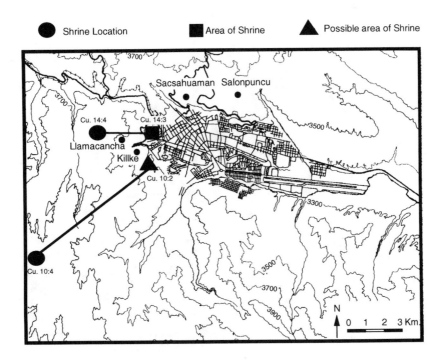

Map 5. The suggested courses of ceques Cu. 10 and Cu. 14. The region between these two ceques contains ceques Cu. 11, Cu. 12, and Cu. 13. The third shrine on Cu. 13 included a set of solar pillars.

month of January according to the clock and course of the sun and the temperature of the earth."[8]

Expanding on his Chinchincalla–December solstice hypothesis, Aveni (1981:308–309) has identified a region on the western slope of Killke where the December solstice sun set, as viewed from the Coricancha. The selection of the Coricancha as the observation point for the December solstice is a reasonable one since this temple represented the center of the ceque system, and Albornoz (1984:204 [ca. 1582]) indicates that at the time of the December solstice much of Capac Raymi was celebrated near it.

Part of our 1990 survey work focused on the area southwest of Cuzco in the area of Killke and the ridge above Llamacancha. This fieldwork identified a possible location for the Chinchincalla pillars on the western shoulder of Killke (Photo 8). This area contained several looters' pits, revealing the remains of a burial, a stone terrace approximately five meters long, and a light scatter of Inca pottery. Excavations were conducted at this site in 1992 to determine

Photo 8. Killke Hill as seen from the Coricancha. Fieldwork in 1990 identified looted burials on Killke near where the sun sets on the December solstice as seen from the Coricancha.

whether it once held one of the solar pillars as described by Cobo. Although no pillar foundations were identified, the test excavations did confirm that the end of the ridge contained several Inca period burials. These burials were composed of single individuals placed in stone-lined pits approximately one meter wide and ninety centimeters deep (Photo 9). Because of the looting, it was difficult to determine whether the burials had originally been visible on the surface.

The location of the burials marks a date in early December as viewed from the center of the Coricancha, and the December solstice as seen from the small plaza—traditionally called Intipata (Terrace of the Sun)—in front of the temple (Figure 6). To mark the December solstice sunset from the interior of the Coricancha, the pillars would have to have been situated approximately fifty meters up the slope from the burials. This area is currently under cultivation and shows no surface remains.[9]

Photo 9. Excavated Burials on Killke. The burials on Killke were composed of single individuals placed in stone-lined pits approximately one meter wide and ninety centimeters deep.

There is, however, another plausible location from which the Inca could have observed the December solstice sunset, one that requires a different position for the pillars of Chinchincalla (Cu. 13:3). The Anonymous Chronicler (1906:151 [ca. 1570]) indicates that from the usnu in Haucaypata the Inca watched the sun set behind pillars on the hill of Picchu during a specific evening in August. This date marked the beginning of the planting season. If the sun was watched from the central plaza of Cuzco in August to start planting, it is possible that it was watched from the same location during the December solstice to conclude planting. Depending on where the usnu was located in the plaza, the sun can be seen to set to the southwest of Cuzco along the hill above Llamacancha on 21 December (Figure 7). This hill is in the archaeologically defined region that contained the thirteenth ceque of Cuntisuyu, and marks an alternative location for Chinchincalla (Cu. 13:3).

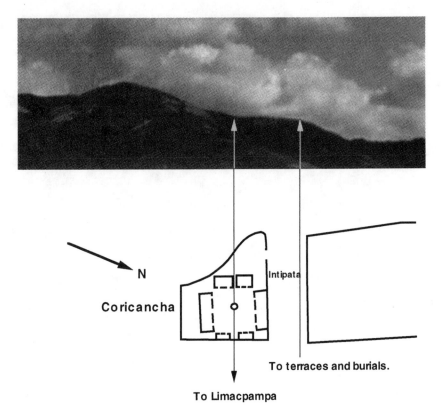

Figure 6. The location of the December solstice sunset as seen from the area of the Coricancha. The sun sets over Killke as seen from the Coricancha, Limacpampa, and Intipata.

Quiancalla and the June Solstice Sunset

The third set of solar towers specifically mentioned by Cobo was on a hill called Quiancalla [Quiangalla]. Cobo places these markers, the ninth shrine on the sixth ceque of Chinchaysuyu (Ch. 6:9), along the Yucay road. Cobo also notes that summer began when the sun reached these markers. He recognized that the December solstice is technically the beginning of summer—and the growing season—in the Andes. However, if Polo de Ondegardo was the original author of Cobo's ceque system account, summer refers to the June solstice and the beginning of the dry season.

There is no location in the Cuzco region currently bearing the name Quiancalla. This toponym, however, is mentioned in several

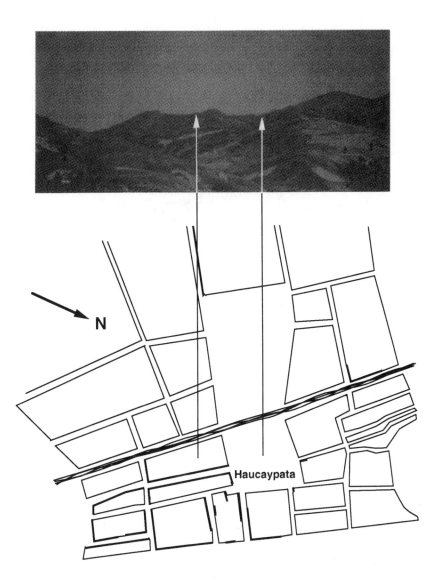

Figure 7. The location of the December solstice sunset as seen from the Plaza de Armas (Haucaypata). At this time, the sun sets over the area of Llamacancha.

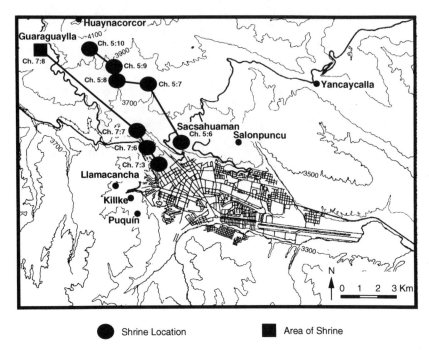

Map 6. The suggested courses of ceques Ch. 5 and Ch. 7. The region between these two ceques contains ceque Ch. 6. The ninth shrine on Ch. 6 included a set of solar pillars.

sixteenth-century land documents as being northwest of Cuzco in
an area intersected by the Inca road to Yucay (Archivo Departamental del Cuzco, Judicial Civil: Leg. 73, 1851: f. 1, 4v [1541]). The
general position of Quiancalla can be further clarified through the
courses of other Chinchaysuyu ceques (Bauer n.d.b). The course of
the fifth ceque of Chinchaysuyu is well documented as ending at a
small spring on the southern slope of Huaynacorcor Mountain, and
the seventh ceque of Chinchaysuyu is known to have projected from
Cuzco toward the small community of Guaraguaylla, near the base
of this mountain (Map 6). A large ridge in this region that descends
from the summit of Huaynacorcor toward the community has been
suggested as a possible area for the Quiancalla pillars, since it dominates the western horizon of the Cuzco Valley and the Inca road to
Yucay passed over it (Aveni 1981:309; Zuidema 1981c:168–169).

As viewed from central Cuzco, the approximate position for the
June solstice sunset on Quiancalla is problematic, since the ridge of
Huaynacorcor is too far north for the sun to be seen setting there on

any date. Accordingly, researchers have examined other locations in the Cuzco environs from which the June solstice sun sets behind the ridge of Huaynacorcor.

In considering from where Quiancalla might have been viewed, Zuidema (1981c:168–169) and Aveni (1981:309) proposed a hypothesis linking this huaca to several others described in Cobo's account of the Cuzco ceque system. They suggest that rather than viewing the June solstice sunset from central Cuzco, it may have been watched from the shrines of Chuquimarca (An. 3:4) and Mantocalla (An. 3:6). These shrines are located east of Cuzco in an area that offers clear views of the Huaynacorcor ridge. We believe that this may be a fruitful line of inquiry.

Cobo describes Chuquimarca, the fourth shrine along the third ceque of Antisuyu, as follows:

> The fourth was called Chuquimarca; it was a temple of the Sun on the hill of Mantocalla, in which they said that the Sun descended many times to sleep. For this reason, in addition to the other things, they offered it children. (Cobo 1980:33 [1653: Bk. 13, Ch. 14])[10]

There are a number of interesting aspects to this brief description of Chuquimarca. First, Chuquimarca is characterized as a sun temple. This suggests that solar observations might have been made there. Second, Cobo mentions that the sun descended at Chuquimarca many times to sleep. This is a possible reference to sunset observations. Third, the hill on which Chuquimarca was located, Mantocalla, was one of the most important hills of the Cuzco region. It is listed in Cobo's document as a huaca on the same ceque as Chuquimarca:

> The sixth was called Mantocallas [sic] which was a hill held in great veneration, on which, at the time of shelling maize, they made certain sacrifices. For these [sacrifices], they placed on said hill bundles of carved firewood dressed as men and women and a great quantity of maize ears made of wood. After great drunken feasts, they burned many sheep with the said firewood, and killed some children. (Cobo 1980:33 [1653: Bk. 13, Ch. 14]).[11]

Molina (1989:69–71 [ca. 1575]) also mentions Mantocalla in his description of the month that contained the festival Inti Raymi. During this month, the ruling Inca and his lords went to Mantocalla, where they were served by female servants called *mamacona*. The celebration lasted several days and was apparently associated with a structure—not just the hill—as the women "remained outside in a court." The festival ended, according to Molina, when the ruling Inca returned to Cuzco at the end of the month.[12] The lunar month described by Molina began on a new moon within a few days of 25 May (Gregorian calendar) and ended at or just after the June solstice.

Unfortunately, no sites in the Cuzco region currently bear the name of Chuquimarca (An. 3:4) or Mantocalla (An. 3:6), but their approximate locations can be deduced by the identification of nearby huacas. The probable locations of huacas along the second (An. 2) and fourth (An. 4) ceques of Antisuyu are presented on Map 7. The area between them held the third ceque of Antisuyu. The identifications of the eighth huaca on the third ceque with the modern community of Yuncaypampa (An 3:8), and the ninth huaca with a nearby mountain pass called Yancaycalla (An. 3:9), are secure. These findings define a region indicated in Map 7 that contains the sun temple of Chuquimarca (An. 3:4) and the hill shrine of Mantocalla (An. 3:6). However, there are a number of different locations in this circumscribed region that may represent the huacas in question.

Photo 10. The Site of Cusilluchayoc, an extensively carved limestone outcrop.

Photo 11. The Site of Salonpuncu (or Lacco). Salonpuncu is a prominent limestone outcrop that has also been extensively carved and contains many fissures that have been enlarged with excellent Inca workmanship.

Upon leaving the city of Cuzco along the royal road of Antisuyu, one climbs to a relatively flat escarpment to a site now called Cusilluchayoc (Photo 10). It is an extensively carved limestone outcrop with the remains of Inca structures along its west side. This impressive site is the nearest possible location to Cuzco for Chuquimarca (An. 3:4). From Cusilluchayoc, the June solstice sunset may be seen over a nearby hill, and the ridge of Huaynacorcor is not visible in this direction. Accordingly, a proposition linking Chuquimarca to Quiancalla fails for this particular site.[13]

About three hundred meters northeast of Cusilluchayoc is a prominent limestone outcrop with a small stream on its northern slope. The outcrop, known by several names including "Salonpuncu" and "Lacco," has also been extensively carved and contains many fissures that have been enlarged with excellent Inca workmanship (Photo 11). Aveni (1981:309) and Zuidema (1986b:188) suggest that this site is the location of Chuquimarca (An. 3:4).

Aveni locates Quiancalla some six kilometers away on the Huay-

Photo 12. View of Huaynacorcor Ridge from Salonpuncu. As viewed from the top of Salonpuncu, the sun sets behind the Huaynacorcor ridge on the June solstices.

nacorcor ridge that corresponds to the June solstice sunset as viewed from Salonpuncu (Photo 12). To be visible at this distance against the glare of the setting sun, the pillars would need to be four to six meters high and one to two meters in diameter. Survey work found no evidence of any pillars in this area of the ridge.[14] If the pillars once stood there, they have been destroyed, the stones carried away, the foundations dug out, and the trenches filled in with dirt. In other words, although the June solstice sunset can be seen on the ridge of Huaynacorcor from Salonpuncu, no archaeological evidence survives to support the suggestion that the actual pillars of Quiancalla once stood there.

Proceeding north from Salonpuncu, one encounters the remains of an Inca road. One branch of this road leads to the ruin now called Pucapucara and the other climbs to the shoulder of a hill, ending at the foundations of several large, but roughly constructed, rectangular compounds (Photo 13). John Rowe (pers. com. 1992) suggests these compounds as a possible location for Chuquimarca or Mantocalla. From the foundations, the June solstice sun sets over a steeply descending portion of the Huaynacorcor ridge, and from a small hill just north of these compounds it sets over the peak of Huaynacorcor. This is the limit of the region containing Chuquimarca and Mantocalla, if they were used to view the June solstice sunset behind Huaynacorcor. A large looters' pit with fragments of human bone and fine Inca ceramics is located on this peak. However, the prominence of any mountain in the Cuzco region is a likely spot to find Inca offerings, and looting at the summit of Huaynacorcor does not provide direct evidence that the Quiancalla pillars were there.

Our archaeological and astronomical research identified another, more speculative, location for the observation point of the June sol-

Photo 13. Rectangular Compound above Salonpuncu. A rough stone foundation marks the end of an Inca road in the northern portion of the region that contained Chuquimarca and Mantocalla.

Photo 14. The Lower End of Huaynacorcor Ridge. A disturbed area on the Huaynacorcor ridge was found near where the sun sets on the June solstice as seen from the Sacsahuaman plain.

stice sunset and the pillars of Quiancalla. It is unrelated to the course of the third ceque of Antisuyu, or to the locations of Chuquimarca and Mantocalla. The lower end of the Huaynacorcor ridge contains an area of extensive disturbance where four pits have been dug one to two meters into the ground (Photos 14 and 15). This disturbed area was identified in 1990 during the survey phase of the project as a possible location for the Quiancalla pillars. However, the 1992 astronomical fieldwork indicated that the June solstice sunset could not be seen at this point from the Chuquimarca-Mantocalla region. Instead, it was found that this area marks the June solstice sunset as viewed from the center of the Sacsahuaman plain.[15] The connection of Sacsahuaman with a possibly looted area and with a solstice sunset point is intriguing, but archival research has not yet yielded evidence suggesting that the Inca celebrated the June solstice feast of Inti Raymi there.[16] Additional research is needed to determine which of these many possibilities was the ob-

Photo 15. Disturbed Area on Huaynacorcor Ridge. The lower end of the Huaynacorcor ridge contains an area of extensive disturbance where several pits have been dug.

servation point of the June solstice sunset, and the position of the Quiancalla pillars (Map 7).

Sunrise Observations

So far only the pillars employed by the Inca to observe sunsets have been discussed in this chapter. A number of chroniclers wrote of pillars marking important sunrises in the Cuzco Valley. Verifying their existence and determining the location of such sunrise markers is difficult because the city is at the northwest end of a long valley and the distance to the southeast horizon is great.

Erecting a pillar capable of marking the December solstice sunrise as viewed from central Cuzco would be physically prohibitive using Inca construction methods. The southeastern horizon—with portions as far as fifty kilometers away—is typically ten times more distant from central Cuzco than the western horizon. The size of

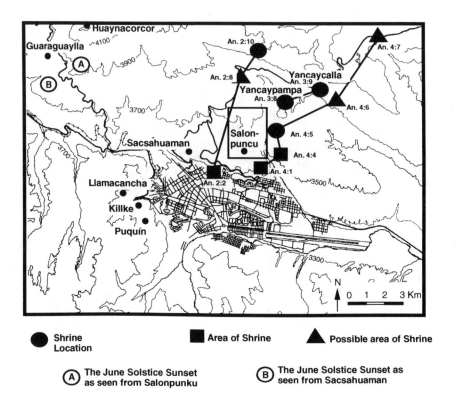

Map 7. The suggested courses of ceques An. 2, An. 3, and An. 4. The region between these ceques contains the sun temple of Chuquimarca (An. 3:4) and the hill shrine of Mantocalla (An. 3:6).

pillars necessary for visibility scales directly with distance, and the December solstice sunrise markers would have had to be thirty meters high to be visible from central Cuzco.

Observations of the sunrise on the June solstice, during the important Inti Raymi festival, could easily have been marked. The June solstice sunrise, as seen from central Cuzco, is over a relatively nearby hill. The ridge where the sun rises, as viewed from the Coricancha, is now developed, and a house is located at the spot where the June solstice sun rises. From the main plaza of Cuzco, the hill that forms the sunrise horizon in June is very close. From the southeast end of the plaza (the cathedral currently occults the sunrise horizon from the center of the plaza), the solstice sunrise occurs near some radio towers. The horizon area, which has been developed over the past few years, contains several areas of light Inca pottery scatters. There are, however, no traces of stone foundations on the hill which might represent those of the solar pillars.

There is evidence to suggest that the June solstice sunrise may have also been honored in a different manner. Zuidema (1982a:439–445) has examined information provided by Molina (1989:68–70 [ca. 1575]) on an annual Inca pilgrimage from Cuzco southeast to the pass of Vilcanota (now called La Raya) that occurred during the time of the June solstice. Molina suggests that the eastward direction of this journey was set because that is where the Inca believed the sun was born. Since a Cuzco-to-La Raya line is too far south to be aligned with the sun, this belief was not based on a physical sunrise alignment. It may have been a symbolic alignment, or simply a note that each day, the sun is born anew in the east.

Zuidema (1981b:331; 1982c:65; 1988b:145) also has hypothesized that the ruling Inca watched the December solstice sunrise over a mountain called Moto from the temple of Puquín Cancha during the Capac Raymi celebrations. This hypothesis is apparently built on two observations made by Molina. The first is that Molina (1989:110 [ca. 1575]) indicates that the ruling Inca went to the temple of Puquín Cancha on the 23rd day of Capac Raymi. The second is Molina's (1989:68 [ca. 1575]) description of the pilgrimage to the pass of Vilcanota, described above. One of the first stops in this pilgrimage was the mountain of Omoto (currently called Moto) at the southeast end of the Cuzco Valley. Combining these data, Zuidema suggests that the ruling Inca observed the December solstice sunrise over Moto Mountain from the site of Puquín Cancha. This proposal, like the suggested Mantocalla-Quiancalla connection, is an interesting one and worth consideration.

Until recently the Puquín Cancha–Moto Mountain hypothesis remained speculative and impossible to test because the location of Puquín Cancha was unknown. In 1990, however, construction on Puquín Hill unearthed several finely worked Inca stone blocks at a depth of more than two meters in an area traditionally known as Inti Cancha. Excavations were conducted at the site by the Instituto Nacional de Cultura in Cuzco, under the direction of Justo Torres in 1990 and 1991, and revealed a large quantity of carved stone blocks, a foundation wall, and several burnt Inca offerings that contained gold objects (Justo Torres pers. com. 1991). These impressive Inca remains on the slope of Puquín are unusual, and given their quality, it is reasonable to suggest that they represent the temple of Puquín Cancha (Photo 16). The probable identification of Puquín Cancha provided an opportunity for us to test in 1992 the Puquín Cancha–

Photo 16. Excavations at Puquín Cancha. Excavations in 1990 and 1991 in the area of Puquín revealed a large quantity of carved stone blocks, a foundation wall, and burnt Inca offerings. These finds may be the remains of the Inca temple called Puquín Cancha.

Moto Mountain hypothesis. Although parts of Moto Mountain are visible from the Puquín site, astronomical measurements indicate that they do not align with the December solstice sunrise. Accordingly, our fieldwork does not support the proposed model.

The Zenith and Antizenith Passages of the Sun

The Zenith Passages

Each morning observers see the sun ascend in the sky until midday when it reaches the meridian (a north/south line dividing the eastern half of the sky from the western half). From this high point, the sun then begins to descend. When the sun crosses the meridian in tropical regions, like Cuzco and most of Tahuantinsuyu, it can pass through a point directly overhead. This point is called the zenith.

The dates on which this happens depend on the latitude of the solar observation. Zenith passage in Cuzco occurs on 13 or 14 February and on 30 October. On these dates, vertical objects in Cuzco cast no shadow at noon.[17]

The only historical account that directly mentions this phenomenon is that of Garcilaso de la Vega (1966:117 [1609: Vol. 1, Bk. 2, Ch. 22]). He correctly connects the zenith passage dates in Quito with the equinoxes. Less direct evidence for Andean interest in the passage of the sun through the zenith comes from terms in early Quechua and Aymará dictionaries (Ziólkowski and Sadowski 1992:199–200) that include words and phrases for describing the sun overhead.[18] Unfortunately, it is unclear whether these terms are meant to describe the biannual zenith passage of the sun, or simply its daily arrival at noon. The existence of words to describe the passage of the sun overhead, and Garcilaso de la Vega's reference to the zenith passage in Quito, suggest that the concept (at least) of a zenith passage was most likely used by Andean peoples. Nevertheless, the scarcity and ambiguity of the data, especially when compared to the abundant information on the solstices, suggest that if the zenith passages were observed in Cuzco, they were of relatively minor importance in the ritual calendar and Inca astronomy.

The passage of the sun through the zenith is not a horizon phenomenon. In other words, it is a notable occurrence to someone casting shadows in the fashion described by Garcilaso de la Vega, but not to an observer focused on the horizon. The passage of the sun through the zenith can be extrapolated to the horizon by observing the position of the sunrise (or -set) on the days that this occurs. Tentative evidence for Inca interest in the sunrise position on the zenith passage date may exist in the window placement in the "Torreón," a building at Machu Picchu that also contains a solstitial alignment (Dearborn and White 1983). The light of the rising sun enters two windows of the Torreón for only a brief period (about a week) on either side of the zenith passage dates. Unfortunately, this feature of the Torreón is not so constraining that it demands a particular date, and it is not known to exist in any other Inca structure.

Zuidema has also proposed that physical alignments marking the sunrise on the dates of zenith passage can be found in the Cuzco Valley. In this case, he has suggested that the last three ceques of Antisuyu (An. 7, An. 8, and An. 9) formed a nearly continuous line which pointed toward the sunrise on the zenith passage date: "The three ceques were very close to the same direction, succeeding each other out from Cuzco and pointing to the zenith sunrise as seen

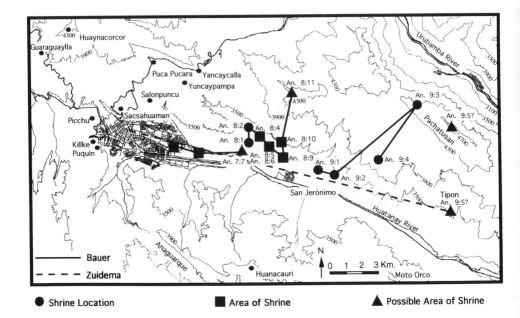

Map 8. The suggested courses of ceques An. 7, An. 8, and An. 9. Ground documentation of shrines does not support the suggestion that the last three ceques of Antisuyu (An. 7–An. 9) formed a ritual line pointing to the zenith sunrise as seen from central Cuzco.

from the Temple of the Sun" (Zuidema 1983b:252). This hypothesis was tested during recent field research on the ceque system. Map 8 depicts the direction of the seventh, eighth, and ninth ceques of Antisuyu as indicated by Zuidema's (1982b:206; 1982c:64; 1990: 70–71; Aveni 1990:53) map of ceques that he believes were used for astronomical measurements, as well as the course of these same ceques as proposed by Bauer's field identification of huacas. The results of this comparison do not support the idea that the last three ceques of Antisuyu formed a ritual line pointing to the zenith sunrise as seen from central Cuzco.

The Antizenith Passages

In 1981, Zuidema developed a hypothesis suggesting that the Inca were interested in the zenith passage of the sun as well as in the time when the sun passes directly underfoot (through the nadir). Although passage of the sun through the nadir is not an observable phenomenon, its timing can be approximated through what Zuidema has called an "antizenith" observation; that is, by noting the days when the sun sets (or rises) 180 degrees from the position where it rose (or set) on the dates that it passed through the zenith. As with the zenith passage, the dates of the antizenith passage vary depending on the latitude. For Quito, the zenith and antizenith dates are coincident on the equinox, while in Cuzco the antizenith (nadir) passages occur around 18 August and 26 April. As these months are consistent with the maize planting and harvest celebrations in Cuzco, for which there is considerable evidence of solar observation, Zuidema proposes that the Inca linked their maize celebrations to the concept of antizenith dates. Because this hypothesis has generated considerable interest (Urton 1980; Anders 1986a; Aveni 1980, 1981, 1989; Urton and Aveni 1983; Krupp 1983, 1991; Hadingham 1984; Ziólkowski and Sadowski 1985; Hyslop 1985; 1990) and debate (Dearborn and Schreiber 1986), we review its strengths and weaknesses below.

To begin with, there are no direct historical references or clear physical remains that indicate that antizenith observations were made by the Inca. Furthermore, the historical references and physical evidence used to support the proposed antizenith observations have shifted over the years. In his initial article on zenith and antizenith observations, Zuidema (1981b:325) states that Inca interest in the zenith (and conversely the antizenith) "can be established unambiguously by two previously unmentioned pieces of evidence." The first piece of evidence is that certain features in the foundation of Muyucmarca (a circular structure with radial interior support walls on the summit of Sacsahuaman) are aligned with the zenith sunrise and the antizenith sunset directions. The second piece of evidence concerns the dates of the zenith and antizenith passages as observed from the Islands of the Sun and the Moon in Lake Titicaca. These islands contain Inca shrines, and from this latitude, the solstices, equinoxes, zenith passage and antizenith passage dates divided the year into eight approximately equal parts. Furthermore, Zuidema (1981b:326) notes that when the Spanish established the cult of the Virgin in 1582 in Copacabana on the shores of Lake Titicaca, they selected 2 February and then 5 August as major festival days. Since these dates are within a few days of the zenith and antizenith passage dates for that region, Zuidema believes that their selection indicates an indigenous recognition of these solar events. While these data are interesting, we would classify them as highly circumstantial, rather than unambiguous, indications of Inca interest in the zenith and antizenith passages.

In the context of this antizenith hypothesis, Aveni (1981:309–316) examined the Anonymous Chronicler's claim that the sun was observed, from the usnu in the central plaza of Cuzco, to set between the central pillars of Picchu at the time of maize planting. Assuming that ceques were straight lines, he proposed a position for the central pillars. From this location he then identified the portion of the central plaza from which sunset observations correspond to the antizenith passage dates. This model-dependent method of positioning the pillars of Picchu is problematic, since it is now known that many of the ceques were not straight (Niles 1987:171–206; Bauer 1992a). Furthermore, the foundations for neither the Picchu pillars nor those of the usnu have been identified.

The conclusions of Aveni concerning the antizenith alignment of the Picchu pillars are challenged by a later article that reexamines the initial antizenith theory (Zuidema 1988b). This study rejects the idea that the central Picchu pillars marked the sunset on the antizenith, and shifts their proposed location up the slope of Picchu to mark a date in early September. In this new study, it is proposed that the northernmost of the four pillars, rather than the central ones, marked the antizenith sunset. This redevelopment of the antizenith hypothesis is based on a combination of readings of incompletely described ritual events in Cuzco, making it difficult to support or oppose. Nevertheless, the dramatic repositioning of pillars on Picchu, and the reassessment of the dates they marked, highlight the incidental nature of the founding assumptions of the antizenith hypothesis.

A continuing element in the antizenith hypothesis (Zuidema 1981b:331–335; 1988b:145) is the suggestion that the Usnu-Picchu line extended twenty-four kilometers southeast to the archaeological site of Tipon (also called Quispicancha). It is proposed that from Picchu, the Inca watched the sunrise over Tipon on the day that the sun passed through the zenith. Reversing this direction, it is also suggested that the Inca witnessed the antizenith sunset over Picchu from Tipon. Our research indicates that the Tipon-Picchu antizenith sunset observation would have been especially difficult for two reasons. First, from Tipon the August sun sets high above Picchu on the slope of a distant mountain called Mama Cimuna (4,342 masl). Because Picchu is far below the horizon, the alignment requires extrapolating the sunset location on the remote Mama Cimuna down to the ridge of Picchu near Cuzco. Second, at this great distance Picchu appears very small, and pillars the size of those described in the chronicles would not have been visible.

Closing the circle, Zuidema (1982b:206; 1982c:64; 1990:70–71) suggests that the Tipon-Picchu alignment is documented unambiguously by the course of the last three ceques of Antisuyu (An. 7, An. 8, and An. 9), believing that these three ceques ran in a straight line from near the center of Cuzco to Tipon and marked the direction of the antizenith sunrise and the zenith sunset. He has also proposed that the path defined by these three continuous ceques formed the course of a maize harvest procession:

> In April, the orientation of the *ceques* of III-3 [An. 7–An. 9] was used in the centripetal direction towards Cuzco to observe the setting of the Sun, an observation that was conducted at the time when the star was going through the nadir, half a year after it had reached its zenith (Zuidema 1981). In the same month of April, there was a tallying of the *huacas* of these *ceques*, and rituals were celebrated that sanctioned the results of the observations, for it was in this direction—along the axis of these *ceques*—that the harvest in procession was brought into Cuzco. (Zuidema 1990:74–75)

Research in the Cuzco Valley provides a means to test aspects of the zenith-antizenith proposal. Again, Map 8 shows that the final three ceques of Antisuyu do not travel in a straight line from Cuzco to Tipon, nor do they form a procession course into Cuzco. In other words, archaeological data do not support the proposition that the corn harvest was brought into the city along a zenith-antizenith–oriented line. Furthermore, evidence for a procession of any form in this direction is extremely circumstantial. Molina states that on the first day of the harvest ceremony, the youths who had been knighted in the previous Capac Raymi ceremony would go to a field called Sausero (Co. 2:3) and bring the maize to Limacpampa (Co. 2:1). Ardiles Nieves (1986) and Bauer (1992a:192) have determined that Sausero was located on the edge of Cuzco near the suburb called San Borja. As can be seen on Map 9, the area of Sausero is too far south for a path connecting it to Limacpampa to be physically aligned with the zenith sunrise, the antizenith sunset, or any other sunrise/set.

In sum, we have presented evidence that supports the belief that the Inca may have practiced zenith observations. Indeed, it would be surprising if a people who were as interested in the sun as the Inca had *not* noted when it reached the highest point in the sky. This solar event is particularly noteworthy (as described by Garcilaso de la Vega) in Ecuador, where the sun reaches zenith on the

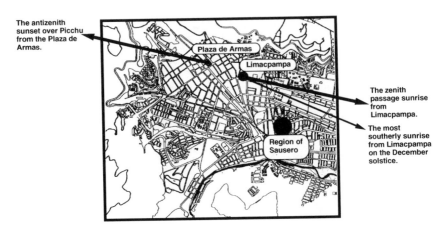

The antizenith sunset over Picchu from the Plaza de Armas.

Plaza de Armas

Limacpampa

The zenith passage sunrise from Limacpampa.

The most southerly sunrise from Limacpampa on the December solstice.

Region of Sausero

Map 9. The antizenith passage and the location of Sausero. A straight line from Limacpampa to Sausero runs to the southeast, but is not physically in the direction of any sunrise. The antizenith sunset is defined by reversing the direction to sunrise on the zenith passage date.

day of the equinox. Researchers, however, have increasingly accepted the idea that the solar observations made during the planting and harvest ceremonies of Cuzco were associated with antizenith passages of the sun. The case that the Inca linked their planting and harvesting observations to a reversal zenith passage sunrise (antizenith) is not supported by established historical or archaeological data from the Cuzco region.

Summary and Discussion

The chronicles' descriptions of the solar pillars of Cuzco, and their continued existence a century after the arrival of the Spaniards, argue that these towers were substantial in size and made of durable materials. A survey of other Inca structures in the Cuzco region, together with Betanzos' claim that they were made of quarried material, suggests that the pillars were constructed of stone. Although numerous researchers have examined the horizons of Cuzco in the past decades, no one has found clear evidence of the towers. The lack of archaeological evidence for these towers is perplexing, since it seems reasonable to expect that they would leave physical remains durable enough to last four hundred years. A possible explanation for their disappearance is that the Spaniards looted and systematically destroyed the towers and their foundations. Such destruction could have been linked to one of the many campaigns that took place between 1539 and 1650 to discover and destroy indigenous forms of religion, or may have simply been part of a search for silver and gold offerings.

In this chapter, the historical accounts of Inca solar observations were compared to our Cuzco field data. The investigation concludes with mixed results. The most consistent information presented in the historic sources is that there were four pillars on Picchu used in some type of solar observation and that the Inca witnessed the arrival of the solstices with the use of such pillars. We are currently unable to determine with certainty the locations or the functions of the Picchu towers, although the Anonymous Chronicler indicates that they were observed from somewhere in the central plaza during the month of August.

Continued investigation of the June solstice sunset pillars and the location from which this sunset was observed is needed, since our research identified a number of possible positions for the pillars and point of observation. If the June solstice sunset observation was made from Haucaypata, then the pillars would have stood on the lower portion of Picchu in an area now covered with houses. If the observation was made from the Coricancha, the solstice pillars would have been located slightly farther up the hill. This is an interesting possibility, since the point on Picchu that marks the June solstice sunset as seen from the Coricancha would also mark an August sunset date as viewed from near the center of the plaza. Although we inspected the area of the June solstice sunset on Picchu, as seen from the Coricancha, several times, and test excavations were conducted there in 1992, no evidence of Inca foundations has been found.[19]

Alternatively, Cobo notes that there were solar pillars on a hill called Quiancalla marking "the beginning of summer," which may have been markers for the June solstice sunset. Our field and archival research indicates that the area of Quiancalla was located on the slope of Huaynacorcor near the community of Guaraguaylla. This position of Quiancalla requires an observation point outside central Cuzco. We currently suggest three distinct locations as possible sites outside the city for the June solstice observations of Quiancalla. The first, following the research of Aveni (1981), is the area around the Inca site of Salonpuncu. This site is, however, more than six kilometers from the Quiancalla area, and there is no evidence of Inca structures on the ridge at the location that marks the June solstice sunset as seen from Salonpuncu. A second possible location is the foundations of a rectangular compound northeast of Salonpuncu. From this region the solstice sun sets near the peak of Huaynacorcor. A third possible observation location is the plain of Sacsahuaman. This plain is located approximately one kilometer closer to the Quiancalla area, and the June solstice sunset point, as seen from the plain, is marked by what appear to be looters' pits. In no case can the sun be observed along any part of the ridge of Huaynacorcor from the central regions of Cuzco, so the pillars of Quiancalla must have been observed from a different location than those of Picchu and Chinchincalla.

Cobo also writes that there was a set of solar pillars on the hill of Chinchincalla. Aveni (1981) suggests that these towers marked the December solstice sunset as viewed from the Coricancha. This would place the pillars southwest of Cuzco on the hill of Killke. Survey and excavation work identified a burial area on the shoulder of Killke near where the pillars would have stood if viewed from the Coricancha. However, no physical evidence for the pillars was found, and confirmation of Aveni's proposal that the pillars of Chinchincalla stood on Killke remains to be provided. Alternatively, archaeological survey results constrain the pillars of Chinchincalla to a region between Killke and a position on the hill above the hamlet of Llamacancha. The December solstice sunset could have been watched over this latter position from the usnu in the central plaza of Cuzco.

Monitoring the motion of the sun was an important expression of the imperial religion that the Spaniards tried to suppress. A system of horizon pillars would have been highly visible and the focus of attention for religious zealots as well as treasure hunters seeking the offerings that might have been buried under them. While remains of the towers were visible nearly a century after the conquest, their destruction probably began during the early conquest period. With their destruction, the solar cult upon which the Inca based their beliefs withered. Chroniclers who arrived later (e.g., Molina) saw only the operation of the more ancient lunar calendar and related it to the cycle of festivals that had marked the Inca year.

5. Stellar Observations

THE SOLAR PILLARS THAT ONCE STOOD on the horizons of Cuzco marked the motion of the sun and incorporated that movement into the ritual organization of Inca society. Sun observations were inextricably linked to ceremony, and they attracted the attention of numerous indigenous and Spanish scholars, resulting in the preservation of a relatively large body of information on solar astronomy. Andean interest in the sky, however, did not end with the setting sun. Historical accounts of stellar observations, though less common and less detailed than those of the sun, exist as well. The accounts of star observations that we will summarize and discuss in this chapter show considerable variation. This variation is hardly surprising, as the accounts record information from across the Andes. It suggests that many aspects of local astronomy continued unchanged even after regions and their peoples became incorporated into the Inca Empire.

This chapter is composed of two sections. First, the early colonial accounts of stellar and planetary observations are presented. Sources include, among others, Polo de Ondegardo [1585], Monzón [1586], Garcilaso de la Vega [1609], Pachacuti Yamqui Salcamayhua [1613], Guaman Poma de Ayala [1615], Avendaño [1617], Arriaga [1621], and Calancha [1638] as well as the anonymous Huarochirí manuscript [ca. 1608]. As has been noted by other researchers (Zuidema and Urton 1976; Urton 1981a; Ziólkowski and Sadowski 1992), a number of late-sixteenth- and early-seventeenth-century lexicons mention individual stars and constellations. Although the lexicons present data in a less narrative format than the standard chronicles of Peru, they contain important information on pre-Hispanic stellar observations. Andean lexicons begin with that of Domingo de Santo Tomás (1951

[1560]) and the *Arte y vocabulario* . . . (1951 [1586]), traditionally credited to Antonio Ricardo, and continue through the later Quechua dictionary of Gonçález Holguín (1989 [1608]) and the Aymará lexicon of the Italian Jesuit Ludovico Bertonio (1984 [1612]). Ziólkowski and Sadowski (1992:167–233) provide an extensive review of the astronomical terms contained in these dictionaries. Our discussion concentrates on Gonçález Holguín's (1989 [1608]) work, since it contains the most complete set of star references.[1]

In the second part of this chapter, we examine several hypotheses relating different archaeological remains in the Cuzco region to stellar observations. These include the alignment of certain features of the Temple of the Sun with the rise of the Pleiades, as well as possible relations between the courses of various ceques and the rise and set positions of specific stars.

Historical Accounts of Celestial Observations

Early colonial references to Inca star watching are scattered through a wide range of documents. These accounts include the standard chronicles of Peru, many of which have been cited in previous chapters, as well as a number of other lesser known works. In this section, we introduce the major Inca star-watching references in chronological order. This compilation serves as a reference base for our interpretations of Inca star watching, presented in the chapter summary.

Before a discussion of the historical sources can begin, it must be noted that the Inca generally made no linguistic distinction between planets and the brightest stars. In Quechua, both are called *chasca* (shaggy hair), while *coyllur* (star) is used for lesser stars (Urton 1981a:107). Gonçález Holguín's (1989:632 [1608]) vocabulary states that the term "Hatun ccoyllur" (great star) was used for *planets*, while Bertonio's (1984: Pt. 1, 369 [1612]) Aymará dictionary contains the term "Hacha huara huara" for *planet star (planeta estrella)*. Four of the five planets that can be seen with the naked eye regularly appear brighter than Sirius, the brightest star in the sky. Of these, Venus can appear nearly fifteen times brighter than Sirius, becoming a prominent object in the morning or evening sky. It is improbable that anyone who regularly watches the sky would fail to identify this small group of bright objects that wander across a background of fixed stars.

Identifying Inca constellations also requires some knowledge of the stellar group names used by the Spaniards of this period. The stars were thought to rotate on the outermost sphere of the universe, and the Spanish cosmographer Zamorano (1585) describes forty-eight constellations known in antiquity. Named constellations included Lira (Lyra), Tauro (Taurus), Cisne (the swan, Cygnus), Delfino (Delphinus), and Centauro (Centaurus), but not the Southern Cross. These formal constellation names were accepted by astronomers and cosmographers all over Europe. Exploration of the Southern Hemisphere and the charting of the southern polar regions led to proposals for new constellations, and in his 1603 atlas, Johann Bayer, a European astronomer who lived from 1572 to 1625, created twelve new constellations for unnamed portions of the southern sky. Bayer followed Ptolemy and included the stars of the Southern Cross in Centaurus. He did, however, draw a cross over the hind legs of the Centaur and mention that there was a modern recognition of this group as a cross (Bayer 1603: Table 41). The names of southern constellations, and their boundaries, varied considerably over the next centuries as scholars came to a consensus, requiring over two hundred years for astronomers to settle on the name Crux for the Southern Cross.

The most frequently cited source on Inca star watching is the 1585 abstract of Polo de Ondegardo's *De los errores y supersticiones de los indios*. The abstract contains the following passage:

Among the stars, as a rule, all of them worshipped the one they call Collca, which we call the Pleiades. And the other stars were venerated especially by those who believed that they were in need of their assistance. For they attributed various offices to various stars. Thus, the Shepherds worshipped and sacrificed to a star they call Urcuchillay, which they say is a sheep [llama] of many colors, which is concerned with the conservation of livestock, and it is understood to be the one that the Astrologers call Lyra. And the same people worship two others close to this one, which they call Catachillay and Urcuchillay, which they claim to be a ewe with a lamb. Others who live in the forests worship another star which is called Chuquichinchay, which they say is a jaguar in whose charge are the jaguars, bears, and pumas. They also worship another star which they call Ancochinchay, which protects other animals. In the same fashion they worship another which they call Machacuay, in whose charge are the Serpents and Snakes, that they may not hurt them, and in general they believed that for each [kind of] animal and bird on earth there was a similar one in the sky who was in charge of its procreation and increase. And thus they dealt with various stars, such as the one they called Chacana, and Topatorca, Mamana and Mirco, and Miquiquiray, and other such. (Polo de Ondegardo 1965a:2–5 [1585: Ch. 1]; translation modified)[2]

Miguel Cabello Balboa (1951:308 [1586: Pt. 3, Ch. 15]) used this abstract as the basis for a short description of Inca star worship. Parts of the abstract were also reproduced by Acosta (1954:143 [1590: Bk. 5, Ch. 4]), Calancha (1981:835–836 [1638: Bk. 2, Ch. 11]), and Murúa (1946:285–286 [ca. 1615: Bk. 3, Ch. 51]).

Cobo almost certainly possessed Polo de Ondegardo's now-lost original 1559 report and used this complete document, rather than the 1585 abstract, in writing his *Historia del Nuevo Mundo*. Accordingly, Cobo's chronicle yields many details of Inca stellar observations that are not present in the surviving 1585 abstract. Cobo records the following information on Inca star worship:

> The worship of the stars was the result of their opinion that the creator had designated a second cause which was to look after the preservation of each kind of thing. In accordance with this belief, they thought that there was a patron in heaven for each of the animals and birds that provided for their preservation and increase. This function was attributed to several constellations of stars. And they thought that all of these patrons came from that group of small stars commonly known as the Pleiades, which these Indians called Collca, and the power that conserved the animals and birds flowed from this group of stars. For this reason it was called "mother," and it was universally considered to be a major *guaca* by all of the *ayllos* and families. They were all familiar with it, and those Indians who were informed about such matters kept better track of its course all year long than that of any of the other stars. However, they did not make use of it for anything else, nor did they mention that it had any other powers. Nevertheless, all the provinces offered great sacrifices to it. The rest of the stars were worshiped only by those who considered that they had need of them, according to the functions that they attributed to them, and they were the only ones who were familiar with them, kept track of them, and made offerings to them. The others did not do any of these things, nor did they feel any obligation to do so. The worship of each star was carried out in the following way.
>
> All herders respected and made sacrifices to the constellation called Lira by the astronomers and known to the Indians as Urcuchillay. They said it was a parti-colored ram that took care of their livestock. Two other small stars that are below it, forming the letter T, were said to be the animal's feet and head. The herders also worshiped another one called Catachillay which is found nearby and is also rather large and yet another smaller one close to it. They pretended that these stars were a llama with its lamb which both came from Urcuchillay.
>
> Those Indians who lived in the forests and *yunca* lands worshiped and

made sacrifices to another star that they called Chuquichinchay, which they say is a tiger [jaguar] and was thought to watch over tigers, bear, and lions. As sacrifices were offered to it, they requested that these wild animals do them no harm. Those who needed to travel through dense woodlands also entrusted themselves to this star for the same reason as those who lived there.

They took great care in worshiping another star called Machacuay. They thought that this star watched over snakes, serpents, and vipers. This is because it looks like a snake when lightning flashes. . . . Finally, they worshiped this star for the same reason as the others: so that serpents and vipers would do them no harm. They also respected another star which they called Ancochinchay. They said it looked after the welfare of other animals.

In short, they identified a star in the sky for every species of animal, and for this reason they worshiped many stars, had names for them, and made sacrifices to them. Here are the names of some of the other stars: Topatoraca, Chacana, Mirco, Mamana, Miquiquiray, Quiantopa, and others. In fact, they had names for all the stars of the first magnitude, the morning and evening star [Venus] and the most noteworthy signs and planets. (Cobo 1990:30–31 [1653: Bk. 13, Ch. 6])[3]

In these passages, Polo de Ondegardo and Cobo introduce a night sky populated with both wild and domestic animals. The economically important llama is represented in the stellar constellation, Urcuchillay. Since *urco* in Quechua is used for male animals, it seems appropriate to suggest that this stellar llama was a male (Gonçález Holguín 1989:357 [1608]). Polo de Ondegardo and Cobo specifically identify this llama with the constellation Lyra, and state that shepherds worshiped it and sacrificed to it (Photo 17). Lyra is an ancient constellation of Mediterranean origin that was accepted across sixteenth-century Europe as widely as it is today (Bayer 1603: Table 9). The most prominent star in Lyra is Vega. It is the fifth brightest star in the sky and lies just outside the Milky Way. While Polo de Ondegardo's abstract suggests that Urcuchillay is an individual star, Cobo's recounting of the full document describes the figure as including nearby stars, "Two other small stars that are below it, forming the letter T, were said to be the animal's feet and head." This indicates that this llama was represented as a star-to-star constellation.[4]

The Polo de Ondegardo and Cobo accounts continue by saying that the herders also worshiped a nearby constellation named Catachillay. Catachillay is said by these authors to have contained a bright star representing a female llama, and a fainter star as her

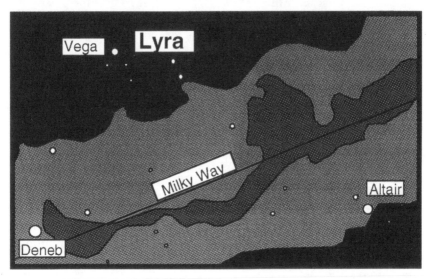

Photo 17. The stars of Vega, Altair, and Deneb. Vega is the brightest star in Lyra, the constellation that Polo de Ondegardo identifies as the llama, Ur-cuchillay. The nearby bright stars Deneb and Altair are the principal candidates for being part of the female llama, Catachillay, which is also described by Polo de Ondegardo. (Photograph by Dennis DiCicco)

lamb. Catachillay must have been (or included) a prominent star, since a poem, recorded by Juan Pérez Bocanegra (1631:710), includes a stanza which mentions Catachillay[5] as rising just before dawn:

Chipchijcachac catachillai	Glittering catachillay
P'uncha pussac quean tupa	Daylight's guide, dawn's aurora,
Cam huacyacpac, manavpa	For you, crier who doesn't listen,
Quecaiquicta hamuynilla	To you despised, just say "come"
Piñascaita quespichillai	Make him forgive my anger,
Susurhuana	*Susurwana*

(TRANSLATION BY BRUCE MANNHEIM IN ZUIDEMA 1982B:216)

There are two very bright stars near Lyra that currently represent the best possibilities for this constellation.[6] The brightest of the two is Altair in the western constellation of Aquila. At the latitude of Peru, it rises at the same time as Vega, and is just across the Milky Way from it. The second star is Deneb in the western constellation Cygnus. Deneb is slightly closer than Altair, but rises about an hour later.

In his Aymará dictionary, Bertonio (1984: Pt. 1, 236; Pt. 2, 38 [1612]) describes Catachillay as "a nebulous star in the Milky Way, or stars above the nebulosity." Altair is on the edge of the Milky Way, but Deneb is in the middle of it, sitting on the edge of a bright nebulous patch (Photo 17). Separately, Bertonio (1984: Pt. 1, 150 [1612]) identifies the name Unuchilla catachilla as "cross of stars" and Catachilla huara huara as a probable reference to the Pleiades (1984: Pt. 1, 107 [1612]).[7] Gonçález Holguín (1989:51, 465 [1608]) writes that Catachillay and Urcochillay were stars of "the cross" and a "star cross." On the other hand, the *Arte y vocabulario . . .* (1951:98, 155 [1586]) states that the terms *katachillay* and *ur'qu-chillay* were used for Venus (el lucero).

The identifications of Catachillay with "the cross" are ambiguous, because there are several constellations called "the Cross." Urton (1980; 1981a:129–150) records numerous cross constellations in modern Quechua astronomy, and they are equally abundant in European astronomy. The stars of the Southern Cross were rediscovered to European astronomers by Alviso de Cadamosto, who saw them while anchored off the coast of Gambia in 1454, and they were again reported in 1501 by Amerigo Vespucci, who called them an almond (Allen 1963:185–189). Acosta (1954:11 [1590: Ch. 5]) and Cobo (1956:27–31 [1653: Bk. 1, Ch. 8]) called these stars the Southern Cross and described their use in timekeeping and navigation. It was called the Southern Cross because a much more ancient and familiar cross already existed in the northern sky.

The northern constellation of Cygnus, which includes the prominent star Deneb, has been called the Cross (Crux major) at least since the time of Gregory of Tours (ca. 575). Gregory (1885 [ca. 575: Ch. 23]) additionally identified a nearby constellation, Delphinus, as Crux minor. Bayer (1603: Table 9) notes that in his day, Cygnus was commonly called the Cross by farmers. This description was common across Europe (von Arnim 1942; Allen 1963:194–195). Although we cannot be sure to which of the many crosses in the northern and southern skies Bertonio and Gonçález Holguín were

Table 3. *The Twenty Brightest Stars*

	STAR	V*a*	Date of Conjunction	DIST	Possible Inca Constellations
1 Sirius	α CMa	−1.5	28 June	9	
2 Canopus	α Car	−0.7	25 June	25	
3 Rigil Kent	α Cen	−0.2	28 Oct	1	Llamacñawin
4 Arcturus	α Boo	−0.1	24 Oct	69	
5 Vega	α Lyr	0.0	27 Dec	19	Urcuchillay
6 Capella	α Aur	0.0	3 June	5	
7 Rigel	β Ori	0.1	5 June	25	Chacana
8 Betelgeuse	α Ori	0.4	15 June	9	Chacana
9 Procyon	α CMi	0.4	10 July	13	
10 Achernar	α Eri	0.5	12 Apr	59	
11 Hadar	β Cen	0.6	18 Oct	1	Llamacñawin
12 Altair	α Aql	0.8	10 Jan	9	
13 Antares	α Sco	0.9	24 Nov	15	
14 Spica	α Vir	0.9	10 Oct	51	
15 Alpha Crucis	α Cru	0.9	23 Sept	0	Mamana or Mirco?
16 Aldebaran	α Tau	0.9	26 May	20	
17 Fomalhaut	α Psa	1.1	24 Feb	65	
18 Pollux	β Gem	1.2	10 July	23	
19 Deneb	α Cyg	1.3	24 Jan	2	Catachillay
20 Beta Crucis	β Cru	1.3	29 Sept	3	Mamana or Mirco?

V: Apparent Visual Magnitude
Conjunction: The table gives the sixteenth century date (Georgian Calendar) on which the sun had the same east/west position in the sky as the star. This date marks the center of the period of invisibility for the star.
DIST: Distance from the center of the Milky Way (degrees)
*a*The traditional method of measuring the brightness of a star is in magnitudes. A first magnitude star is approximately 2.5 times brighter than a star of second magnitude, and the visual limit is about sixth magnitude. The brightest star in the sky is Sirius at magnitude of −1.5.

Photo 18. The Pleiades, a cluster of stars of which six or seven are visible to the unaided eye. They are whitish in appearance and spread over a degree of sky. The inhabitants of Peru called them several names, including Collca and Oncoy. Two stars called Chuchucoyllor were near the Pleiades and may be among the stars of Taurus or Perseus. (Photograph by Dennis DiCicco)

referring, an identification with the older Northern Cross, Cygnus, is consistent with the statements of Polo de Ondegardo and Cobo that Urcuchillay was located in Lyra and Catachillay was nearby.

Many Andean animals were believed to have celestial counterparts. Cobo specifically states that "they had names for all of the stars of the first magnitude," so we may assume that most, if not all, of the brightest stars (Table 3) were named. In the above passages, Polo de Ondegardo and Cobo call the Pleiades—Las Siete Cabrillas (the Seven Kids [Goats]) to the Spaniards—the Collca (storehouse), a name confirmed by Gonçález Holguín (1989:440 [1608]).[8] Cobo's complete version provides more information on this constellation than does Polo de Ondegardo's summary. Cobo indicates that this asterism was the mother of all stars (Photo 18).[9] Cobo also states that considerable effort was made to track and to understand the movements of the Pleiades across the sky, and that all the provinces offered sacrifices to it. As will be discussed below, the Pleiades were also known by several other names.

Polo de Ondegardo and Cobo list a number of stars without presenting any additional description, among them Mamana and Mirco.

Gonçález Holguín (1989:225 [1608]) again presents us with the ambiguous identification of Maman Mircu as "some stars in the area of the Cross" and includes a myth fragment under "mirccuni," suggesting that these stars (Maman Mirccuc) represent ones who eat their parents (Table 4). Again, we cannot be sure if Gonçález Holguín refers to the Northern Cross (Cygnus) or the Southern Cross. If the association with the Southern Cross is correct, the stars could be Alpha and Beta Crucis, which are among the twenty brightest stars of the sky (Table 3 and Photo 19). Urton's ethnographic work in the village of Mismanay (1981a:100) identifies the constellation of Maman Mircu with some stars in Puppis, a constellation far from either Cross. Puppis contains no bright stars but lies between Sirius, the brightest star in the sky, and Canopus, the second brightest. The discrepancy between the crosses of Gonçález Holguín, and the identification found by Urton is not entirely surprising. In many instances, Urton (1981a:100–105) obtained multiple identifications in which informants from different villages used different stars for a constellation. Complete homogeneity is not to be expected in village-level astronomy.

The star presented by Polo de Ondegardo and Cobo as Chacana may be identified by information contained in Gonçález Holguín's dictionary. This source specifically states that "Chaccana" referred to the Tres Marías (Three Marys), or what we call Orion's belt (Photo 20). However, it must also be noted that Gonçález Holguín's vocabulary contains some references that contradict information found in Polo de Ondegardo's and Cobo's accounts. Gonçález Holguín (1989:117 [1608]) writes that a star named "Chhoque chinchay" was part of the llama constellation (Table 5), whereas Polo de Ondegardo and Cobo, as well as most other chroniclers, associate this star with large cats such as jaguars.[10]

We have very little information for the other stars listed by Polo de Ondegardo and Cobo. The star An'qochinchay (Ancochinchay) is also listed in the *Arte y vocabulario* . . . (1951:142 [1586]) as "a star worshiped by the Indians." But the names Topatorca (Topatoraca), Miquiquiray, and Quiantopa[11] are not found in other independent historical documents.[12]

The Milky Way, which the Inca called *mayu* (river), is brightest and thickest around the constellation of Sagittarius. At the latitude of Peru, this constellation passes high overhead, resulting in a more prominent display than is visible to European or North American observers. Recognized today as a vast disklike assemblage of stars, the Milky Way is visible only as a glowing band of light crossing the sky on a dark evening. In this disk, huge clouds of interstellar dust

Table 4. *Selected Star References from Gonçález Holguín (1989 [1608])*

Aranyak huarachazca. Luzero de la mañana. (p. 33)	Aranyak huarachazca. Morning star.
Catachillay, o vrcuchillay. El cruze. (p. 51)	Catachillay, or urcuchillay. The cross.
Coyllur. Estrella. (p. 70)	Coyllur. Star.
Ccoyllur chipchic. Estrella muy reluziente. (p. 70)	Ccoyllur chipchic. Very bright star.
Chaccana. Tres estrellas que llaman las tres marias. (p. 90)	Chaccana. Three stars called the Three Marys [Orion's belt].
Chhasca ccoyllur. Luzero del dia. (p. 98)	Chhasca ccoyllur. Day star.
Chhoque chinchay, o llama. Vna estrella que parece al carnero. (p. 117)	Chhoque chinchay, or llama. A star that looks like a sheep.
Maman mircu. Vnas estrellas caue el cruzero. (p. 225)	Maman mircu. Some stars in the area of the cross.
Mirccuni. Comer a su padre o madre, que por ser peccado estupendo le dieron vocablo proprio, y en el cielo fingieron vna estrella contraria a este peccado y que influye contra los que lo hazen, que llaman, Maman mirccuc cuyllur, que dize, Estrella de los que comen a su padre o madre. (p. 242)	Mirccuni. To eat one's father and mother, since it is a great sin, they gave it its own word, and in the sky they pretended there was a star against this sin, and which would influence against those who did it, which they called Maman Mirccuc cuyllur, which means star of those who eat their father or mother.
Paccarik chhascca. El luzero de la mañana. (p. 266)	Paccarik chhascca. The morning star.
Cabrillas del cielo. Collca cuyllur, o ccapac collcca cuyllur. (p. 440)	The Pleiades. Collca cuyllur [storehouse star], or ccapac collcca cuyllur [royal storehouse star].
Cruzero estrellas. Catachillay orcochillay. (p. 465)	Star cross. Catachillay urcuchillay.
Luzero de la mañana. Chazca coyllur. (p. 570)	Morning star. Chazca coyllur.
Luzero de la noche. Chissichascca. (p. 570)	Evening star. Chissichascca.

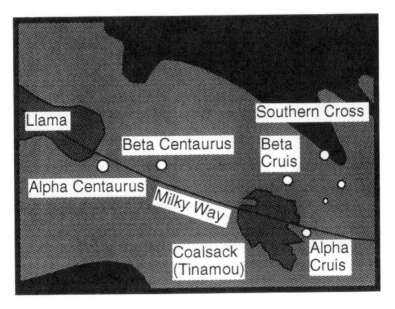

Photo 19. The Southern Cross and Alpha and Beta Centauri. Alpha and Beta Centauri form the eyes of the dark lane identified as a llama. The Coalsack (Yutu) is a dark spot on the Milky Way near the Southern Cross. (Photograph by Dennis DiCicco)

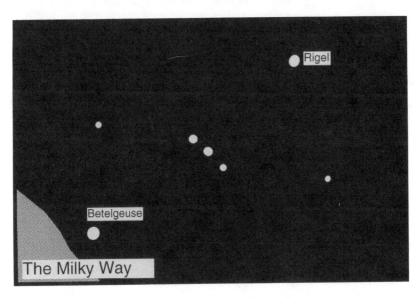

Photo 20. The stars of Orion. The Spanish knew the belt stars of Orion as the Three Marys. These stars are referred to as Chacana by Polo de Ondegardo, Gonçález Holguín, and other early writers. (Photograph by Dennis DiCicco)

Table 5. *Tentative Identifications of Inca Constellations*

Stellar Constellations

Inca Constellation	Region[a] of the Sky	Principal Stars	Distance from Milky Way (in degrees)
Urcuchillay	Lyra	Vega	20
Catachillay	Cygnus	Deneb	2
Chacana	Orion	Betelgeuse and Rigel	9 25
Chuchucoyllor	Taurus or Perseus	?	?
Collca (also called Oncoy)	Taurus	The Pleiades	23

Dark Constellations

Yacana	A dark lane between Scorpius and Centaurus. The constellation may include the bright stars Alpha and Beta Centauri as the eyes of the llama (Llamacñawin).
Yutu	The Coalsack near the Southern Cross.

[a]We include the modern constellation name only to indicate the part of the sky where the Inca constellation was located.

obscure the more distant stars, causing dark rifts to appear along this nebulous band. The Inca identified figures within these dark areas of the Milky Way. José Acosta (1954:7–8 [1590: Bk. 1, Ch. 2]), a Jesuit priest and naturalist, furnishes a description of these dark figures in his *Historia natural y moral de las Indias* (Natural and moral history of the Indies):

> I speak not only of the shining and resplendent parts . . . but much more for other dark and black spots that are in the sky. Because we really see in it things like spots, that are very noticeable, which I do not remember ever having seen in the heavens when I was in Europe, and here, in this other hemisphere, I have seen them very clearly. These spots are of the color and form of the eclipsed moon, and resemble it in their blackness and darkness. They travel fixed to the same stars and always of the same form and size.[13]

At the time of Acosta, the rifts of the Milky Way had received little attention from European astronomers. The great Jesuit astronomer Christoph Clavius made an early reference to the rifts in a 1596 edition of his *Commentary on Sacrobosco's Sphere*, which was incorporated in 1612 into his large work *Opera Mathematica*. He used these rifts to provide evidence that the Milky Way was fixed in shape and rotated with the stars (Lattis 1994). Without naming his source, Clavius reports the observation of "a certain learned and religious man passing his life in the province of Peru," who wrote that "near that pole there appear dark places in the night sky as if the heaven had been perforated."[14]

Most European constellations are formed by grouping stars in a region of the sky. The resulting figure is arbitrary, but serves to identify and name that region. In addition to "star-to-star" constellations, the Inca identified figures within the rifts, or dark areas, of the Milky Way, especially representations of various animals. The most famous of these is a llama and her lamb. The form associated with a constellation is seldom compelling, so it is not surprising that Spaniards, or indigenous people trained in European schools in the New World, had trouble seeing these figures. For example, Garcilaso de la Vega wrote:

> They fancied they saw the figure of an ewe with the body complete suckling a lamb in some dark patches spread over what the astrologers call the milky way. They tried to point it out to me saying: 'Don't you see the head of the ewe?' 'There is the lamb's head sucking'; 'There are the bodies and their legs.' But I could see nothing but the spots, which must have been for want of imagination on my part. (Garcilaso de la Vega 1966:119 [1609: Vol. 1, Bk. 2, Ch. 23]).[15]

These dark figures, formed by interstellar dust, are generally absent from Western astronomy. Urton (1981a:109) has termed them "dark cloud constellations." Just as they did in the sixteenth century, these dark cloud constellations still represent major features of the night sky for Andean villagers.

A unique text to survive from the early colonial period of Peru is the Huarochirí manuscript. This document was written sometime between 1598 and 1608 by a bilingual scribe from the Huarochirí region, a mountainous area of central Peru. It is one of the few works composed by an indigenous author and written almost entirely in Quechua. As the anonymous author discusses the mythology of the region, he offers information on certain stars and constellations, in particular a dark constellation called the Yacana, which represented a llama:

How Something Called the Yacana Comes Down from the Sky to Drink Water. We Shall Also Speak about the Other Stars and Their Names

They say the Yacana, which is the animator of llamas, moves through the middle of the sky. We native people can see it standing out as a black spot.

The Yacana moves inside the Milky Way. It's big, really big. It becomes blacker as it approaches through the sky, with two eyes and a very large neck.

This, we know, is what native people call the Yacana.

They say if a man was in luck and fortunate, the Yacana would fall right on top of him while it drank water from some spring.

As its woolly bulk pressed down upon him, someone else would pluck out some of its wool.

That apparition would occur at night.

In the morning, at daybreak, the man would look at the wool he'd plucked out. Examining it he'd see the wool to be blue, white, black, and brown, of every hue, thickly matted together.

If he had no llamas, he'd worship at the place where he had seen the apparition and plucked the wool, and trade for some llamas right away. After worshiping he'd trade for a female and a male llama.

Just from the two he'd bought, two or three thousand llamas would soon come.

In old times the Yacana revealed itself this way to a whole lot of people all over this province.

In the middle of the night, when no body is aware of it, the Yacana drinks all the water out of the ocean. If the Yacana failed to drink it, the waters would quickly drown the whole world.

A small dark spot goes before the Yacana, and, as we know, people call it the Tinamou [or Yutu].

This Yacana, they say, has a calf. It looks just as if the calf were suckling.

Also, we know there are three stars in a straight line.

They call these the Condor, the Vulture, and the Falcon.[16]

Next are the ones we call the Pleiades;[17] if they come out <crossed out:> [very] at their biggest people say, "This year we'll have plenty." But if they come out at their smallest people say, "We're in for a very hard time."

> They call another constellation, which stands out as a perfect ring, the Pihca Conqui.
>
> Certain other stars always appear very large.
> People give them the names Poco Huarac, Villca Huarac, and Cancho Huarac.
> In the old times, people, or at least some few of them, reportedly used to worship them, saying, "These are the animators, the makers."
> The rest still worshiped these stars as they were rising, spending the appropriate nights in sleepless vigil, but said, "We'll hold the other huacas in higher honor."
> This is all we know. (*Huarochirí Manuscript* 1991:132–133 [ca. 1608: Ch. 29])

Through this passage we again see a night sky populated with animals. The anonymous author of the Huarochirí manuscript pays particular attention to a llama suckling its calf. This constellation, however, appears to be different from the star-to-star llama constellations described by Polo de Ondegardo and Cobo. This time, a llama is represented as a large dark cloud constellation. The llama has two large eyes, presumably stars. The ethnographic work of Urton (1981a:185–188) provides a modern identification of this llama as a dark lane stretching from Scorpius to Centaurus. It ends near the two bright stars called "Llamacñawin" (eyes of the llama), or Alpha Centauri (Rigil Kent) and Beta Centauri (Hadar), the third and eleventh brightest stars in the sky. Besides being the progenitor of herds, the llama constellation may also be associated in Andean mythology with rain (Urton 1981a:54–65; Zuidema and Urton 1976). This dark cloud llama constellation should not be confused with the T-shaped stellar llama constellation described by Polo de Ondegardo and Cobo, since it is located approximately 90 degrees from Lyra (Photo 21).

The anonymous author of the Huarochirí manuscript states that a constellation that "comes before" the llama was called the Yutu. This is a partridgelike bird sometimes called Tinamou, after the Carib name. Again, the ethnographic work of Urton (1981a:181–185) provides an identification of this constellation. It is the Coalsack, a dark spot in the Milky Way southeast of the Southern Cross, which, as implied in the document, rises some hours before the dark llama and Alpha and Beta Centauri (Photo 19).

The Huarochirí manuscript mentions that there were three stars in a straight line, each named for a different bird (a condor, a vulture, and a falcon). It also describes the careful observation of the

Photo 21. The Dark Cloud Constellation of the Llama. A dark lane between Scorpius and Centaurus was seen as a llama, and the dark region below it was seen as its lamb. Alpha and Beta Centauri form the eyes of the llama. (Photograph by Dennis DiCicco)

Pleiades at dawn and indicates that their brightness was used in forecasting harvests. Moreover, the anonymous author states that there was a set of stars that formed a perfect ring, called the Pihca Conqui, and he mentions several other stars for which no descriptions are offered: Poco Huarac, Villca Huarac, and Cancho Huarac.[18]

Juan de Santa Cruz Pachacuti Yamqui Salcamayhua was an indigenous writer of the early seventeenth century. Born between Cuzco and Lake Titicaca sometime after the Spanish invasion, Pachacuti Yamqui Salcamayhua wrote in a mixture of Spanish, Quechua, and Aymará. Like the works of Guaman Poma de Ayala and the Huarochirí manuscript, Pachacuti Yamqui Salcamayhua's chronicle presents unique information on Inca astronomy, not recorded by European writers. The most acclaimed aspect of his work is an elaborate drawing said to depict a wall of the Coricancha. This drawing is an invaluable reference for understanding the Andean cosmology (Figure 8). A number of features on the left side of the wall are considered masculine in the Andean world, with corresponding

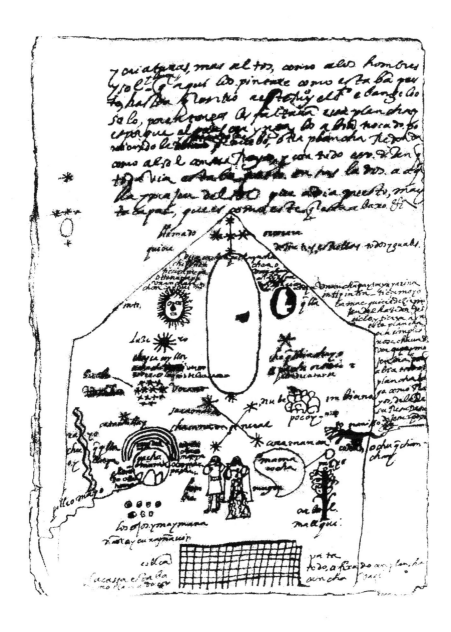

Figure 8. Pachacuti Yamqui Salcamayhua's drawing representing a wall of the Coricancha. The drawing has been interpreted as showing the masculine features of the Andean world on the right side and the feminine features on the left. Of the approximately twenty separate figures in the drawing, eight appear to be astronomical.

feminine features on the right (Isbell 1978:207–210). Of the approximately twenty separate figures in the drawing, eight appear to be astronomical. Along with prominently placed icons of the sun and moon, there are six figures that appear to be stellar or planetary. Several of these astronomical references have been interpreted by scholars, beginning with Lehmann-Nitsche (1928), as constellations.

At the peak of the gabled wall outline is a cross of five stars sitting above an oval. The cross is made of three stars in a row with single stars above and below them. The three stars in a row are labeled "Orcorara, which means three stars all equal."[19] This is reminiscent of the "three stars in a straight line" mentioned in the Huarochirí manuscript. Bertonio (1984: Pt. 2, 379 [1612]) translates the Aymará word *Orcorara* as "a large flock, or a crowd of men or animals." This cross of five stars is thought to represent the stars of Orion (Lehmann-Nitsche 1928:79; Isbell 1978:207). The three stars of Orion's belt are distinctive because of their nearly equal brightness and their straight alignment. Perpendicular to that line and below it (as viewed from Peru) is Betelgeuse, the eighth brightest star in the sky. An equal distance above the belt is Rigel, the seventh brightest star.

Directly under the oval in Pachacuti Yamqui Salcamayhua's drawing is a set of five stars, four of which are in the shape of a cross labeled "Chacana in general" and "Saramama" (maize mother);[20] the fifth is located slightly to one side. These stars are thought to symbolize the Southern Cross (Lehmann-Nitsche 1928:106–110), and indeed the drawing bears a striking resemblance to the five brightest stars of the Southern Cross. However, it should be noted that Pachacuti Yamqui Salcamayhua's label may suggest that this pattern of stars represents celestial crosses "in general" and not a specific constellation (Urton 1980:90; 1981a:132).

The right side of Pachacuti Yamqui Salcamayhua's drawing contains the moon, an evening star named Chuquechinchay,[21] winter clouds, water, and a catlike animal called Chuquechinchay. The position of the catlike animal among the celestial figures suggests a relationship to Chuquichinchay, Polo de Ondegardo's and Cobo's star representing jaguars. This suggestion is supported elsewhere in Pachacuti Yamqui Salcamayhua's chronicle (1950:242 [1613]) where he describes Chuquechinchay as "an animal of many colors which is said to be the lord of the Otorongos (large cats)."[22]

The left side incorporates the sun, a morning star labeled both "Luzero" and "Chasca Coyllur,"[23] a cluster of summer stars, and an isolated star called "Catachillay." The parallel morning and evening stars of the drawing may be Venus (Lehmann-Nitsche 1928:113–

115). The star cluster below the evening star could be interpreted as the Pleiades. Given the importance attached to the Pleiades in all other accounts, their omission would be surprising. Finally, on the left side of the figure are also representations of the world, springs, and lightning.

Another indigenous writer who provides information on the names of various stars is Guaman Poma de Ayala:

> These rumors the Indian women told and the philosophers told who know that in the stars there are men and women and sheep with their young and partridges and hunter and herder, grinding stone, lion, deer. And from the comets they know that which will occur, good and bad sign: *cuyllorcona, Chasca Cuyllor, Oncoy Cuyllor, Caza Cuyllor, Pacari Cuyllor, Uara Uara.*[24]

Besides giving a general term for stars, *cuyllorcona,* and the name of a currently unidentified star, Caza Cuyllor (hunter star?),[25] Guaman Poma de Ayala seems to refer to two morning stars, Chasca Cuyllor and Pacari Cuyllor, both of which may have been Venus. He mentions a star called Uara Uara, but Bertonio (1984: Pt. 1, 233; Pt. 2, 149, 379 [1612]) states in his Aymará dictionary that this term simply means "star." Guaman Poma de Ayala also gives general descriptions of stars and constellations that are known from other writers: the llamas and their calves, the partridge (Yutu), and the lion (Chuquichinchay), as well as lesser-known ones such as the herder (*pastor*), the grinding stone (*batán*), and the deer (*uenado*). Guaman Poma de Ayala (1980:62, 238 [1615:79, 264 (266)]) also clearly depicts the sun, moon, and a single star in two of his drawings (Figures 9 and 10). Elsewhere in his chronicle he notes that the star in these figures was "el Luzero" and that the Inca called it Chasca Cuyllor (Guaman Poma de Ayala 1980: 63, 161, 236, 239, 272 [1615: 80 (80) 185 (187), 263 (265), 265 (267), 299 (301)]). The term *luzero* (or *locero*) can be used for any bright star, but it is most frequently applied to Venus.

Guaman Poma de Ayala (1980:546, 831 [1615: 577 (591), 885 (899)]) also mentions a star called Oncoy Cuyllor (sick star), a star also noted in the writings of Pablo Joseph de Arriaga. In 1621 Arriaga published his now-famous work *La extirpación de la idolatría en el Perú* (The extirpation of idolatry in Peru). Within this detailed account of native religion, Arriaga furnishes the following reference to the Oncoy constellation:

> After the confessions are made in the solemn celebrations, of which there are three each year. The principal close to the celebration of

Figure 9. The Inca's coat of arms, according to Guaman Poma de Ayala, contained emblems of the Sun, Moon, Venus, and the shrine of Pacariqtambo.

Figure 10. Idols of the Inca. Guaman Poma de Ayala shows the Inca and his wife praying to the Sun, Moon, Venus, and the shrine of Pacariqtambo during the month of Capac Raymi.

> Corpus Christi, or at the same time, which they call Oncoy Mitta,
> which is when the Pleiades, which they call Oncoy, appear. They wor-
> ship [this constellation] so that the corn does not dry up.[26]

Arriaga states that the Oncoy constellation was the Pleiades and
that its observance was associated with maize production.[27] Furthermore, he indicates that in the postconquest era the worship of
this constellation was linked to its appearance around the time of
Corpus Christi.[28] The movable feast of Corpus Christi occurs on the
ninth Sunday following Easter, or the tenth Sunday following the
first full moon after the vernal equinox, a date that moves between
31 May and 28 June. This is close to the time in early June when the
Pleiades can be seen to rise before the sun.

Some studies present a specific date for the heliacal rise of the
Pleiades. The first day when a star can be seen rising before the sun
will vary depending on the atmospheric conditions and the lunar
phase. In the early sixteenth century, the sun passed nearest the
Pleiades in mid-May. By early June, the sun would have moved far
enough that the Pleiades, of rather modest brightness, could be seen
in the predawn sky. The author of the Huarochirí manuscript (1991:
132–133 [ca. 1608]) described just such a morning vigil watching for
a star to appear, and Urton's (1981a:118, 119) ethnographic work
finds such activities occurring today in rural villages. Urton (pers.
com. 1993) also suggests that Oncoy can mean "pregnant"; unfortunately, this modern usage of the word cannot be confirmed in any of
the sixteenth- or seventeenth-century lexicons. If in Inca times Oncoy also meant "pregnant," then the relation between the term Oncoy and the Pleiades as "the mother of all stars," as suggested by
Cobo, becomes clear.

Elsewhere in his work, Arriaga provides a list of specific questions which village leaders were to be asked during an anti-idolatry
campaign by the Spaniards. One of the questions concerned star
worship:

> Whether they know of any person or persons who have worshiped the
> sun, moon, or the stars they call Oncoy, which are the Pleiades, or the
> stars they call chacras, which are the three Marys, or the morning star
> which they call Pachahuárac or Coyahuárac. (Arriaga 1968b:165 [1621])[29]

Arriaga preserved important information in this question.[30] He repeats his identification of the Inca constellation of Oncoy with that
of the Pleiades, and he offers two names for the morning star (i.e.,
Venus): Pachahuárac and Coyahuárac. Furthermore, he provides

what appears to be an alternate name for the Andean constellation Chaccana (or Chacana [Orion's belt]), calling it "chacra" (field).

Garcilaso de la Vega also offers insights into Andean star watching. Although he was not educated in Andean astronomy and was unaware of the numerous stars named by other chroniclers, Garcilaso de la Vega (1945:110 [1609: Vol. 1, Bk. 2, Ch. 21]) does present information on both Venus and the Pleiades in the following passage:

> They called the sun *Inti*, the moon *Quilla*, and the planet Venus *Chasca*, which is "curly" or "mane," from its many rays. They watched the Pleiades because they look so close together and different from the other stars, which caused them admiration, but for no other reason. And they did not watch the other stars, because they had no need to do so and knew not of what is gained by watching them. Nor did they have names for particular stars, other than those already mentioned. In general they called them *cóillur*, which means star. (Garcilaso de la Vega 1966:115 [1609: Vol. 1, Bk. 2, Ch. 21])[31]

Slightly later in his chronicle, Garcilaso de la Vega (1966:120 [1609: Vol. 1, Bk. 2, Ch. 23]) discusses further the importance of Venus[32] in Inca astronomy:

> Regarding the star Venus, which sometimes they saw in the evening and sometimes at dawning, they said that the Sun, as lord of all the stars, order it to go near him, sometimes before him and sometimes behind, because it was more beautiful than the rest.[33]

There are several additional early colonial descriptions of native star watching. These brief references support the information presented above concerning the importance of Venus, the Pleiades, and Orion's belt in Inca astronomy.[34] In an account from the Guamanga area (modern Ayacucho), the following information is provided by Luis de Monzón (1881:204–205 [1586]) on Andean star worship:

> And by order of the Incas they worshipped the sun and the moon and the stars and especially the morning star, which in their language is called *auquilla*, and the Pleiades, which in their language is called *larilla*, and other large stars.[35]

Monzón's description furnishes unique names for the morning star (auquilla) and the Pleiades (larilla). Apparently the villagers of the Guamanga area worshiped many of the same stars as the people in the rest of the Andes, but they had different names for them.

From another part of the Guamanga area comes a report, *Misión de las provincias de los Huachos y Yauyos*, written by an anonymous Jesuit in 1613. This account, influenced by the anti-idolatry campaigns of the Huarochirí region, discusses various huacas of the region. It notes that there were four major celebrations in the year, one of which was related to when the Pleiades[36] appear:

> One was when the Oncoy, which are the Pleiades, first appears and is seen in their hemisphere.[37]

Fernando de Avendaño, a priest who lived in Lima and several other locations in Peru during the early seventeenth century, also recorded information on native star knowledge.[38] A letter written by Avendaño on 3 April 1617 contains this description:

> The Indians worship two classes of Idols, some fixed, like hills and cliffs and high snow-covered peaks, and the sun, moon, and the stars, the Pleiades, and the Three Marys, and the thunder and lightening, and the ocean and springs; the other [class] are movable, like those they have in their fields.[39]

Here Avendaño mentions two constellations that have been noted by other early colonial writers: the Pleiades and the Three Marys (Orion's belt). Elsewhere in the same letter, Avendaño (1904:381 [1617]) states that the Pleiades were called Oncoimita:

> . . . and the major [celebration] of the year was for Corpus Christi, which is when the Pleiades were best seen and they called it Oncoimita, and they have particularly dedicated this time, because it is when the maize freezes and crops are spoiled.[40]

Like Arriaga, Avendaño indicates that the Pleiades were watched during Corpus Christi and were worshiped to promote a successful maize harvest.

The late, 1638, work of Calancha (1981:835 [1638: Bk. 2, Ch. 11]) also includes a brief passage that mentions Venus as well as the Pleiades:

> They worshipped the stars, the morning star and the evening star Venus; the Pleiades that they call *Collca*.[41]

Elsewhere in his chronicle, Calancha stresses the importance that the Pleiades had in defining a year for the north coast populations (the Pacasmayos and Yungas) of Peru:

They do not count the year by Moons or by the course of the Sun, but rather from the rise of the stars which we call the Cabrillas (the Pleiades) and which they call Fur. The reason for this is found in a long fable, which is none of my concern. It was a law that they counted the year thusly, because these stars gave them food and nurtured their crops, for their livelihood, therefore, they had to begin the year from the time they saw it appear and it gave them sustenance. (Calancha 1981:1244–1245 [1638: Bk. 3, Ch. 2]; translation by Urton and Aveni 1983:222)[42]

Calancha (1981:1243 [1638: Bk. 3, Ch. 2]) also mentions Orion's belt (las Marías) and includes rare information on north coast star mythology:

Divine for them were two stars that they called Patá, which we call The Marys, and many of these Indians today tell (and many perhaps believe) that the star in the middle is a thief, and villain and bastard, that the Moon chose to punish and sent to the two stars to take it with them (this is what Patá means) and handed it over to vultures which are those buzzards formed by the four stars which are a ways below The Marys. And in memory of this exemplar punishment these seven stars are in the sky recalling the blame and the punishment.[43]

In connection with Calancha's information on Orion, Donnan (1978:95) has noted that a figure being consumed by buzzards while tied to a post is common in the iconography of the early north coast Moche (Figure 11). The association of such figures (Larco Hoyle 1938–1939: Fig. 215; Hocquenghem 1987: Fig. 29) with the stars of Orion requires a continuity of myth and imagery that lasts for nearly a millennium. Though this is a long time, it is no longer than that found for the common European recognition of the stars of Cygnus as a Cross.

From 1656 to 1664 a series of anti-idolatry campaigns were conducted in the north central highlands of Peru, in the region of Cajatambo. Duviols (1986) has published many of the native "confessions" that resulted from these investigations as recorded among the papers of the Archbishop of Lima. Star worship is mentioned in more than forty separate testimonies. For example, one villager indicated that the stars were worshiped two times a year (Ysabel Llupay Vilca 1656: fol. 12v, in Duviols 1986:97). Other individuals (e.g., Hernando Chaupiscon 1658: fol. 20, in Duviols 1986:160) indicated that Venus (el lusero) was called "Chachaguaras" and that it was associated with *curacas* (local lords). Furthermore, one informant stated that the Pleiades were called "Pugllaiguaico" (Pedro

Guamanbilca 1658: fol. 66, in Duviols 1986:227). The most detailed statement concerning native star worship is given by Hernando Hacaspoma:

> And likewise they adore the morning star which they called atungara [Hatunhuarac] as creator of the elder and leaders and likewise two small stars, which travel with the Pleiades, which they called Chuchuco[y]llor as creators of the *chuchus* and *chacpas* which are those that are born feet first and those of twins which they say are children of the idols and huacas.
>
> And likewise they worship the seven stars called the Pleiades and called in their language Oncoicoillur, the stars that appear when the frost begins around Corpus and San Juan so that their fields will not freeze and so that there will be no disease and pests and they said this prayer: *paoc yaya oncoiyaya ama micuita cagahum ama micuita rachachum* powerful lord which has much food and property do not permit the frost to spoil our fields.[44]

Hacaspoma suggests that Venus was called "the great star" (Hatunhuarac). He also indicates, like so many other writers, that the Pleiades were associated with maize, and that these stars were watched near the time of Corpus Christi. In addition, Hacaspoma describes a constellation called "Chuchucoyllor" as two stars that traveled close to the Pleiades.[45] Although the brevity of this description makes a definitive identification of these two "small" stars impossible, the proximity to the Pleiades suggests that they are among the stars of Taurus or the southern part of Perseus (Photo 18).[46]

Finally, Bertonio's Aymará dictionary (1984: Pt. 1, 236; Pt. 2, 161, 226 [1612]) provides several additional names that were used for the Pleiades, including Hucchu, Vel Vicchu, and Mucchu.

These brief citations conclude our review of early colonial accounts of stellar and planetary observations. The named objects identified as planets, stars, and constellations recorded in these accounts are summarized in the Appendix.[47] Before discussing these accounts, however, we examine several theories that suggest that specific archaeological sites in the Cuzco region served as star observation points.

The Ceque System and the Stars

The Inca built a series of towers on the hills surrounding the capital to mark the annual movement of the sun along the horizon. It is also clear that they were interested in the appearance, disappear-

Figure 11. Buzzards consuming a malefactor bound to a post was a popular motif among Moche artisans a thousand years before Calancha's information relating this image to Orion. (Based on a drawing by Hocquenghem 1987: Fig. 29)

ance, and movement of various stars. From these known facts, it is possible to propose that the Inca may also have built markers, or used natural features, to locate the rise and set of certain stars. In this section, we explore various hypotheses that connect archaeological remains in Cuzco with Inca star watching.

Unlike the sun, stars rise and set at fixed positions throughout the year. This being the case, a single point on the horizon can serve as a near permanent marker of an individual star's rise or set position.[48] For approximately half the year, a star can be observed to rise sometime during the night, and for the remainder of the year, it rises during the day and will become visible in the sky only after sunset. From Peru, most stars are not visible on days when the sun has the same right ascension (east/west coordinate in the sky) as the star. This period of invisibility follows the last evening on which the star still can be seen after sunset, referred to as a "heliacal set." Eventually the sun moves past the star, and the period of invisibility ends with the first morning the star can be seen rising before the dawn, known as a "heliacal rise."

The duration of a star's invisibility depends on its brightness, how close the sun passes to it, the amount of extraneous light present in the sky (which changes with the phases of the moon), and the transparency of the atmosphere. When the atmospheric transparency is low (due to humidity, for example), stars must rise higher before becoming visible, and will appear fainter when first seen. These conditions may explain the passage in the Huarochirí manuscript (1991: 133 [ca. 1608: Ch. 29]) which states, "if they [the Pleiades] come out . . . at their biggest people say, 'This year we'll have plenty.' But if they come out at their smallest people say, 'We're in for a very hard time.'" Variations in atmospheric conditions as well as changes in the ambient light level due to the lunar phase and position will alter the altitude at which the Pleiades, or any star, can be seen in the dawn or dusk sky. As a result, the period of invisibility will change from year to year. For the Pleiades, a disappearance from the night sky lasting forty to fifty days is quite reasonable.

Guiding the eye to the correct location will help to detect a star when it first rises, particularly when a heliacal rise of a faint star (or group of stars) is competing with the brightening of the predawn sky. One of the easiest ways to guide the eye is with some immovable point of reference, like a window or a wall. This method could be used by village star watchers who make observations for their own purposes, or by a small number of priests who would report their observations to others. It is also possible to construct or select a horizon feature to mark a stellar position and aid in observing stellar appearance. It is important to remember that to use the fiducial effectively, it must be visible at low light levels. As with the observation of a sunrise on a distant horizon, it is probably easier to find an observation location from which natural features can be used than it is to construct the necessary large horizon markers needed in star watching. Such natural horizon markers could be used by a large group of watchers.

Ceques as Astronomical Sight Lines

Zuidema (1980, 1981b, 1982a–c, 1983a–b, 1988b) has proposed that many of the ceques formed straight lines and that some ceques are astronomically aligned. In a detailed hypothesis concerning Inca star watching, he propounds that certain ceques of the Cuzco region were used as stellar sight lines. For stars that have an annual period of invisibility, the first morning rise and last evening set can be used to define a "star season." Zuidema (1982b, 1983b) incorporates four of these seasons into a complex model of a calendrically functioning ceque system. This hypothesis has been developed through years of investigation and requires some background information to be understood.

The first step in understanding the ceque–star season hypothesis is to assume certain ceques of Cuzco were straight lines. Cobo (1980:15 [1653: Bk. 13, Ch. 13]) begins his description of the ceque system by stating that "From the Temple of the Sun as from the center there went out certain lines which the Indians call ceques . . . ," and he proceeds to list the huacas of each ceque in an order proceeding away from the Coricancha. Cobo's description of the Cuzco ceque system can be compared with Cristóbal de Molina's (1989: 126–128 [ca. 1575]) description of the Capac Cocha ritual. This celebration was not linked to any particular month, but was performed for important events like the coronation of a new Inca. During a Capac Cocha event, offerings were gathered in Cuzco and then redistributed to all the huacas of the empire. The individuals who made the offerings are said to have traveled to the huacas in straight lines (Molina 1989:127 [ca. 1575]). Zuidema (1977a:231) has extrapolated from Molina's account of the Capac Cocha ritual to argue that the huacas of certain ceques in the Cuzco system formed straight lines and were used in making astronomical observations.

The proposition that some ceques formed sight lines that were astronomically aligned has become widely accepted and has influenced the findings of other researchers. Sherbondy (1982, 1986, 1987) and Van der Guchte (1984, 1990) have conducted fieldwork in the Hanan Cuzco region to identify the locations of certain huacas. These researchers have concluded their investigations with detailed maps illustrating the projection of ceques as straight lines across Chinchaysuyu and Antisuyu. The straight-line hypothesis has also been reinforced by the many hypothetical reconstructions of the system that have been published (see Chávez Ballón 1970; Wachtel 1973; Sherbondy 1982, 1986; Urton 1984; Van der Guchte 1984, 1990; Zuidema 1964, 1977a, 1983b, 1990; Aveni 1990; Farrington 1992).

According to this model of the system, the various ceques radiated from the Temple of the Sun to mark specific points on the Cuzco horizon, and some of these points were linked to specific star rises and sets. Zuidema (1982b, 1983b) has proposed that the sixth,

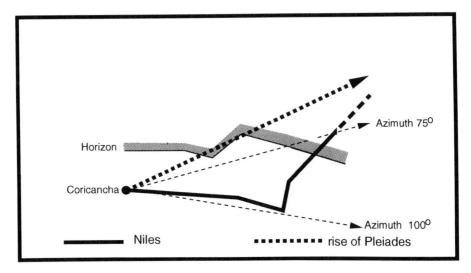

Figure 12. The course of ceque An. 5 (following the work of Niles). As viewed from the Coricancha, the shrines of the fifth ceque of Antisuyu (An. 5) are spread across 25 degrees of azimuth and cross the horizon at a location more than 10 degrees from the rise of the Pleiades.

eighth, and ninth ceques of Chinchaysuyu (Ch. 6, Ch. 8, and Ch. 9) were aligned with the sets of Vega, the Pleiades, and Betelgeuse respectively; the fifth and sixth ceques of Antisuyu (An. 5 and An. 6) with the rise of the Pleiades and Betelgeuse; and the first ceque of Cuntisuyu (Cu. 1) with the rise of Beta Centauri. All of these were important stars for the Inca (Table 5 and Appendix). The beliefs that the ceques of Cuzco ran in straight lines and that certain ceques of the system were aligned with the rise and set positions of specific stars are intriguing ideas and worth exploring.

A test of the physical straightness of the Cuzco ceques can be made using the huaca identifications proposed by Niles (1987:181–190) based on her archaeological investigation of the fifth ceque of Antisuyu (An. 5)—a ceque which Zuidema suggests was aligned with the rise of the Pleiades. Niles' shrine identifications are based on huaca descriptions provided by Cobo, surviving place names, and the courses of Inca roads. Precise locations, descriptions, and photographs are given for each candidate. The ceque defined from these proposed huaca identifications is far from straight, and the shrines of An. 5 are spread across 25 degrees of azimuth as viewed from the Coricancha (Figure 12) and cross the horizon at a location more than 10 degrees from the rise of the Pleiades.

After intensive survey work in the Cuzco Valley, both Niles (1987:

171–206) and Bauer (1992a, 1992c) have determined that An. 5 is not exceptional and that many of the ceques did not form straight lines. These studies suggest that certain huacas and their respective ceques are found in locations radically different from those predicted by the straight-line representation of the ceque system. In addition, the studies indicate that ceques changed directions as they zigzagged their way across the landscape. If this is the case, then it would be difficult for the ceques themselves to have formed sight lines radiating from the center of Cuzco to mark specific star rises and sets on the horizon. This point is illustrated in Figure 13, which uses the fieldwork of Bauer (n.d.b) to plot the courses of ceques Ch. 6, Ch. 8, Ch. 9, An. 5, An. 6, and Cu. 1. The directions of the associated stellar rises and sets as viewed from the Coricancha (the origin of the ceques), as well as the approximate horizon line, are also included on this figure. It can be seen that the range of azimuths subtended by huacas of individual ceques often exceeds 30 degrees. This angle is so broad that there appears to be no significant physical basis for the association of these ceques to specific stars.

Individual Huacas as Star Fiducials

While ceques were not actually straight lines, it might be suggested that a direction is defined by a single important huaca on the horizon. Documents suggest that if any star or constellation was marked it would have been the Pleiades, thus we use them as a test. The ceque that Zuidema (1982b) believes was aligned to the set of the Pleiades was Ch. 8, for which the horizon was marked by the solar pillars, Sucanca (Ch. 8:7). As discussed in chapters above, the pillars of Sucanca were on Picchu, but their precise location cannot currently be determined.

Zuidema (1982b:211–212) supports the proposed alignment of Ch. 8 to the set of the Pleiades with the name of the tenth huaca of this ceque, Catachillay (Ch. 8:10), which he claims refers to the Pleiades.[49] The identification of Catachillay with the Pleiades contradicts nearly all of the early colonial documents from Peru, which state that the Pleiades were called Collca or Oncoy by the Inca. The exception is Bertonio's (1984: Pt. 1, 107, 150, 236; Pt. 2, 38 [1612]) Aymará dictionary, which provides multiple identifications for the name Catachillay, including one in which the Pleiades are mentioned. As has been discussed above, Catachillay is the name used by Polo de Ondegardo and Cobo to identify a constellation of a female llama. These writers specifically indicate that the star of Catachillay was near the constellation Lyra which is some 110 degrees

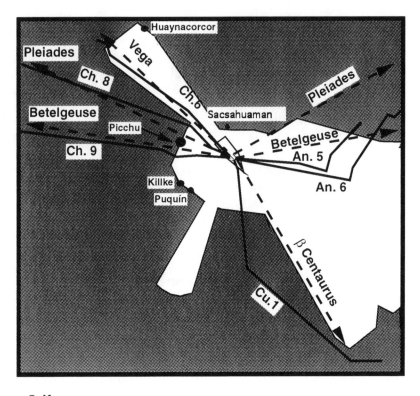

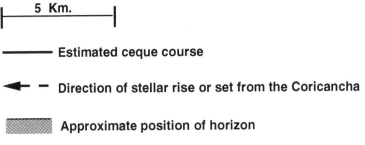

Figure 13. The physical relation between ceques and the rise and set positions of stars. The estimated courses of ceques Ch. 6, Ch. 8, Ch. 9, An. 5, An. 6, and Cu. 1 are compared to the direction for the sets of Vega, the Pleiades, and Betelgeuse and the rises of the Pleiades, Betelgeuse and Beta Centauri.

across the sky from the Pleiades and sets nearly 17 degrees farther north.

It has also been proposed that the fifth ceque of Antisuyu (An. 5) was aligned with the rising point of the Pleiades. In support of this, Zuidema (1982b:216) uses the seventeenth-century Quechua poem recorded by Pérez Bocanegra that describes the rise of Catachillay. The poem ends with the name *susurwana*. Zuidema (1982b:215–218) associates the root of this word, *susur*, with the eighth huaca of An. 5, named Susumarca (An. 5:8), and suggests that this shrine marked the direction of the Pleiades rise. Zuidema believes that this huaca lies somewhere near the Hacienda Susurmarca, northeast of Cuzco.[50] Niles (1987:197) agrees with this general position of Susumarca (An. 5:8), and Bauer has identified a specific spring in the area as the most likely candidate. Its azimuth, approximately 75 degrees, is nearly 10 degrees from where the Pleiades rise as viewed from the Coricancha. This is too far away to be useful in guiding the eye to the position of the Pleiades rise. It should also be noted that neither the huaca Catachillay (Ch. 8:10) nor that of Susumarca (An. 5:8) could have served to actually mark the rise or set of the Pleiades, not only because of their locations in the landscape but also because neither is situated on a horizon.

In sum, at the close of our archaeological and astronomical research in the Cuzco region we found no clear evidence to support the proposition that certain ceques or individual shrines of the Cuzco ceque system are aligned with the rise and set positions of specific stars. The relationships between Inca sites and stellar observations merit further exploration, along the lines of studies like those of Hyslop (1985) at the Inca installation of Incahuasi in the Cañete Valley. Future studies, however, must not assume that the alignments proposed for Cuzco are known.

The Coricancha and the Rise of the Pleiades

Unlike solar observations, which used horizon pillars, there is no direct historical documentation stating that the Inca constructed monuments to mark the heliacal rises and sets of any stars. Nevertheless, Cobo's (1990:30 [1653: Bk. 13, Ch. 6]) comment that people kept better track of the Pleiades than of any other star, as well as Arriaga's (1968a:213 [1621: Ch. 5]), Avendaño's (1904:381 [1617]) and Hacaspoma's (1656: fol. 14–14v, in Duviols 1986:151) descriptions linking an important feast held near the time of Corpus Christi to the rise of the Pleiades, demonstrates Inca interest in observing the rise of this group of stars. This interest may still survive, as Randall (1982) has proposed a link between Corpus Christi, the rise of the Pleiades, and one of today's major Andean pilgrimage celebrations, Coyllor Riti (snow star). Given that the Inca, and other Andean peoples, were interested in observing the Pleiades, researchers working in Cuzco have been interested in investigating possible observation points for these stars. Among the various positions tested, the Coricancha is currently the most plausible.

Information presented by various chroniclers on the principal temple of the Inca, the Coricancha, has been discussed by Rowe (1944:26–41). Within its walls, this temple is said to have held a shrine to the stars. If this is the case, then it is possible that the Inca watched particular star rises or sets from this temple. In 1976 and 1980, Aveni and Zuidema recorded a series of astronomical measurements in the Coricancha. They found that the southwest wall of the courtyard faced an azimuth of 66° 44' or slightly more than 20' north of the position where the Pleiades rose in A.D. 1500 (Zuidema 1982b:214). From this Zuidema (1982b:214) suggests that the heliacal rise of the Pleiades was observed from this temple area (Figure 14), and he pays particular attention to a passageway that enters the courtyard through the southwest wall. The northeastern side of the courtyard had two gabled rooms, but the section of wall across from the passage was between the rooms and therefore had no gables to obscure the horizon.

We tested these alignments and measured the orientation of the passageway. The exact azimuth for the passageway depends on which side of the hallway is measured, but on average it marks a horizon position slightly north of that defined by the southwest wall of the Coricancha (Zuidema 1982b:214). However, the difference is insignificant when one takes into consideration that the stars of the Pleiades are spread across a degree of sky. Though not aligned to the precise spot where the Pleiades rose in A.D. 1500, the orientation of this passageway is close enough to guide an observer to the proper region of horizon. Andean interest in the Pleiades makes it plausible to suggest that the Inca watched the Pleiades rise from the Coricancha, but it cannot be known with certainty. Nor can it currently be assumed with any assurance that the orientation of the Coricancha was set for this observation.

Summary of Inca Star Watching

The documentary fragments of Inca stellar astronomy reveal a night sky filled with animal images frequently associated with the processes of reproduction. We propose that this plethora of animals was

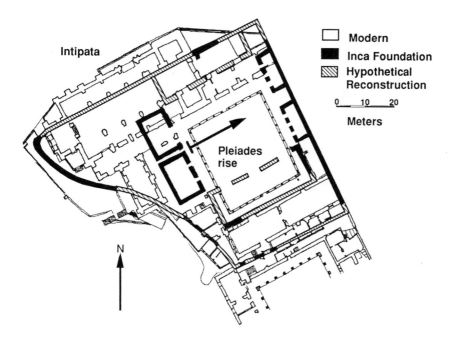

Figure 14. Santo Domingo, the Coricancha, and the rise of the Pleiades. Aveni and Zuidema found that the southwest wall of the courtyard of the Coricancha faced 20' north of the direction where the Pleiades rose in A.D. 1500. (Base map from Gasparini and Margolies 1980:46)

a precipitate of a general pan-Andean, folk astronomy that, unlike solar worship, underwent little change during the growth of the Inca Empire (Photo 22). While bright (large) stars are considered the principal candidates for stars named by the Inca, striking groups, such as the rather faint Pleiades, were also important.[51] The considerable variations found among the star names suggest that there was no systematic attempt by the Inca to impose a centralized, state-controlled stellar astronomy on conquered peoples.

Preeminent among the observed stars were the Pleiades. They had several names, including Collca and Oncoy as well as Larilla, Fur, and Pugllaiguaico. Cobo, copying from Polo de Ondegardo, writes that this cluster was considered to be the mother of all stars and that "those Indians who were informed about such matters kept better track of its course all year long than that of any of the other stars." The Pleiades were believed by the Inca to be associated with maize production, and their appearance and disappearance were observed with great interest. This custom continues today as villagers

Photo 22. The Milky Way. Andean sky watchers saw the Milky Way as a river (mayu). At the latitude of Peru, the thickest and brightest part of the Milky Way (the Sagittarius-Scorpius region) passes prominently overhead.

examine the brightness of the Pleiades for information concerning the maize harvest (Urton 1981a:119).

Less is known about the functioning of planets in Inca astronomy, although it is clear that Venus was closely watched. Because Venus orbits the sun closer than the earth does, it can only be seen in the evening or in the morning. Venus, like the Pleiades, bore a number of names, including Chasca Cuyllor, Pacaric Chasca, Pacari Cuyllor, Auquilla, Pachahuárac, Chachaquaras, and Atungara. The identification of Venus in historical texts, however, should be considered tentative, since, as Urton (1981a:166–167) notes, some of these names refer to bright evening and morning stars as well as to Venus.

In spite of the dearth of information on Inca constellations, historical and ethnographic research permits some identifications (Table 5). The Andean star constellations representing a male and female llama, Catachillay and Urcuchillay, are particularly intriguing. Zuidema (1982b:211–212, 219–224) associates the name Catachillay with two different constellations. He uses one of Bertonio's multiple entries to relate Catachillay to the Pleiades. Our review of the historic materials on Inca star watching does not support this

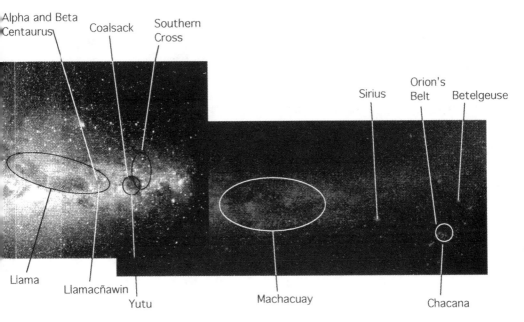

Animal constellations were identified with darker portions of the Milky Way as well as with groups of stars. (Photograph by Dennis DiCicco)

identification, as it contradicts the detailed accounts of Polo de Ondegardo and Cobo that describe Catachillay and the Pleiades as two distinctly separate constellations. Elsewhere in the same study, Zuidema (1982b:219–224) associates Catachillay and Urcuchillay with Alpha and Beta Centauri. Again, there are no direct historic references to support this association. Alpha and Beta Centauri are near the end of a dark rift in the Milky Way. Ethnographic research by Urton (1981a: 54–65, 103) and Zuidema (1983b; Zuidema and Urton 1976) has convincingly identified this dark cloud as the llama described by Garcilaso de la Vega. Alpha and Beta Centauri are then consistent with being the bright stars that were described as form-ing the eyes of that llama in the Huarochirí manuscript. This dark cloud llama constellation, called the Yacana, is situated in the area of Centaurus and should not be confused with the llama constella-tions named Urcuchillay and Catachillay, which were made up of at least five stars in a completely different part of the sky. Polo de On-degardo states that Urcuchillay was in Lyra, and Cobo writes that it included two smaller stars forming a T. These writers indicate that Catachillay, a female llama and her calf, was located near Urcuchillay and was made up of one large and one small star. Polo de Ondegardo's and Cobo's descriptions of Catachillay, coupled with Bertonio's description of it as a nebulous star in the Milky Way, and Gonçález Holguín's identification of it as some star in the cross, strongly suggest that the female star llama was in Cygnus.

Another tentative identification is the constellation that Polo de Ondegardo called Chacana. Gonçález Holguín indicates that this constellation represented what the Spaniards referred to as "the Three Marys," or Orion's belt. Arriaga and Avendaño provide additional information, confirming that Orion's belt was an important Andean constellation, and ethnographic work by Urton documents that it is still called Chacana in the region of Cuzco. The identification of stars in Orion with the stars at the top of Pachacuti Yamqui Salcamayhua's drawing of a wall in the Coricancha is also plausible. His figure would seem to be a remarkably accurate representation of Orion's belt plus the bright stars Betelgeuse and Rigel. Pachacuti Yamqui Salcamayhua's name for this constellation is Orcorara, which, he writes, was three stars of equal brightness. It is even possible, although highly speculative, that the three stars of the belt could have been those called the Condor, the Vulture, and the Falcon in the Huarochirí manuscript. Testimonies from the area of Cajatambo suggest another Andean constellation, called Chuchucoyllor, was located in the region of Taurus or Perseus, since it is described as two stars near the Pleiades.

Two other possible dark cloud constellations identified in the work of Urton (1981a, 103–105) are the Machacuay (snake) and Yutu (also called the partridge by Guaman Poma de Ayala). The Machacuay is believed to be a black streak between Canis Major near η CMa (Adhara) and the Southern Cross.[52] The Yutu is described in the Huarochirí manuscript as a small dark spot that goes before the llama. Urton suggests that this constellation corresponds to the dark cloud constellation, known to us as the Coalsack, located near the Southern Cross.

Additional stars mentioned in more than one source included Mamana mircu and Choquechinchay. Mamana mircu is briefly mentioned by Polo de Ondegardo, and Gonçález Holguín states that this star ate its parents. Choquechinchay is described by Polo de Ondegardo, Cobo, and Pachacuti Yamqui Salcamayhua as a large cat. Although Urton (1981a) and Lehmann-Nitsche (1928) have some data on these constellations, their identifications are still open to investigation.

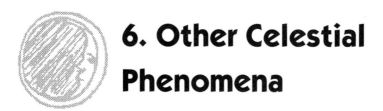

6. Other Celestial Phenomena

THE SLOW CYCLES OF THE SUN, moon, planets, and stars are regular and dependable features in an otherwise changing world. Superimposed on the order of these progressions are other unpredictable and transient celestial events. There are atmospheric phenomena that appear in the sky that may not have been distinguished by the Inca from astronomical phenomena. Among these are rainbows, lunar halos, noctilucent clouds, and sun dogs.[1] In mountainous regions, the flashes of light from distant thunderstorms that can be seen above the horizon may also have been classed with astronomical events.[2] Watchers of the night sky likewise are familiar with phenomena like meteors,[3] fireballs, and less-frequent novae or supernovae. While a regular observer will readily recognize the differences between meteors, noctilucent clouds, and comets, an individual who only casually looks at the sky may not.

Bright comets and eclipses are dramatic and highly visible events. People who look to the sky for omens cannot ignore the sudden appearance of these unexpected celestial occurrences.[4] To the Inca, as to many ancient cultures, comets and eclipses were occasions for concern and fear. These unusual celestial events left deep impressions on those who witnessed them, and they invariably found their way into history and myth. In some instances, the inclusion of astronomical phenomena in precontact accounts can help date events in Inca history (Ziółkowski 1985). At the very least, these accounts provide evidence that indigenous astronomers were interested in a broad range of celestial phenomena. This chapter will present and discuss the available information from the conquest and early colonial eras on eclipses and comets.[5]

Eclipses

The daily appearance of the sun is one of the most reliable events of our world. Few events are as "wrong" as its disappearance in the middle of a clear day. On such occasions, the sky takes on aspects of twilight, and the planets and bright stars become visible. The sun itself is surrounded by a pale corona extending several times its radius, and bright red arcs appear at the rim of the black spot that is the sun itself. Every year, there are two to five solar eclipses. Some are partial, others annular (this is a "ring eclipse," where the apparent size of the moon is smaller than that of the sun), and others are total. Averaged over time, the earth experiences 1.5 central (annular or total) eclipses each year. Because only a small fraction of the earth's surface experiences these eclipses, they can be considered uncommon events. Any particular spot on the earth's surface experiences a total solar eclipse once every few centuries.[6] Between the years 1440 and 1570, some 27 annular or total eclipses of the sun, and approximately twice as many partial eclipses, crossed the territory of Tahuantinsuyu (Table 6 and Figure 15).

Lunar eclipses are slightly less frequent than solar eclipses. The annual number of events ranges between zero and three, but they are visible over large areas. A lunar eclipse can be seen from any spot on the earth's surface nearly every year, and the Spaniards in the New World witnessed these events along with the indigenous populations.[7] Cobo notes how some Spanish priests would predict the coming of lunar eclipses as a means to convince the local population that such events were simply a natural phenomenon.

> The Spaniards have acquired the reputation of being very wise because the Indians are extremely impressed by the fact that we are capable of predicting the eclipses with such precision that we let them know not only the night that one will occur but even the exact time that it will begin, the amount of the moon that will be darkened, and how long it will last. Since they do not understand the causes of such an admirable phenomenon, they are struck dumb when they see that we can predict an eclipse. (Cobo 1990:30 [1653: Bk. 13, Ch. 6])[8]

Information on eclipses was available to the Spaniards in a number of resources. For example, the almanac of Zamorano (1585:232–242) provides the necessary information to calculate the hour of eclipses at many locations in the Americas, including Cuzco.

The sun provides the energy to grow crops, and it was universally

Table 6. *The Total and Annular Solar Eclipses between 1440 and 1570 That Passed through Tahuantinsuyu*

Julian Date			Type	Comments
1444	May	17	annular	Sun partially eclipsed at sunset
1445	Oct	30	total	Southern Chile
1459	July	29	total	Near Quito
1460	Jan	23	annular	Southern Chile
1467	Aug	29	annular	Central Chile
1470	Dec	22	annular	Colombia
1471	June	18	total	Southern Chile at sunrise
1485	Mar	16	total	Near Quito
1488	Jan	13	annular	Sun partially eclipsed at sunset
1492	Apr	26	annular	Colombia
1498	June	19	annular	Southern Chile
1499	Dec	2	total	Central Chile
1510	Nov	1	annular	Colombia
1513	Aug	30	total	Near Cuzco
1514	Feb	24	annular	Northern Chile
1521	Sept	30	annular	Northern Chile at sunrise
1524	July	30	total	Southern Ecuador/Northern Peru
1535	Dec	24	total	Central Chile
1538	Apr	28	total	Sun partially eclipsed at sunset
1539	Apr	18	total	Southern Ecuador
1542	Feb	14	annular	Southern Ecuador near sunset
1543	July	31	total	Northern Chile in the morning
1550	Sept	10	total	Near Quito
1553	July	10	annular	Southern Ecuador
1563	Dec	15	total	Southern Chile near sunrise
1567	Oct	2	total	Central Chile
1568	Mar	28	annular	Central Peru

Data from Oppolzer (1962).

accepted in the Andes as a major deity. The unexpected total or partial obscuring of the sun, or his wife the moon, seemed to threaten the safety of the world. The real physical danger of blindness from watching a partially eclipsed sun may have supported the general concerns about the eclipses.[9] Polo de Ondegardo, Cobo, Garcilaso de la Vega, and Arriaga provide consistent descriptions of Inca responses to these events, including wailing and dog beating.[10] Polo de Ondegardo gives the following account of the indigenous reaction to eclipses and comets:

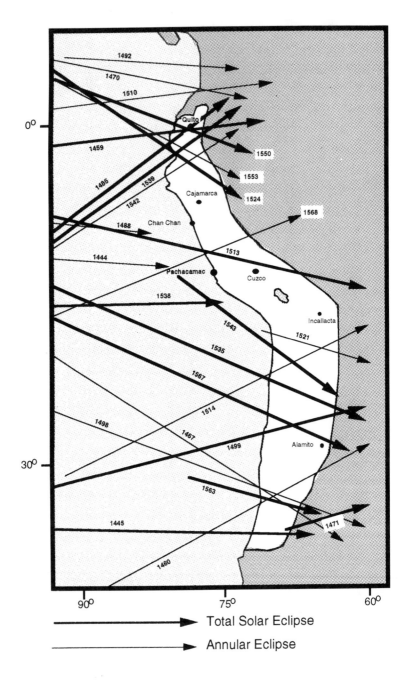

Figure 15. The total and annular solar eclipses between 1440 and 1570 that passed through Tahuantinsuyu.

When there is an eclipse of the sun or of the moon, or when a comet appears, or a flash in the skies, they shout and weep, ask other people to shout and weep, and make the dogs bark or howl by beating them. They also walk in processions around their homes at night with lighted torches and perform other ceremonies, so that the evil that they fear and that they regard as a bad omen will not befall them. (Polo de Ondegardo 1965d:204 [1567])[11]

Cobo provides a slightly longer commentary on solar and lunar eclipses, some of which seems to be based on his observations of eclipses during his prolonged stay in Peru:

They felt that the eclipse of the Sun was a grave matter, and when an eclipse occurred, they consulted with their diviners about its significance. Once they were certain of the effects implied by the eclipse, they made large and expensive sacrifices, including in them several images of gold and silver. In addition they would kill much livestock and many boys and girls. Normally, the sorcerer would pretend that the eclipse foretold the death of some prince and indicated that the Sun went into mourning because he had nothing to do in the world. When this happened, all of the women dedicated to the Sun would go on long fasts, wear clothing that showed their sadness, and offer frequent sacrifices. . . .

They had as many foolish ideas about the eclipse of the Moon as they did about that of the Sun. They said that when there was an eclipse of the Moon a [mountain] lion or a serpent was attacking in order to tear her apart, and for that reason they shouted at the top of their voices and whipped their dogs so that they would bark and howl. The men made ready for war by blowing their trumpets, beating their drums, and yelling as loud as they could. They hurled arrows and spears at the Moon, and they made menacing gestures with their spears, as if they were going to wound the lion and the serpent. They said that this was done to frighten the lion and the serpent so that they would not tear the Moon apart.

This they did because they understood that if the lion accomplished his aim, the world would be left in darkness. This custom was so ingrained in their minds that even though they have been Christians for many years and always heard sermons against this custom, they have not forsaken it entirely. In fact they still shout loudly when there is an eclipse of the moon. (Cobo 1990:27, 29 [1653: Bk. 13, Chs. 6 and 7])[12]

Garcilaso de la Vega was born in Cuzco in 1539 and lived there for twenty years. During that time, four total or annular solar eclipses

crossed the territory that had been Tahuantinsuyu. The path of totality for the solar eclipse of 1543 passed south of Cuzco, and as
viewed from that city, about 80 percent of the sun would have been
covered. The center line of the eclipses of 1542, 1550, and 1553
passed north of Cuzco, but again, most of the sun was covered. In
this period, there were fourteen lunar eclipses visible in Cuzco
(weather permitting), and some of them were witnessed by Garcilaso de la Vega. These are his comments on eclipses:

> They observed the eclipses of the sun and moon, but without under-
> standing their causes. When there was a solar eclipse, they said the Sun
> was angry at some offense committed against him, since his face ap-
> peared disturbed like that of an angry man, and they foretold, as as-
> trologers do, the approach of some grave punishment. When the moon
> was eclipsed, they said she was ill as she grew dark, and thought that if
> she disappeared altogether, she would die and the sky would fall in and
> crush them all, and that the end of the world would come. When a lunar
> eclipse began, they were seized with fear and sounded trumpets, bugles,
> horns, drums, and all the instruments they could find for making a
> noise. They tied up their dogs, large and small, and beat them with
> many blows and made them howl and call the moon back, for according
> to a certain fable they told, they thought that the moon was fond of dogs
> in return for a service they had done her, and that if she heard them cry
> she would be sorry for them and awake from the sleep caused by her
> sickness. . . .
>   They assessed the sickness of the Moon by the extent of the eclipse. If
> it was total, they could only think she was dead, and they feared every
> moment that she would fall and they would perish. Then they wept and
> wailed with more sincerity, as people who were face to face with death
> and the end of the world. As they saw the Moon gradually recovering
> her light, they said she was getting better from her sickness, because
> Pachacámac, the upholder of the universe, had restored her to health
> and commanded that she should not die so that the world should not
> perish. When she was quite bright again, they congratulated her and
> thanked her for not having fallen. All this concerning the moon I have
> seen with my own eyes. (Garcilaso de la Vega 1966:118–119 [1609:
> Vol. 1, Bk. 2, Ch. 23])[13]

Arriaga, the famous extirpator of idolatry, provides a similar description of Inca reactions to lunar eclipses. Although it is known
that Arriaga had read Garcilaso de la Vega's chronicle, Arriaga indicates that he had also personally witnessed these frightened responses to lunar eclipses:

What they used to do during eclipses of the moon, which are called
quillamhuañum, meaning "the moon dies," or *quilla tutayan*, "the
moon grows dark," they still do, whipping the dogs, beating drums, and
shouting through the town to bring the moon back to life. (Arriaga
1968b:60 [1621: Ch. 6]; translation modified)[14]

These passages record the general alarm that was engendered by
unexpected changes in the sun or moon. Pedro Pizarro (1921:393–
394 [1571]) described a reaction to a specific solar eclipse. Ziólkowski (1985:156–160) has identified this as the solar eclipse of 31 July
1543 and elaborates on Pizarro's account. The eclipse was interpreted by the inhabitants of the *encomienda* of Lucas Martínez as a
sign that the sun was unhappy with their mining of a vein of silver,
and in spite of threats, the natives refused Martinez's demands to
continue work. Pizarro's account demonstrates how such extraordinary astronomical events dramatically influenced native lives.

In general, solar and lunar eclipses are frequent enough that they
can be recognized without reliance on a long historical record. They
were interpreted to represent the near death of these celestial objects, and as extraordinary and visually compelling events, they
attract great attention. This must be particularly true for people
who recognize the sun and the moon as paramount forces in their
world.[15]

Comets

Several comets are discovered every year. Most never become visible to the naked eye, but every few years one does. A bright comet
is a striking and unmistakable object moving slowly through the
sky. Depending on its brightness and orbit, it may be visible for a
few days or for several months. Unlike planets, which are always
observed within 9 degrees of the ecliptic, comets can be seen in any
part of the sky. Additionally, their motion among the background
stars can be much higher than that of the planets or the sun. On oc-
casion, they can be seen to move over 10 degrees in a night. While
comets are very distinctive objects, the name has been applied by
inexperienced observers to a wide range of events from aurorae and
noctilucent clouds to bright meteors.

Some chronicles record information on what seem to be pre-
Hispanic appearances of comets.[16] One reference is provided by Pachacuti Yamqui Salcamayhua (1950:242 [1613]), who states that
several comets were seen in the Cuzco region near the time of
Amaru Topa's birth. Although Amaru Topa was the eldest son of

Pachacuti Inca Yupanqui (the ninth Inca), he did not become Inca at the death of his father. Instead, he became an important Cuzco administrator for his younger brother Topa Inca Yupanqui, who was chosen to succeed his father as ruler of the empire:

> In that time they say that news arrived of a miracle in Cuzco, of something like a *yauirca* or *amaru* that had emerged from the mountain of Pachatusan, a very fierce beast, half a league long and thick, and two and a half fathoms in width, and with ears and fangs and whiskers; and it came by Yuncaypampa and Cinca, and from there it entered the lake of Quibipay. Then two *sacacas* of fire came out of Asoncata, and [one] passed Pontina [mountain] of Arequipa; and the other came down to and passing Guamanca, where there are three or four very high mountains covered with snow, those in which they say that there are animals with wings, and ears, and tails and four feet, and on top of their backs many spines like a fish; and from afar they say that it appeared to them [to be] all fire.[17]

While it would be interesting to identify the comets described by Pachacuti Yamqui Salcamayhua, we know too little about the date of Amaru Topa's birth. There were seven comets with three or more recorded sightings observed between 1430 and 1470. The apparition of Halley's comet in 1456 was very bright and has over 150 recorded sightings.

Two independent descriptions exist of a comet being seen on the eve of Atahualpa's death in Cajamarca. The first of these was written by Francisco de Xérez, secretary to Francisco Pizarro, who was present in Cajamarca during Atahualpa's execution. Xérez's report on the initial conquest was published in 1534 immediately after his return to Spain. His comments on the event are as follows:

> Now I want to tell a remarkable thing, and it is, that twenty days before this happened, . . . one night when Atahualpa was making merry with some Spaniards, talking with them, suddenly a sign appeared in the sky, in the direction of Cuzco, like a fiery comet, that lasted much of the night. At seeing this sign Atahualpa said that very soon a great lord of that land would die.[18]

Cieza de León also mentions a comet sighting near the time of Atahualpa's death. He states that a sign was seen in the sky during Atahualpa's imprisonment in Cajamarca, and that an earlier sign had been seen near the death of Huayna Capac, Atahualpa's father.[19] Cieza de León suggests that he received his information from an eye witness who saw the Cajamarca comet.[20] This may be true since Cieza de León is known to have interviewed a number of the "original conquistadors" during his stay in Cuzco in 1550. According to Cieza de León:

> When Atahualpa was taken prisoner in the province of Cajamarca, some Spaniards still alive who were with . . . Francisco Pizarro, who captured him, saw a green sign as thick as an arm and the length of a lancet descend from the midnight sky. And while the Spaniards were observing it, Atahualpa heard about it, and it is said that he asked them to let him out so that he could see it. And when he did, a great sadness came over him which lasted all the next day. And when the governor, Don Francisco Pizarro, asked him why he was so said, he answered, "I have seen the sign in the sky, and when my father Huayna Capac died, a similar sign was seen." Fifteen days later Atahualpa was dead. (Cieza de León 1976:316 [1553: Bk. 1, Ch. 65])[21]

Atahualpa was taken prisoner by Pizarro on 16 November 1532 in Cajamarca and was executed there on 26 July 1533. Xérez and Cieza de León indicate that the sign was seen in the sky about two weeks before Atahualpa's death. European records describe a comet that appeared as bright as Jupiter on 8 July 1533 (Pingré 1783:488). Chinese records follow its movement from the beginning of July through mid-September. This comet was bright enough and well enough observed that an orbit has been calculated for it (Marsden 1975:9).

The comet that Cieza de León associated with Huayna Capac's death is less firmly identified. It is not mentioned by Xérez, and the information is, at best, thirdhand (coming from Atahualpa to an unnamed Spaniard and then to Cieza de León). Furthermore, it is based on Atahualpa's ability to identify the astronomical event preceding Huayna Capac's death as a comet, distinct from other transient events like a fireball. Assuming Atahualpa's statement was indeed factual, Ziółkowski (1985:161–167) and Dearborn (1986:17–19) have identified the likely date for Huayna Capac's death.

The date of Huayna Capac's death is significant in understanding the last days of the Inca Empire. When the Spaniards arrived in 1532, they found the Inca Empire engaged in a bloody civil war that followed the sudden death of Huayna Capac. Accounts of the civil war taken from Atahualpa's followers claim that before Huayna Capac's death, he divided the empire between his sons Atahualpa and Huascar (Rowe 1978). After some years, a civil war began. Cieza de León sets the death of Huayna Capac at 1526. This is consistent with the story told by Atahualpa loyalists who suggest that the war began because of Huascar's greedy desire to control the whole empire. Followers of Huascar claim that Huayna Capac died after the first appearance of the Spanish forces, and that the civil war resulted from Atahualpa's attempt to usurp the northern portion of the empire. In this vein, Cobo (1979:159 [1653: Bk. 12, Ch. 17]) reports that Huayna Capac was alive when the Spaniards first arrived in Túmbez. Pizarro arrived at Túmbez on his second voyage to South America, which occurred from 1527 to early 1528. Accordingly, while the year of Huayna Capac's death is not known, researchers place it between 1525 and 1530 (Rowe 1978).

A list of comets for which orbits have been determined does not record any comet between 1506 and 1531 (Marsden 1975). It is therefore necessary to consider reports of cometlike sightings that are less accurate and less dependable. The dates and events of interest were recorded in the classic compilation of comet and cometlike occurrences by Pingré (1783), and are provided in Table 7 with

Table 7. *Candidates for the Comet That Appeared near the Time of Huayna Capac's Death*

1526 August
Appeared like a flaming sword. Visible from 23 August until 7 September.

1527 August 11
Appearing at approximately 4:00 A.M. and visible for less than two hours of a single day, this object appeared like a "hand with an épée." In the same year, another observer described a fireball that some called a comet. The brief duration of this sighting suggests that it does not record a comet. Noctilucent clouds are often produced by sunlight illuminating the high vapor trail for an hour or two prior to sunrise or after sunset. In temperate latitudes, such clouds are most often seen in the summer months.

1528 January
Beginning on the 11th and lasting for ten days, this comet was observed in Pisces, and so was visible to the Inca. Pingré disputes the position, but believes that it was visible in the Southern Hemisphere.

1529 August
Four comets were reported with tails pointing to the "four quarters of the earth." The validity of this impossible (as reported) occurrence was doubted by the seventeenth-century Dutch astonomer Hevelius. Pingré suggests that it was an aurora, which would not have been visible in Peru.

Data from Pingré (1783).

commentary. Possible comet sightings occurred in August through September of 1526 and January of 1528. The 1528 sighting was visible in the constellation of Pisces, and so was certainly visible in Peru. Arguments can be made supporting both of these dates, but Pachacuti Yamqui Salcamayhua's account (1950:265 [1613]) places Huayna Capac's death shortly after Capac Raymi, the festival month associated with the December solstice. This supports the 1528 date for the death of Huayna Capac presented in Cobo's account.

Summary

The celestial phenomena discussed in this chapter are not commonplace, yet they are frequent enough that good sky watchers will see them and wonder about their significance. As unpredictable events to the Inca, comets and eclipses could not be incorporated into the ritual fabric of the annual calendar. Nevertheless, when witnessed, these transient features of the sky had to be interpreted. Since comets and eclipses were unexpected and disrupted the regular cycles of the other celestial objects, they were interpreted as ominous events. Thus it was sadly fitting that during his captivity in Cajamarca, Atahualpa, the last independent Inca to rule in the Andes, should see a comet across the night sky of Tahuantinsuyu, as did his father before him.

7. An Overview of Inca Astronomy and Calendrics

THE INCA AND OTHER ANDEAN PEOPLES lived in a complex world influenced by many powerful supernatural forces. These forces were believed to exist as anima in both terrestrial and celestial objects. The inclusion of astronomical objects in this cosmology is hardly surprising, as half of the visible world is sky, and the sun dominates the day as the brightest object in nature. Andean agriculture began millennia before the rise of the Inca, and all farmers know of the importance of sunlight in the seasonal cycle. Moreover, the need to respond to the seasonal cycle is biological. That cycle is driven by the sun, and mirrored by other objects of the sky. Recognition of this relationship provides a basis for accepting the power of the sun and other astronomical objects.

Long before the Inca polity came into existence, Andean peoples knew the sun as a provider of warmth, light, and the seasons. Pre-Inca offerings, such as those made on islands of Lake Titicaca, may record the great antiquity of solar worship in the Andes. Optimal planting dates vary from place to place, but the general motion of the sun, and its periods, was familiar to all groups who came under Inca control. Much attention was also given to the moon and stars. The steady waxing and waning of the moon defined periods of approximately 29.5 days, and the reappearance of the Pleiades in the morning sky heralded the beginning of a new agricultural cycle. Other stars were thought to influence the health and reproductive success of animals, particularly the llama. Even wild animals had celestial patrons, and humans asked these stars for protection.

Against this background of folk astronomy, the Inca state developed, evolving its own vision of Andean astronomy as the polity grew to control much of western South America. Of all the supernatural patrons that the Inca might have taken, the sun was the one that was recognized and accepted along the entire length of the Andes. The Inca successfully grasped control of existing beliefs in the sun and developed them. Using information included in a variety of late-sixteenth- and early-seventeenth-century historical sources we have presented a summary of what is known of Inca astronomy. The source documents range from the Quechua writings of indigenous authors that expounded upon the celestial world to Spanish texts calling for the destruction of native Andean religions. None of the accounts, however, was written specifically as an astronomical treatise. Information on Andean sky watching was included in the documents almost parenthetically as the writers attempted to record the history, organization, and religion of the vanquished Inca Empire.

Our analysis is also built on archaeological and astronomical research conducted in the Cuzco region. This fieldwork includes an extensive survey of Inca shrines in the Cuzco Valley. Astronomical measurements were taken from the Coricancha, the most sacred sun temple of the empire, as well as from a number of other locations in the Cuzco area. This field research complements the historical data, providing information on specific archaeological sites and the astronomical alignments associated with them.

We have little doubt that astronomy provided an important focus for Inca imperial organization, and that their astronomical knowledge included elements for which direct historical or physical evidence no longer exists. We find, however, little support for the detailed, astronomically based hypotheses suggested in some recent research projects. Rather than having a highly complex calendar system, we believe that the Inca developed and used a practical and relatively simple one. Within this calendar system, the solar motion was marked with pillars on the Cuzco horizon and was watched during the large celebrations in the city. These ceremonies, centered on the Cuzco pillars, highlight the importance that astronomical observations held in Inca society as a method of reckoning time as well as publicly reaffirming the legitimacy of Inca rule.

The Spanish accounts offer information on only a few definite solar observations. The most commonly described observation is the sun's arrival at a solstice. The December solstice may have marked the beginning of a new year and occurred in association with Capac Raymi, the month during which the young nobles of Cuzco were initiated into manhood. The June solstice was marked by a festival dedicated to the sun itself, Inti Raymi. Besides these solar observations, a particular sunset in August was designated as the beginning of the planting season. Other events that the Inca may have observed were the equinoctial and zenith passages of the sun; however, these are not well documented and Inca interest in their occurrence remains speculative. Whether or not specialists, like the yanca described in the Huarochirí manuscript, used light and shadow casting to monitor the motion of the sun is also open to debate, but it is certain that the Inca built pillars at the junction of the earth and sky to mark specific sunrises and -sets during large public observations.

As manifestations of imperial ritual, the solar pillars represent an important source of information on the social organization of Cuzco and the empire. Cobo states that there were fourteen pillars in the Cuzco region, marking the first day of each month of the year. On the other hand, Garcilaso de la Vega states that there were sixteen. Available accounts provide specific information on three locations with a total of eight pillars. The possible existence of six additional pillars is suggested in the same accounts, but their locations on the Cuzco horizon are not well documented. There were two pillars marking the June solstice sunset on a hill called Quiancalla, to the northwest of Cuzco. There were probably four pillars, also situated to the northwest of Cuzco, on the hill of Picchu. These pillars marked an August sunset date and possibly the June solstice sunset as seen from central Cuzco. Accounts of these pillars suggest that there may have been four additional pillars on a hill to the northeast of central Cuzco that were used to observe sunrises in conjunction with the Picchu markers. Two additional pillars stood to the southwest of Cuzco, on a hill called Chinchincalla. They may have marked the December solstice sunset. The possible existence of two more pillars is suggested by Polo de Ondegardo's claim that a "middle of March" (Julian calendar) feast was marked by the passage of the sun between some columns. Although the location of the pillars is not given, the reference to the middle of March suggests that they may have been related to the equinoxes.

Our archaeological and astronomical work in the Cuzco region concluded with mixed results concerning the solar observations of the Inca. The most abundant information presented in the sources concerns the four solar pillars on Picchu. Depending on the account, the Inca marked either the beginning of the planting season or the arrival of a solstice with these pillars. The location of Picchu is suitable for marking dates between March and September, as viewed from either the Haucaypata or the Coricancha. Because the documentary information on these pillars is ambiguous, and physical evidence for them has not been found, we are currently unable to determine their exact locations or functions. Without additional historical or archaeological evidence, the dates marked by these pillars remain speculative.

Our research on the pillars of Quiancalla supports an earlier proposal by Aveni and Zuidema that these marked the June solstice. While there is uncertainty regarding the precise position of these pillars, the likely identification of Quiancalla with the ridge of Huaynacorcor requires the existence of more than one location in the confines of the Cuzco Valley from which solar observations were made. To watch the sun set over the ridge of Huaynacorcor, it is necessary to travel east of the city. Molina's (1989 [ca. 1575]) account places the ruling Inca at a site called Mantocalla, east of Cuzco, on the June solstice. The general location of Mantocalla has been identified, but currently we are unable to suggest where the solar observations were made from or where the Quiancalla pillars once stood.

We also investigated the location of the Chinchincalla pillars. Survey data indicates these pillars were positioned on a hill called Killke or on an adjacent hill to the north. From the Coricancha, the December solstice sun sets over Killke (Aveni 1981). From the central plaza of Cuzco, it occurs over the adjacent hill, above an area known as Llamacancha. Although excavations on Killke located a terraced area including burials near where the pillars would have to have been situated to be viewed from the Coricancha, unambiguous structural remains of the solar markers have not been found, and their positions remain to be identified.

A convenient, easily manageable time unit for dividing the year is available by observing lunar phases, but agricultural utility requires that the calendar stay in phase with the seasons. Since twelve lunar months consist of 354 days—11 days short of a solar year—a twelve-month lunar calendar rapidly loses synchrony with a solar year. Simple sky watching can provide the necessary fiducial for maintaining synchrony between these calendars. Observation of a single solstice determines when it is necessary to include an additional intercalation month to synchronize the lunar phases with the solar year. Accounts from Peru that were based on information gathered after 1570 give clear evidence of a twelve-month lunar calendar that began with the first new moon including or following a solstice. It is highly probable that such a calendar was used long before the Inca Empire came into existence.

When the Inca co-opted the power of the sun, they took control of time itself. The establishment of a single set of pillars to mark a solstice formalizes the lunar-solar calendar described above. Extension of this system by establishing more pillars to mark months or festivals leads to an inherent conflict in the coordination of the solar motion with lunar phases. The simplest resolution of this conflict is to elevate the importance of the sun by developing a calendar based purely on solar motion. There is documentary evidence to suggest that such a calendar was used in Cuzco at the height of the Inca Empire.

The earlier chroniclers, Betanzos and Polo de Ondegardo, describe a calendar in which the months were defined by solar observations. These solar months would have had fixed lengths of thirty or thirty-one days. The impact of such an imperial solar calendar on the popular lunar calendar is minimal since lunar phases can be integrated into it for designating festivals. In the case of the Inca, the first new moon that rose during a solar month could be given the name of that month. On average, once every three years two new moons will rise during a single fixed month, leading to an unnamed intercalated lunar period.[1]

Monitoring the motion of the sun was an imperial expression of religion that the Spaniards tried to suppress. A system of horizon pillars would have been highly visible and the focus of attention for religious zealots as well as treasure hunters seeking the offerings that might have been buried beneath them. The introduction of Christianity after the Spanish invasion and the probable destruction of the solar pillars eliminated the mechanical basis of the solar calendar.

Stellar observations made by the Inca also have been discussed. It is certain that the Inca watched with great interest the movements of the Pleiades that they called, among other names, Collca and Oncoy. These stars were, and still are, observed for information concerning the maize harvest. The Inca also watched the movement of Venus, which appears at times as a bright star in the morning sky and at other times in the evening. Along with the Pleiades and Venus, the Inca observed a number of other stars. Stellar constellations for which reasonable identifications can be proposed include Chacana (the belt of Orion), Urcuchillay (the stars around Vega), Catachillay (a region around Deneb in Cygnus), and Chuchucoyllor (a region near the Pleiades). In addition to stellar constellations, the Inca recognized the dark lanes in the Milky Way as constellations. The best known of these is a llama and its lamb. Described by Garcilaso de la Vega and the author of the Huarochirí manuscript, this llama is recognized today as a dark lane extending along the Milky Way from Scorpius to Centaurus. The stars Alpha and Beta Centauri represented the llama's eyes (Llamacñawin), and are still widely recognized today. Possible identifications are also available for the dark constellations of the Yutu (the Coalsack near the Southern Cross) and the Machacuay (a less-prominent dark lane between the Southern Cross and Canis Major). A host of other Inca constellations remain only as names.

Inca observations of eclipses and comets also have been briefly discussed in this book. As disruptions in the orderly flow of nature, these phenomena were considered dangerous. Individual and state reactions to their occurrence provided security against the perceived threat. Of particular interest is a statement by Cieza de León that suggests that comets were seen on the eve of Atahualpa's death as well as on that of his father, Huayna Capac. A review of likely comet sightings confirms the existence of a bright comet near the time of Atahualpa's death in July of 1533. The comet that may have been seen at the time of Huayna Capac's death is not clearly documented, but the best candidate for it dates to January of 1528.

This work provides a reference base for the major historical descriptions of Inca astronomical practices. In addition, we have presented our interpretations of those historical descriptions, complemented with archaeological research from the Cuzco area. We emphasize that astronomy and the coordination of the calendar by the state are important issues in the study of ancient complex societies. In their roles as divine heads of state and the masters of the society's rituals, the rulers controlled time as well as the processes of societal reproduction. The rulers gained prestige and access to cosmogonic powers through rituals, and the state was inscribed into the very structure of social order.

The utilization of astronomy is not limited to the place or time of the Inca. Many ancient societies watched the movements of the celestial bodies across the sky with great interest. The observations of the sun, moon, planets, and stars formed basic tenets of their calendar systems, ritual celebrations, and cosmologies. The study of ancient astronomy should not be simply an inquiry into indigenous understandings of celestial objects, but an investigation of native social organizations and the foundations for elites' claim to authority and power. We propose that the expansion of Cuzco from a village community to an imperial capital required changes in the social organization of the Inca. Concurrent with the growth of the empire, there developed a new class of elites that claimed the sun as their ancestor and patron. New ceremonies developed during this period, encoding the new rights and duties of each member of the society. Development of a ritual calendar, which reinforced the ruling Inca's role as the paramount religious authority and which was largely based on solar and lunar sightings, helped to justify the status of the emperor. The ruling Inca, divine descendant of the sun, was seen to have access to ethereal knowledge and powers through which he controlled or interacted with universal forces. The unique position of the ruling Inca, as mediator between the Sun and the people of the Andes, provided him with eminent powers and proved to be an important component element of Inca statecraft.

Astronomical knowledge is fragile, yet it was a critical element in the social organization of many ancient cultures. In the case of the Inca, participation in large public astronomical observations in conjunction with elaborate ceremonies provided visible links to their origin myth and helped to strengthen the ruling elite's claim to dynastic power. The foundations of Inca sun worship and society were shattered with the arrival of the Spaniards and the subsequent executions of Atahualpa (1533) and Topa Amaru (1572). The deaths of these Incas, the conquest of the empire, and the replacement of sun and huaca worship with Christianity, marked the end of indigenous rule in the Andes. The destruction brought about by the Spaniards was so thorough that within mere decades the imperial monuments of the Inca, including the horizon pillars of Cuzco, were in ruins. With the introduction of the European calendar and Catholic ritual cycle much of Andean astronomy was transformed or abandoned altogether. As a new structure of time—a European one—was imposed on the Andes, the solar pillars, the timepieces of the Inca, ceased to apply. Inca time management and social organization were governed by Spanish ritual, and were forever altered.

Cuzco and the surrounding area have witnessed tremendous change since the Inca astronomical observations and public rituals were made and recorded. The Inca Empire and the Spanish Empire that displaced it no longer exist. Cuzco has been transformed from a sacred city of ruling elites to a center of tourism. Much of the hilly terrain of Cuzco now bears the scars of deforestation and overcultivation. Perhaps the only features that have not changed in the five centuries since the Spanish invasion are the cyclic movements of the sun and moon. The intimate bond between astronomical apparatus, time, and the social order in the Inca Empire is just a starting place in the study of Inca astronomy, and investigators are encouraged to probe beyond the current data. To the extent that such research establishes new directions of inquiry and investigation, our understanding of the Inca, their empire, and the Andean past will advance.

Appendix

Selected Star References from Early Colonial Sources (1585–1653)

Reference	Notes	Source
Ancochinchay *	protects other animals	Polo de Ondegardo (1965b: 2–5 [1585: Ch. 1])
An'qochinchay	a star worshiped by the Indians	*Arte y vocabulario . . .* (1951:142 [1586])
Aranyak huarachazca	morning star	Gonçález Holguín (1989:33 [1608])
Atungara (Hatunhuarac)	the morning star	Hacaspoma (1656: fol. 14–14v, in Duviols 1986:151)
Auquilla	morning star	Monzón (1881:204–205 [1586])
Batán		Guaman Poma de Ayala (1980:831 [1615:885 (899)])
Cabrillas	*See* Pleiades	
Cancho Huarac		*Huarochirí Manuscript* (1991:133 [ca. 1608: Ch. 29])

(continued)

* This information was copied from Polo de Ondegardo's work and can be found in Cabello Balboa (1951:308 [1586: Pt. 3, Ch. 15]), Acosta (1954:143 [1590: Bk. 5, Ch. 4]), Cobo (1990:30–31 [1653: Bk. 13, Ch. 6]), Calancha (1981:835–836 [1638: Bk. 2, Ch. 11]), and Murúa (1946:285–286 [ca. 1615: Bk. 3, Ch. 51]).

Reference	Notes	Source
Casador		Guaman Poma de Ayala (1980:831 [1615:885 (899)])
Catachillay *	a llama with a lamb	Polo de Ondegardo (1965b: 2–5 [1585: Ch. 1])
	the Cross	Gonçález Holguín (1989:51 [1608])
	star cross	Gonçález Holguín (1989:465 [1608])
	star cross	Bertonio (1984: Pt. 1, 150 [1612])
	the Pleiades (Cabrillas)	Bertonio (1984: Pt. 1, 107 [1612])
	a nebulous star in the Milky Way	Bertonio (1984: Pt. 1, 236; Pt. 2, 38 [1612])
		Pachacuti Yamqui Salcamay-hua (1950:226 [1613])
		Pérez Bocanegra (1631:710)
Caza Cuyllor		Guaman Poma de Ayala (1980:831 [1615:885 (899)])
Chacana *		Polo de Ondegardo (1965b:2–5 [1585: Ch. 1])
Chaccana	The Three Marys (Orion's belt)	Gonçález Holguín (1989:90 [1608])
Chacana en general		Pachacuti Yamqui Salcamay-hua (1950:226 [1613])
Chachaguaras	Venus (el lusero), associated with local lords	Chaupiscon (1658: fol. 20, in Duviols 1986:160)
Chacras	the Three Marys (Orion's belt)	Arriaga (1968a:273 [1621])
Chakana	the Three Marys (Orion's belt)	Arte y vocabulario . . . (1951: 114 [1586])
Chasca	Venus	Garcilaso de la Vega (1945: 115 [1609: Vol. 1, Bk. 2, Ch. 21])

Reference	Notes	Source
Chasca Cuyllor	day star (Venus)	Guaman Poma de Ayala (1980:831 [1615:885 (899)])
Chasca Coyllur	morning star (Venus)	Pachacuti Yamqui Salcamayhua (1950:226 [1613])
Chazca coyllur	morning star (Venus)	Gonçález Holguín (1989:570 [1608])
Chhasca ccoyllur	day star (Venus)	Gonçález Holguín (1989:98 [1608])
Chissichascca	evening star (Venus)	Gonçález Holguín (1989:570 [1608])
Ch'oqe chincha	certain stars	Arte y vocabulario . . . (1951:146 [1586])
Chuchucoyllor	two stars near the Pleiades, creators of chuchus and chacpas	Hacaspoma (1656: fol. 14–14v, in Duviols 1986:151)
Chuquechinchay	an evening star, a catlike animal	Pachacuti Yamqui Salcamayhua (1950:226 [1613])
Chuquichinchay *	worshiped by mountain people, was a jaguar	Polo de Ondegardo (1965b:2–5 [1585: Ch. 1])
Chhoque chinchay	a star, looks like a sheep [llama]	Gonçález Holguín (1989:117 [1608])
Collca *	the Pleiades (Cabrillas)	Polo de Ondegardo (1965b:2–5 [1585: Ch. 1])
	the Pleiades (Cabrillas)	Calancha (1981:835 [1638: Bk. 2, Ch. 11])
	the Pleiades (Cabrillas), called mother	Cobo (1990:30–31 [1653: Bk. 13, Ch. 6])
Collca cuyllur, or Ccapac collcca cuyllu	the Pleiades (Cabrillas)	Gonçález Holguín (1989:440 [1608])
Condormi	one of three stars in a straight line	Huarochirí Manuscript (1991:133 [ca. 1608: Ch. 29])

(continued)

Reference	Notes	Source
Coyahuárac	morning star (Venus)	Arriaga (1968a:273 [1621])
Fur	Pleiades (Cabrillas)	Calancha (1981:1244–1245 [1638: Bk. 3, Ch. 2])
Guamantapas	one of three stars in a straight line	Huarochirí Manuscript (1991:133 [ca. 1608: Ch. 29])
Hombres and mugeres		Guaman Poma de Ayala (1980:831 [1615:885 (899)])
Hucchu	Pleiades (Cabrillas)	Bertonio (1984: Pt. 1, 236; Pt. 2, 161 [1612])
Huara Huara	star	Bertonio (1984: Pt. 1, 236; Pt. 2, 149 [1612])
Katachillay	Venus (el lucero)	Arte y vocabulario . . . (1951:98, 155 [1586])
Larilla	Pleiades (Cabrillas)	Monzón (1881:204–205 [1586])
León		Guaman Poma de Ayala (1980:831 [1615:885 (899)])
Llama	stellar constellation in Lyra	Polo de Ondegardo (1965b:2–5 [1585: Ch. 1])
	T-shaped stellar constellation in Lyra	Cobo (1990:30–31 [1653: Bk. 13, Ch. 6])
	a dark spot in the form of a llama with two eyes and a large neck, called Yacana	Huarochirí Manuscript (1991:132–133 [ca. 1608: Ch. 29])
	a dark spot in the form of a llama	Garcilaso de la Vega (1945:123 [1609: Vol. 1, Bk. 2, Ch. 23])
		Guaman Poma de Ayala (1980:831 [1615:885 (899)])
Machacuay *	protects serpents and snakes	Polo de Ondegardo (1965b:2–5 [1585: Ch. 1])
Mamana and Mirco *		Polo de Ondegardo (1965b:2–5 [1585: Ch. 1])

Reference	Notes	Source
Maman Mirccuc	stars that eat their mother or father	Gonçález Holguín (1989:242 [1608])
Maman Mircu	some stars in the area of the cross	Gonçález Holguín (1989:225 [1608])
Miquiquiray *		Polo de Ondegardo (1965b:2–5 [1585: Ch. 1])
Mucchu	Venus	Bertonio (1984: Pt. 1, 236; Pt. 2, 226 [1612])
Oncoicoillur	Pleiades (Cabrillas)	Hacaspoma (1656: fol. 14–14v, in Duviols 1986:151)
Oncoimita	Pleiades (Cabrillas)	Avendaño (1904:381 [1617])
Oncoy	Pleiades (Cabrillas)	*Misión de las provincias de los Huachos y Yauyos* (1919: 183, 188 [1613])
Oncoy	Pleiades (Cabrillas)	Arriaga (1968a:201, 213, 223 [1621: Chs. 2, 5, and 8]; 1968b:165 [1621])
Oncoy Cuyllor		Guaman Poma de Ayala (1980:546, 829, 831 [1615: 577 (591), 883 (897), 885 (899)])
Orcochillay	*See* Urcuchillar	
Orcorara	three stars all equal	Pachacuti Yamqui Salcamayhua (1950:226 [1613])
Orion	*See* Tres Marías	
Pacari Cuyllor		Guaman Poma de Ayala (1980:831 [1615:885 (899)])
Paccarik Chhascca	morning star (Venus)	Gonçález Holguín (1989:266 [1608])
Pachahuárac	morning star (Venus)	Arriaga (1968a:273 [1621])
Pastor		Guaman Poma de Ayala (1980:831 [1615:885 (899)])

(*continued*)

Reference	Notes	Source
Perdises	*See* Tinamou and Yutu	Guaman Poma de Ayala (1980:831 [1615:885 (899)])
Pihca Conqui	stands out as a perfect ring	*Huarochirí Manuscript* (1991:133 [ca. 1608: Ch. 29])
Pleiades (Cabrillas)	called Collca *	Polo de Ondegardo (1965b: 2–5 [1585: Ch. 1])
	called Larilla	Monzón (1881:205 [1586])
	called 'Qoll'qa	*Arte y vocabulario . . .* (1951:172 [1586])
		Huarochirí Manuscript (1991:133 [ca. 1608: Ch. 29])
	called Collca cuyllur, or Ccapac collcca cuyllur	Gonçález Holguín (1989:440 [1608])
		Garcilaso de la Vega (1945: 115 [1609: Vol. 1, Bk. 2, Ch. 21])
	called Hucchu, Mucchu, Vel Vicchu	Bertonio (1984: Pt. 1, 236; Pt. 2, 161, 226 [1612])
	called Oncoy	*Misión de las provincias de los Huachos y Yauyos* (1919: 183, 188 [1613])
		Pachacuti Yamqui Salcamayhua (1950:226 [1613])
		Avendaño (1904:380 [1617])
	called Oncoimita	Avendaño (1904:381 [1617])
	called Oncoy	Arriaga (1968a:201, 213, 223 [1621: Chs. 2, 5, and 8]; 1968b:165 [1621])
	called Collca	Calancha (1981:835 [1638: Bk. 2, Ch. 11])
	called Fur	Calancha (1981:1244–1245 [1638: Bk. 3, Ch. 2])
	called mother	Cobo (1990:30–31 [1653: Bk. 13, Ch. 6])
	called Oncoicoillur	Hacaspoma (1656: fol. 14–14v, in Duviols 1986:151)
	called Pugllaiguaico	Guamanbilca (1658: fol. 66, in Duviols 1986:227)

Reference	Notes	Source
Poco Huarac		Huarochirí Manuscript (1991: 133 [ca. 1608: Ch. 29])
Pugllaiguaico	Pleiades (Cabrillas)	Guamanbilca (1658: fol. 66, in Duviols 1986:227)
'Qoll'qa	Pleiades (Cabrillas)	Arte y vocabulario . . . (1951:172 [1586])
Quiantopa	left out of the 1585 abstract of Polo de Ondegardo	Cobo (1990:31 [1653: Bk. 13, Ch. 6])
Suyuntuytapas (Vulture)	one of three stars in a straight line	Huarochirí Manuscript (1991: 133 [ca. 1608: Ch. 29])
Tinamou	See Yutu and Perdises	
Topatorca *		Polo de Ondegardo (1965b: 2–5 [1585: Ch. 1])
Topatoraca		Cobo (1990:31 [1653: Bk. 13, Ch. 6])
Tres Marías (Orion's belt)	called Chakana	Arte y vocabulario . . . (1951:114 [1586])
	called Chaccana	Gonçález Holguín (1989:90 [1608])
		Avendaño (1904:381 [1617])
	called Chacras	Arriaga (1968a:273 [1621])
Uenado		Guaman Poma de Ayala (1980:831 [1615:885 (899)])
Urcuchillay *	worshiped by shepherds, a llama in Lyra	Polo de Ondegardo (1965b: 2–5 [1585: Ch. 1])
	several stars forming a T	Cobo (1990:30–31 [1653: Bk. 13, Ch. 6])
	the Cross	Gonçález Holguín (1989:51 [1608])
	star cross	Gonçález Holguín (1989:465 [1608])
Ur'quchillay	Venus (el lucero)	Arte y vocabulario . . . (1951: 98 [1586])

(continued)

Reference	Notes	Source
Uara Uara		Guaman Poma de Ayala (1980:831 [1615:885 (899)])
Villca Huarac		Huarochirí Manuscript (1991: 133 [ca. 1608: Ch. 29])
Vel Vicchu	Venus	Bertonio (1984: Pt. 1, 236; Pt. 2, 226 [1612])
Venus	morning star, called Auquilla	Monzón (1881:204–205 [1586])
	called katachillay ur'quchillay	Arte y vocabulario . . . (1951: 98, 155 [1586])
	morning star, called Aranyak huarachazca	Gonçález Holguín (1989:33 [1608])
	day star, called Chhasca ccoyllur	Gonçález Holguín (1989:98, 266 [1608])
	morning star, called Chazca coyllur	Gonçález Holguín (1989:570 [1608])
	morning star, called Paccarik chhascca	Gonçález Holguín (1989:266 [1608])
	evening star, called Chissichascca	Gonçález Holguín (1989:570 [1608])
	called Chasca	Garcilaso de la Vega (1945: 115 [1609: Vol. 1, Bk. 2, Ch. 21])
	evening and morning star	Garcilaso de la Vega (1945: 123 [1609: Vol. 1, Bk. 2, Ch. 23])
	morning star, called Chasca Coyllur	Pachacuti Yamqui Salcamayhua (1950:226 [1613])
	evening star, called Chuquechinchay	Pachacuti Yamqui Salcamayhua (1950:226 [1613])
	Pacari Cuyllor	Guaman Poma de Ayala (1980:831 [1615:885 (899)])
	day star, called Chasca Cuyllor	Guaman Poma de Ayala (1980:831 [1615:885, (899)])
		Guaman Poma de Ayala (1980:62, 63, 238 [1615:79, 80, 264 (266)])

Reference	Notes	Source
	morning star, called Pachahuárac or Coyahuárac	Arriaga (1968a:273 [1621])
	morning and evening star	Calancha (1981:835 [1638: Bk. 2, Ch. 11])
	morning and evening star	Cobo (1990:31 [1653: Bk. 13, Ch. 6])
	morning star, called Atungara (Hatunhuarac)	Hacaspoma (1656: fol. 14–14v, in Duviols 1986:151)
	called Chachaguaras, associated with local lords	Chaupiscon (1658: fol. 20, in Duviols 1986:160)
Yacana	a black spot in the form of a llama with two eyes and a large neck	*Huarochirí Manuscript* (1991:132–133 [ca. 1608: Ch. 29])
Yutu	small dark spot that preceeds the Yacana	*Huarochirí Manuscript* (1991:133 [ca. 1608: Ch. 29])

Notes

1. The Inca and the Sky

1. For additional information on native American astronomy we recommend papers in Aveni (1980), and for more information on the Inca, we suggest Hemming (1970), D'Altroy (1992), and Bauer (1992b). For a summary of astronomical research on the Inca conducted outside of the Cuzco region, see Hyslop (1990:223–243).

2. The Quechua terms, toponyms, and personal names contained in this work are written according to their Hispanicized spelling as found in the Spanish chronicles and on modern maps. The English and Spanish plural form *s* is used in this text rather than the Quechua form (*kuna* or *cuna*).

3. "Y todo lo que hasta aquí os hemos dicho yo y los Ingas mis antepasados, que adorásedes al sol, Punchau, y á las guacas, ídolos, piedras, rios, montes y vilcas, es todo falsedad y mentira. Y cuando os decíamos que entrábamos á hablar al sol, y que él decia que hiciésedes lo que nosotros os decíamos y que hablaba, es mentira; porque no hablaba, sino nosotros, porque es un pedazo de oro, y no puede hablar; y mi hermano Titocuxi me dijo que cuando quisiese decir algo á los indios, que hiciesen entrase solo al dicho ídolo Punchau, y no entrase nadie conmígo; y que el dicho ídolo Punchau no me habia de hablar, porque era un poco de oro, y que despues saliese y dijese á los indios que me habia hablado y que decia aquello que yo les quisiese decir, porque los indios hiciesen mejor lo que les habia de mandar; y que á lo que habia de venerar, era lo que estaba dentro del sol Punchau, que es de los corazones de los Ingas mis antepasados" (Salazar 1867: 280 [1596]).

4. Atahualpa was garroted.

5. "Del templo del sol salian como de centro ciertas lineas, que los indios llaman, ceques; y hacianse quatro partes conforme a los quatro caminos Reales que salian del cuzco: y en cada uno de aquellos ceques estauan por su orden las Guacas, y adoratorios que hauia en el cuzco, y su comarca,

como estaciones de lugares pios, cuya veneracion era general a todas" (Cobo 1980:14 [1653: Bk. 13, Ch. 13]).

6. Zuidema (1964) has developed an alternative numbering system for the ceques and huacas of Cuzco.

7. Bollaert (1865:275) also provides some interesting observations on Andean star watching.

8. For high-latitude sites with low horizons, refraction can cause a significant correction to the position at which the sun will first appear, but this is not a factor in Cuzco. Nevertheless, we included a standard refraction correction.

The typical uncertainty in azimuth found from repeated observations of the sun was 0.03 degrees. Independent observations from a site to the horizon, and from near that horizon location back to the site, were frequently made. Simple comparison of these "to and from" observations give a mean difference of 0.09 degrees. This difference includes a shift in the position to and from which observations were made. For example, several observations required determining the direction of looters' pits on ridges several kilometers away. As the pits themselves were not visible, known trees, buildings, and outcrops near the looters' pits were sighted. The back measurements, however, were from the pits to the original location. Corrections for known offsets to our locations reduce the mean difference between the "to and from" observations to less than 0.05 degrees, consistent with the uncertainty obtained from repeated solar sights. In the cases presented here, this uncertainty corresponds to spatial offset of less than five meters (either at the horizon or at the site), a negligible difference compared to the uncertainty regarding the precise spot from which ancient observations were made.

9. This document has been mistakenly attributed to Cristóbal de Molina (el Almagrista).

10. ". . . y éstos todos eran orejones muy ricamente vestidos con mantas y camisetas ricas de argentería y brazaletes y patenas en las cabezas, de oro fino y muy relumbrantes, los cuales hacían dos hilas, que cada una tenía más de trescientos señores; y en manera de procesión, los unos del un lado y los otros del otro, estaban muy callados y esperando a que saliese el Sol, y aún no había salido bien, cuando así como comenzaban ellos a entonar con gran orden y concierto un canto, entonándole con menear cada uno de ellos un pie, . . . y como el Sol iba saliendo, más alto entonaban su canto.

"El Inca tenía su tienda en un cercado con una silla y escaño muy rico y apartado un poco de la hila de éstos; y al entonar, levantábase con gran autoridad y poníase en el principio de todos y era él el primero que comenzaba el canto, y como él hacía, hacían todos; . . . y así se estaban estos cantando desde que salía el Sol hasta que se encubría del todo, y como hasta el medio día el Sol iba saliendo, ellos iban acrecentando las voces, y de medío día abajo las iban menguando, teniendo gran cuenta con lo que el Sol caminaba" (Segovia 1943:51–52 [1553]).

2. Historical Accounts Concerning Inca Solar Astronomy and the Year

1. See Ziólkowski and Sadowski (1992) for a similar summary of documentary information on Andean astronomy.

2. Gonçález Holguín (1989:269 [1608]) defines *Pachacta unanchani* as "to mark the time to do something."

3. ". . . mes de noviembre llamó este señor Cantaraiquis en este mes comienzan a hacer la chicha que han de beber en el mes de diciembre y enero do comienza el año y hacen la fiesta de los orejones según que la historia os ha contado a los cuales meses Ynga Yupangue nombró en la manera que ya habeis oído . . . cada mes de estos tenía treinta días y que el año tenía trescientos y sesenta y porque andando el tiempo no perdiesen la cuenta destos meses y los tiempos en que habían de sembrar e hacer las fiestas . . . que había hecho aquellos Pacha Unan Chac que dice relojes los cuales habían hecho en estos diez días que se tardó en no les querer declarar lo que ya habeis oído los cuales relojes hizo en esta manera que todas las mañanas e tardes miraba el sol en todos los mese[s] del año mirando los tiempos del sembrar y coger y ansi mismo cuando el sol se ponía y ansi mesmo miraba la luna cuando era nueva e llena e menguante los cuales relojes hizo hacer de cantería encima de los cerros más altos a la parte do el sol salía y a la parte de se ponía . . . en lo más alto de los cerros hizo hacer cuatro pirámides mármoles de cantería las dos de en medio menores que las otras dos de los lados y de dos estados de altor cada una cuadradas e apartada una de otra una braza salvo que los dos pequeños de en medio hizo más juntos que del uno al otro habrá media braza y cuando el sol salía estando uno puesto do Ynga Yupangue se paró para mirar y tantear éste [sol] derecho sale y va por el derecho y medio de los dos pilares y cuando se pone lo mismo por la parte do se pone por donde la gente común tenían entendimiento del tiempo que era ansi de sembrar como de coger . . . los relojes eran cuatro a do el sol salía y otros cuatro a do se ponía do se diferenciaban los transcursos y movimientos que ansi el sol hace en el año" (Betanzos 1987:73–74 [1551: Pt. 1, Ch. 15]).

4. Beginning with the December solstice, the sun rise and set position is seen to move north then south along the horizon. Over the course of the year, the sun sets at a particular spot on the horizon two times in a year, sometime in the winter/spring and then again on a date in the summer/fall.

5. "Por otra estaua el cerro de Carmenga, de donde salen a trecho ciertas torrezillas pequeñas, que siruían para tener cuenta con el mouimiento del sol, de que ellos mucho se preciaron" (Cieza de León 1984:258 [1553: Pt. 1, Ch. 92]).

6. "A todo el mundo llaman 'Pacha', conoçiendo la buelta quel sol haze y las creçientes y menguantes de la luna. Contaron el año por ello, al qual llaman 'guata' y lo hazen de doze lunas, teniendo su quenta en ello. Y usaron de unas torrezillas pequeñas, que oy día están muchas por los collados del Cuzco algo ahuzadas para por la sonbra quel sol hazía en ellas entender en las sementeras y en lo que ellos más sobre esto entienden" (Cieza de León 1985:78 [1554: Pt. 2, Ch. 26]).

7. Some of this information was copied by Cobo (1979:251–256; 1990: 27–28 [1653: Bk. 12, Ch. 37; Bk. 13, Ch. 5]).

8. "El año partieron en doze meses por las lunas: y los demás días que sobran cada año los consumían con las mismas lunas. Y á cada luna, ó mes tenían puesto su mojón ó pilar al derredor de [el] Cuzco donde llegaua el Sol aquel mes. Y estos pilares eran adoratorios principales, á los quales ofrecían diuersos sacrificios y todo lo que sobraua de los sacrificios de las Huacas, se lleuaua á estos lugares que se llamauan Sucanca, y el que es principio de Invierno, Puncuy [Pucuy] sucanca, y el principio de veraño, Chirao sucanca. Al año nombran, Huata en la Quichua, y en la Aymará de los Collas, Mara. A la luna y mes llaman Quilla, y en la Aymará, Pacsi.

"Cada mes del año tenían diuersas fiestas, y sacrificios por su orden, como lo ordenó Pachacuti Ynca. El qual hizo que el año començasse desde Diziembre, que es quando el Sol llega á lo último de su curso al Polo Antártico de acá" (Polo de Ondegardo 1916b:16–17 [1585: Ch. 7]).

9. "Mediado el mes de Marzo, a my quenta, según la que ellos dan por las lunas contando el discurso del Sol por aquellos pilares o topos que llamauan ellos, *Saybas*, que están en torno de la Ciudad del Cuzco, las rrepartía el Ynga ó su lugar tenyente, habiéndose hecho vna fiesta solene para ello en esta forma, que de allí se tomauan mugeres para el Sol" (Polo de Ondegardo 1916c:91–92 [1571]).

10. Cobo also refers to these solar pillars while discussing the offerings made to huacas in the Cuzco region (Cobo 1990:114 [1653: Bk. 13, Ch. 21]).

11. Cobo was the last known chronicler to use the original version of this report.

12. "Conocieron nuestro año solar por la observancia de los solsticios, y empezábanlo por el solsticio estival deste hemisferio antártico, que es a los 23 días de diciembre, y se acababa en el mismo punto donde había comenzado, con que venía a ser su año del mismo número de días que nosotros le damos, excepto la cuenta de los bisiestos o días intercalares, que no alcanzaron.

"Por lo cual, no se puede averiguar qué certidumbre y fijeza tenían en su año, ni aun pienso yo que andaban en esto tan puntuales que dejasen de tener muchos yerros, no embargante que pusieron los mejores medios que supieran para concertarlo y tener cuenta y razón con los tiempos; y así, para que fuese cierta y cabal su cuenta, usaban desta traza: que por los cerros y collados que están alrededor del Cuzco tenían puestos dos padrones o pilares al oriente y otros dos al poniente de aquella ciudad, por donde salía y se ponía el sol cuando llegaba a los trópicos de Cancro y Capricornio; y al tiempo que salía y se ponía en derecho de los pilares de la banda del sur, mirado desde la dicha ciudad, tenía por principio el año. Porque, estando como está aquella ciudad en altura de catorce a quince grados australes, entonces era cuando el sol más se le apartaba por aquella banda, desde donde, volviendo a la equinoccial, pasaba por su cenit; y cuando más se le alejaba por esotro lado del setentrión, salía y se ponía por cima de aquellos pilares, que por aquella parte señalaban su mayor apartamiento; y vuelto de allí al punto de donde partió del trópico de Capricornio y señal de los primeros pilares, concluían el año; al cual llamaban *huata* en la legua quichua, y *mara* en la aimará.

"Componíanlo de doce meses, y éstos contaban por lunas, y así llaman con un mismo nombre al mes y a la luna, que es en la lengua quichua o del Cuzco, *quilla,* y en la aimará, *pacsi.* Los días que sobraban cada año los consumían con las mismas lunas. Así, a la parte del oriente como del poniente, adonde tenían puestos los padrones por donde salía y se ponía el sol cuando llegaba a los trópicos entre el uno y el otro mojón o padrón tenían puestos otros, cada uno en el paraje que llegaba el sol aquel mes; los cuales pilares todos juntos se decían *sucanca,* y eran adoratorios principales a quien ofrecían sacrificios al tiempo que a los demás. A los dos pilares que eran principio del invierno, donde mediaba el año, llamaban *pucuy-sucanca,* y a los otros dos que señalaban el principio del verano, *chirao-sucanca.* Todos los meses eran iguales en días, y cada uno tenía su nombre propio" (Cobo 1956: 142 [1653: Bk. 12, Ch. 37]).

13. "De la adoración que hacían al sol resultaron catorce adoratorios universalmente venerados: éstos eran los padrones o pilares llamados *Sucanca,* que señalaban los meses del año. Los cuales eran tenidos en mucho, y hacíanseles sacrificios cuando a las demás *guacas* y lugares señalados para este efecto. La forma de sacrificar en estos adoratorios era, que después de llevados los sacrificios a las otras *guacas* por el orden que corrían los *ceques,* como se dirá en su lugar, lo que sobraba se ofrecía en estos padrones, porque no estaban en el orden que los demás adoratorios, por seguir el que el sol lleva en su curso; y cada uno acudía con el sacrificio al adoratorio déstos que caía más cerca del *ceque* que tenía a cargo" (Cobo 1956:158 [1653: Bk. 13, Ch. 5]).

14. "En la serranía más alta, á vista de la ciudad del Cuzco, á la parte del Poniente, hicieron quatro pilares á manera de torrecillas, que se pudían sojuzgar de á dos y tres leguas, en paraje de ducientos pasos desde el primero al postrero, y los dos de en medio auía cincuenta pasos del vno al otro, y los dos de los cabos rrepartidos por su quenta á propósito de sus fines; de manera que, entrando el Sol por el primer pilar, se apercebían para las sementeras generales, y començauan á sembrar legumbres por los altos, por ser más tardíos; y entrando el Sol por los dos pilares de en medio, era el punto y el tiempo general de sembrar en el Cuzco, y era siempre por el mes de Agosto. Es ansí, que, para tomar el punto del Sol, entre los dos pilares de en medio tenían otro pilar en medio de la plaça, pilar de piedra muy labrada, de vn estado en alto, en vn paraje señalado al propósito, que le nombrauan Osno, y desde allí tomauan el punto del Sol en medio de los dos pilares, y estando ajustado, hera el tiempo general de sembrar en los valles del Cuzco y su comarca" (Anonymous Chronicler 1906:151 [ca. 1570]).

15. Two leagues is approximately 10 km. At that distance one meter corresponds to 0.3' of arc or 1/100th of a lunar diameter. While some people can see things this small, an object would have to be well over 1' of arc to be prominent at this distance. This suggests a minimum height of three to four meters for the pillars.

16. "La luna del mes de Agosto llamauan Tarpuyquilla. Este mes no en-

tendían en otra cosa más de sembrar, generalmente, ansí el pobre como el rrico, ayudándose vnos con otros. Y este mes de Agosto entraua el Sol por medio de las dos torrecillas, de las quatro que por los Yngas estaua señalado, como se a tratado atrás.

"La luna del mes de Setiembre llamauan Cituaquilla. Este mes se juntauan en el Cuzco todos los yndios de toda la comarca, y juntos todos en la plaça principal, llamada Haocaypata, y allí hazían sus sacreficios al Sol con muchas cerimonias, en vn pilar de piedra que tenían en medio de la plaça, . . . llamado Osno" (Anonymous Chronicler 1906:158 [ca. 1570]).

17. For additional information on the usnu in the central plaza of Cuzco see Zuidema (1980), Aveni (1981:310-317), and Hyslop (1990:38-40, 69-74).

18. "Y para que el tiempo del sembrar y del coger se supiese precisamente y nunca se perdiese, hizo poner en un monte alto al levante del Cuzco cuatro palos, apartados el uno del otro como dos varas de medir, y en las cabezas dellos unos agujeros, por donde entrase el sol á manera de reloj ó astrolabio. Y considerando adonde heriá el sol por aquellos agujeros al tiempo del barbechar y sembrar, hizo sus señales en el suelo, y puso otros palos en la parte que corresponde al poniente del Cuzco para el tiempo del coger las mieses. Y como tuvo certificados estos palos precisamente, puso para perpetuidad en su lugar unas colunas de piedra de la medida y agujeros de los palos, y á la redonda mandó enlosar el suelo, y en las losas hizo hacer ciertas rayas niveladas conforme á las mudanzas del sol, que entraba por los agujeros de las colunas, de manera que todo era un artificio de reloj anual, por donde se gobernaban para el sembrar y coger. Y diputó personas que tuviesen cuenta con estos relojes y notificasen al pueblo los tiempos y sus diferencias, que aquellos relojes señalasen" (Sarmiento de Gamboa 1906: 67-68 [1572: Ch. 30]).

19. An earlier work by Molina called *Historia de los Incas* (History of the Inca) has been lost.

20. The Spaniards used the word *carnero* (sheep) to describe llamas and alpacas.

21. "Y luego por la mañana enbiavan un carnero a *Guanacauri,* que es la huaca principal que ellos tienen como en la *historia de los Yncas* está dicho, en donde le matavan y quemavan los *tarpuntaes,* que heran los que tenían cargo de dar de comer a las huacas; y mientras lo quemavan, al salir del Sol por la mañana, yban muchos yncas y caciques y, arrancando la lana del dicho carnero, antes que le quemasen, andavan dando bozes alrededor del sacrificio con la lana en las manos, diciendo: 'O Hacedor, Sol y Trueno, sed siempre moços y muntipliquen las jentes y estén siempre en paz' y a mediodia, por la misma orden, quemavan otro carnero en *Curicancha* en el patio de la dicha Casa del Sol, que agora es claustro de los frailes del Senor Sancto Domingo; y al entrar del Sol llevavan otro al cerro llamado *Aepiran* [or *Aepitan*], porque sobre él se pone el Sol" (Molina 1989:67-68 [ca. 1575]).

22. "Alcançaron también los solsticios del verano y del invierno, los cuales dexaron escritos con señales grandes y notorias, que fueron ocho torres que labraron al oriente y otras ocho al poniente de la ciudad del Cozco,

puestas de cuatro en cuatro, dos pequeñas de a tres estados poco más o menos de alto en medio de otras dos grandes: las pequeñas estavan diez y ocho o veinte pies la una de la otra; a los lados, otro tanto espacio, estavan las otras dos torres grandes, que eran mucho mayores que las que en España servían de atalayas, y éstas grandes servían de guardar y dar viso para que descubriessen mejor las torres pequeñas. El espacio que entre las pequeñas havía, por donde el Sol passava al salir y al ponerse, era el punto de los solsticios; las unas torres del oriente correspondían a las otras del poniente del solsticio vernal o hiemal.

"Para verificar el solsticio se ponía un Inca en cierto puesto al salir del Sol y al ponerse, y mirava a ver si salía y se ponía por entre las dos torres pequeñas que estavan al oriente y al poniente. Y con este trabajo se certificavan en la Astrología de sus solsticios" (Garcilaso de la Vega 1945:111 [1609: Vol. 1, Bk. 2, Ch. 22]).

23. "Las cuales dexé en pie el año de mil y quinientos y sesenta, y si después acá no las han derribado, se podría verificar por ellas el lugar de donde miravan los Incas los solsticios, a ver si era de una torre que estava en la casa del Sol o de otro lugar" (Garcilaso de la Vega 1945:111–112 [1609: Vol. 1, Bk. 2, Ch. 22]).

24. "Escriviéronlos con letras tan groseras porque no supieron fixarlos con los días de los meses en que son los solsticios, porque contaron los meses por lunas, como luego diremos, y no por días, y, aunque dieron a cada año doze lunas, como el año solar ecceda al año lunar común en onze días, no sabiendo ajustar el un año con el otro, tenían cuenta con el movimiento del Sol por los solsticios, para ajustar el año y contarlo, y no con las lunas. Y desta manera dividían el un año del otro rigiéndose para sus sembrados por el año solar, y no por el lunar" (Garcilaso de la Vega 1945:111 [1609: Vol. 1, Bk. 2, Ch. 22]).

25. "Y ancí al andar del rruedo del sol de uerano, enbierno desde el mes que comiensa de enero. Dize el filósofo que un día se acienta en su cilla y señoría el sol en aquel grado prencipal y rreyna y apodera dallí.

"Y acimismo el mes de agosto, el día de San Juan Bautista, se acienta en otra cilla; en la primera cilla de la llegada, en la segunda cilla no se menea daquella cilla. En este su día prencipal descansa y señoría y rreyna de allí ese grado. El tersero día se menea y se aparexa todo su biaxe un minuto muy poco; por eso se dize que se aparexa su biaje.

"Y de ese grado ua caminando cada el día cin descansar como media hora hacia la mano esquierda mirando al la Mar [d]e Norte de la montaña, los seys meses desde el mes primero de enero, *Capac Raymi, Camay Quilla;* febrero, *Paucar Uaray, Hatun Pocoy Quilla;* marzo, *Pacha Pocuy Quilla;* abril, *Ynga Raymi, Camay Quilla;* mayo, *Atun Cusqui, Aymoray Quilla;* junio, *Haucay Cusqui Quilla;* julio, *Chacra Conacuy Quilla.*

"De este mes de agosto comiensa otra ues, desde la silla principal de la silla segunda principal, que estas dos cillas y casas tiene muy apoderado que cada mes tiene cada su cilla en cada grado del cielo; el sol y la luna ua ciguiendo como muger y rreyna de las estrellas. Cigue al hombre que ua apuntando y rreloxo de los meses del año: agosto, *Chacra Yapuy Quilla;* setienbre, *Coya Raymi Quilla;* utubre, *Uma Raymi Quilla;* nouienbre, *Aya Marcay Quilla;* dezienbre, *Capac Ynti Raymi Quilla.* Se acaua todo el mes al rruedo del andar del sol, comensando otra ues de enero. En este dicho mes se cienta en su cilla como dicho es y así ua cada año" (Guaman Poma de Ayala 1980:830 [1615:884 (898)]).

26. ". . . se sigue el gran varrio de Carmenga, por donde sale el Camino, que llaman de Chinchasuio a toda la tierra de auajo, a Lima Quito y todas las demas prouincias, que caen a la vanda del Norte: En la Cumbre del serro de Carmenga auia muchas torresillas a trechos que seruian para tener cuenta con el mouimiento del sol, y su declinacion, en que eran muy cuidadosos y curiosos" (Vázquez de Espinosa 1948:515 [1628: Pt. 2, Bk. 4, Ch. 76]).

27. "Este rey hizo junta de sus sabios y astrólogos, y todos, con el mismo rey, que sabia mucho, hallaron puntualmente los solsticios. Era una manera de reloj de sombras, y por ellas sabian cual dia era largo y cual corto, y cuándo el sol iba y volvia á los trópicos. A mí me enseñaron cuarto paredes antiquísimas sobre un cerro, y un criollo, gran lenguaraz y verídico, me certificó servia de reloj este edificio á los indios antiguos. Por ser este príncipe tan sabio en los movimientos de los astros, llamó al mes de diciembre, en que nació, *Capac Raymi,* de su mismo nombre; y luégo llamaron al mes de junio *Citoc Raymi,* como si dijéramos, solsticio mayor y menor" (Montesinos 1882:70–71 [1630: Ch. 12]).

28. "La nouena Guaca era un cerro llamado, Quiangalla, que esta en el camino de yucay, donde estauan dos mojones, o pilares que tenian por señal que llegando alli el sol era el principio del verano" (Cobo 1980:24 [1653: Bk. 13, Ch. 13]).

29. "La setima se decia, sucanca, era un cerro por donde viene la acequia de Chinchero, en que hauia dos mojones por señal que quando llegaua alli el sol, hauian de començar a sembrar el maiz. el sacrificio que alli se hacia se dirigia al sol, pidiendole que llegase alli a tiempo que fuese buena sazon para sembrar, y sacrificauanle carneros, ropa, y corderillos pequeños de oro, y plata" (Cobo 1980:26 [1653: Bk. 13, Ch. 13]).

30. "La tercera, Chinchincalla, es un cerro grande, donde estauan dos mojones, a los quales quando llegaua el sol, era tiempo de sembrar" (Cobo 1980:58 [1653: Bk. 13, Ch. 16]).

31. "También alcançaron los equinocios y los solenizaron muy mucho. En el de março segavan los maizales del Cozco con gran fiesta y regozijo, particularmente el andén de Collcampata, que era como jardín del Sol. En el equinocio de setiembre hazían una de las cuarto fiestas principales del Sol, que llamavan *Citua Raimi.* . . . Para verificar el equinocio tenían colunas de piedra riquíssimamente labradas, puestas en los patios o plaças que havía ante los templos del Sol. Los sacerdotes, cuando sentían que el equinocio estava cerca, tenían cuidado de mirar cada día la sombra que la coluna hazía. Tenían las colunas puestas en el centro de un cerco redondo muy grande, que tomava todo el ancho de la plaça o del patio. Por medio del cerco echavan por hilo, de oriente a poniente, una raya, que por larga esperi-

encia sabían dónde havían de poner el un punto y el otro. Por la sombra que la coluna hazía sobre la raya veían que el equinocio se iva acercando; y cuando la sombra tomava la raya de medio a medio, desde que salía el Sol hasta que se ponía, y que a medio día bañava la luz del Sol toda la coluna en derredor, sin hazer sombra a parte alguna, dezían que aquel día era el equinocial. Entonces adornavan las colunas con todas las flores y yervas olorosas que podían haver, y ponían sobre ellas la silla del Sol, y dezían que aquel día se asentava el Sol con toda su luz, de lleno en lleno, sobre aquellas colunas" (Garcilaso de la Vega 1945:112 [1609: Vol. 1, Bk. 2, Ch. 22]).

32. The statement that the gnomon cast no shadow at all on the equinox is suggestive of a zenith passage date, but in the passage below Garcilaso de la Vega correctly recognized that the zenith passage falls near the equinox only as one approaches the latitude of Quito.

33. Molina (1989:73–75 [ca. 1575]) agrees with Garcilaso de la Vega on the importance of this festival, and places it in a lunar month corresponding to September in the Gregorian calendar.

34. "Y es de notar que los Reyes Incas y sus amautas, que eran los filósofos, assí como ivan ganando las provincias, assí ivan esperimentando que, cuanto más se acercavan a la línea equinocial, tanto menos sombra hazía la coluna al medio día, por lo cual fueron estimando más y más las colunas que estavan más cerca de la ciudad de Quitu; y sobre todas las otras estimaron las que pusieron en la misma ciudad y en su paraje, hasta la costa de la mar, donde, por estar el sol a plomo (como dizen los albañíes), no hazía señal de sombra alguna a medio día. Por esta razón las tuvieron en mayor veneración, porque dezían que aquéllas eran assiento más agradable para el Sol, porque en ellas se assentava derechamente y en las otras de lado" (Garcilaso de la Vega 1945:112 [1609: Vol. 1, Bk. 2, Ch. 22]).

35. "Fué éste muy sabio y gran astrólogo; halló los equinoccios, que los indios llaman *illaris*, y por su causa llaman al mes de mayo *Quilla Toca Corca*; como si dijéramos, equinoccio vernal; y al de setiembre *Camay Tupac Corca*, que es equinoccio autumnal. Asimismo partió el año comun en cuatro partes y tiempos, conforme á los cuatro puntos de los solsticios y equinoccios" (Montesinos 1882:72 [1630: Ch. 12]).

36. Guaman Poma de Ayala provides several descriptions of light casting by the Inca:

"Y lo ciguin en el senbrar la comida, en qué mes y en qué día y en qué ora y en qué punto por donde anda el sol. Lo miran los altos serros y por la mañana de la claridad y rrayo que apunta el sol a la uintana. Por este rreloxo cienbra y coxe la comida del año en este rreyno" (Guaman Poma de Ayala 1980:210 [1615:235 (237)]).

"Y para no herrar la ora y día, se ponían a mirar en una quebrada y miraua el salir y apuntar del rrayo del sol de la mañana como uiene por su rroedo, bolteando como rreloxo. Entienden de ello y no le engaña un punto el rreloxo de ellos, que seys meses boltea a lo derecho y otros says a lo isquierdo buelbe" (Guaman Poma de Ayala 1980:234 [1615:260 (262)]).

"Y para sauer las oras y minutos, dize el astrólogo que apunta muy de mañana el rrayo del sol, y la claridad se a de uer de una uentana; la claridad adonde da o que se ponga a mirar an serro por donde sale y anda y buelbe y se acienta, que allí no hierra el punto y camino del sol" (Guaman Poma de Ayala 1980:830 [1615:884 (898)]).

3. The Year

1. The Christian celebration of Easter, for example, is celebrated on the first Sunday after the first full moon on or after the March equinox.

2. Interpreting the full relation between Inca social organization and the calendar is a difficult and complex task that goes beyond our aims here. We refer readers to an edited volume on Inca time keeping (Ziólkowski and Sadowski 1989).

3. For another statement on solar observations made by the *yanca*, see *The Huarochirí Manuscript* (1991:78 [ca. 1608: Ch. 10]).

4. "Y aunq(ue) el mes es conocido. no lo es precissam(en)te el dia. y p(ar)a conoscer q(uan)do ha de ser / se assienta el Yañac en cierta p(ar)te y aguarda al salir del Sol. y mira si comiença a asomar por cierta p(ar)te de vn / cerro. que ya tienen marcada. y en llegando el sol a la señal de auiso a los officiales" (Taylor 1987:93).

5. Guaman Poma de Ayala also provides a brief description of a specialist from the Lucana region:

"Que los yndios filósofos, astrólogos que sauen las oras y domingos y días y meses, año, para senbrar y rrecoger las comidas de cada año.

"Llamado Juan *Yunpa* del pueblo de Uchuc Marca, Lucana, tenía el horden de filusufía y conocía de las estrellas y del rruedo del andar del sol y de las horas y meses, año" (Guaman Poma de Ayala 1980:830 [1615: 884 (898)]).

6. Also see Albornoz (1984:203–204 [ca. 1582]).

7. "Estos años y meses que daban por cuenta, eran meses y años lunares, dando a cada mes de una conjunción de luna a otra; y destos meses lunares daban doce al año, dando su nombre a cada mes" (Callapiña, Supno, y otros Quipucamayos 1974:21 [1542/1608]).

8. This is also inconsistent with the proposed use of "sidereal" lunar months described near the close of this chapter.

9. Ziólkowski and Sadowski (1989, 1992) provide an extensive list of the dates of new moons during Inca times. In the years just prior to Molina's account, the mid- to late-1570s, new moons fell near mid-May in 1569, 1572, and 1574.

10. Pedro Gutiérrez de Santa Clara (1963:225 [ca. 1600]) provides a list of months similar to those mentioned by Fernández, suggesting that one of these authors copied from the other (Ziólkowski and Sadowski 1992:77).

11. Cieza de León (1976:277 [1553: Pt. 1, Ch. 101]) suggests that the Collas of the Lake Titicaca region had a year of ten months. This is not, however, confirmed by other writers.

12. "Porque ni contaban por años sus edades ni la duración de sus he-

chos, ni tenían algún tiempo de punto señalado para medir por él los sucesos, como contamos nosotros desde el Nacimiento de Nuestro Señor Jesucristo, ni jamás hubo indio, ni apenas de halla hoy, que sepa los años que tiene, ni menos los que han pasado desde algún memorable acaecimiento acá. Lo que suelen responder cuando se les pregunta de cosas pasadas, como sean ya de más de cuatro o sies años, es que aquello acaecio *ñaupapacha*, que quiere decir antiguamente; y la misma respuesta dan a los sucesos de veinto años atrás que a los de ciento y de mil, salvo que cuando la cosa es muy antigua, lo dan a entender con cierto tonillo y ponderación de palabras" (Cobo 1956:142–143 [1653: Bk.12, Ch. 37]).

13. However, a date near 15 or 16 August usually would have been in the eighth month.

14. "Sin estos sacrificios cuotidianos, le hacían otros generales a ciertos tiempos, plegarias y ayunos. Particularmente le ofrecían cada mes el suyo, cuando llegaba a las señales o pilares que señalaban los meses" (Cobo 1956: 202 [1653: Bk. 13, Ch. 21]).

15. If both the sunset and sunrise horizons are marked, then fourteen locations must be marked.

16. The eighteen-year precession of the lunar orbit causes a small shift in the apparent path of the moon from month to month.

17. Zuidema (1977a) has also presented an argument for the 328-day period based on the decomposition of the number 328 into 8 and 41. These numbers are important to Zuidema since he believes that a "sacred" week for the Inca was 8 days and that the ceque system held 41 ceques.

4. Seats of the Sun: The Solar Pillars of Cuzco

1. Over a period of a year the sun rise and set position is seen to move north, then south along the horizon. Accordingly, the sun sets at a particular spot on the horizon two times in a year, once in the winter/spring and then again on a date in the summer/fall.

2. Peter Frost brought these pillars to our attention.

3. Defining twelve approximately equal-length months with solar horizon positions requires marking seven locations (if all observations are to be made from one place). From the central portions of Cuzco, three positions on Picchu can mark the June solstice, one month before and after the solstice (22 May/21 July), and two months before and after the solstice (21 April/21 August). From the central plaza the equinoxes (21 March/22 September) can also be marked on the southern slope of Picchu.

4. If one-step paces were used, then the outer pillars would have been approximately 175 meters apart, and the inner pillars would have been separated by 35 meters.

5. We note that the apparently conflicting claims of the Anonymous Chronicler and Betanzos regarding the use of the pillars on Picchu are consistent if they refer to observations made from different locations. Betanzos describes (Pachacuti) Inca Yupanqui's use of the four pillars on Picchu by saying that he "stood in a place" to watch the sun rise and set for deter-

mining the solstice. The Anonymous Chronicler uses what seems to be the same four pillars to mark a date in August as viewed from the plaza, Hau-caypata. Both of these statements could be true if the pillars of Picchu were observed from more than one location.

6. Descriptions of each huaca in the Cuzco ceque system are currently being prepared by Bauer (n.d.b).

7. If we accept that Chinchincalla marked the time to begin planting, the location from which the sun could be observed to set behind it was approximately two kilometers south of the Coricancha.

8. "Y comiensan a senbrar el mays hasta el mes de enero, conforme el rrelojo y rruedo del sol y del temple de la tierra" (Guaman Poma de Ayala 1980:225 [1615:251 (253)]).

9. The December solstice sunset can also be seen on the west shoulder of Killke from Limacpampa. We find this alignment interesting, since it is known from Cobo (1980:35 [1653: Bk. 13, Ch. 15]) that this Hurin Cuzco plaza, like its pair in Hanan Cuzco (Haucaypata [Plaza de Armas]), contained an usnu where the young men made their first sacrifices during the Huarachikoy ritual of Capac Raymi.

10. "La quarta se decia, chuquimarca, era un templo del sol en el cerro de Mantocalla; en el qual decian que bajaua a dormir el sol muchas veces, por lo qual allende de lo demas le ofrecian niños" (Cobo 1980:32 [1653: Bk. 13, Ch. 14]).

11. "La sesta se decia, Mantocallas [sic], que era un cerro tenido en gran veneracion, en el qual al tiempo de desgranar el maiz hacian ciertos sacri-ficios; y para ellos ponian en el dicho cerro muchos haces de leña labrada vestidos como hombres, y mugeres; y gran cantidad de maçorcas de maiz hechas de palo, y despues de grandes borracheras quemauan muchos car-neros con la leña dicha, y matauan algunos niños" (Cobo 1980:32 [1653: Bk. 13, Ch. 14]).

12. Copying Molina, Cobo (1990:142–143 [1653: Bk. 13, Ch. 28]) also states that the ruling Inca celebrated Inti Raymi at Mantocalla.

13. For completeness, we note that there is a large looters' pit on the highest point on the Yancacalle ridge that marks the June solstice sunrise as seen from near Cusilluchayoc.

14. In the general area corresponding to the June solstice sunset as viewed from the north end of Salonpuncu, there is a small pit. It is recent, approxi-mately a meter across, and less than a meter in depth, and there are no arti-facts near it.

15. Zuidema (1977a:257) has noted that the northwest horizon as seen from Sacsahuaman is within the area thought to contain Quiancalla.

16. Cieza de León (1976:154 [1554: Pt. 2, Ch. 51]) claims that the "for-tress" of Sacsahuaman was also a house of the sun, but he gives no infor-mation on what celebrations took place there.

17. On the equator the dates of the zenith passages correspond with the equinoxes. At other latitudes they do not.

18. Two early dictionaries provide possible terms for the zenith passage. The first is by Gonçález Holguín (1989:341[1608]), who lists these entries:

"Intim ticnurayan. El sol esta en el zenit" (The sun in the zenith); "Intim ticnuy cumun. El sol passa de medio dia o abaxa" (The sun passing midday or below); and "Ttikçuy cun intiticnumanta. El sol va declinando despues de medio dia" (The descent of the sun after midday). Given the contexts of these definitions, we suggest that Gonçález Holguín has used the term *zenith* in place of *meridian*.

The second dictionary to provide possible names of the zenith passage is by Bertonio (1984:473 [1612]): "Llegar el sol al Zenith: Inti sunaquero puri" (Arrival of the sun at the zenith). We find this definition ambiguous and are not sure if Bertonio is referring to the zenith passage or to a noon observance.

19. During 1992, test excavations were dug on the hills of Picchu and Killke in possible pillar locations. These excavations used one-by-one-meter grid systems and were dug in arbitrary ten-centimeter levels until sterile subsoil was reached. The test squares on Picchu recovered no prehistoric remains. The work on Killke yielded several burials and fragments of Inca pottery. It should be noted, however, that the Coricancha is a large complex, resulting in correspondingly large areas on Picchu and Killke for marking a solstice. The excavations tested only a small portion of these areas.

5. Stellar Observations

1. Additional linguistic information on Andean stellar astronomy can be gained from the many modern Quechua dictionaries. We recommend Middendorf (1890), Lira (1944), and Cusihuamán (1976), among others.

2. "Entre las estrellas comunmente todos adorauan á la que ellos llaman, Collca, que llamamos nosotros las cabrillas. Y las demás estrellas eran veneradas por aquellos particularmente que les parecía que auían menester su fauor. Porque atribuyan á diuersas estrellas diuersos oficios. Y assí los Ouejeros hazían veneración y sacrificio á vna estrella que ellos llaman, Vrcuchillay, que dizen es vn carnero de muchos colores, el qual entiende en la conseruación del ganado, y se entiende ser la que los Astrólogos llaman Lyra. Y los mismos adoran á otras dos que andan cerca della que llaman, Catuchillay y Vrcuchillay. Que fingen ser una oueja con vn cordero. Otros que viuen en las montañas adoran otra estrella que se llama Chuqui chinchay que dizen que es vn Tigre á cuyo cargo están los Tigres, Ossos, y Leones. También adoran otra estrella que se llaman Ancochinchay, que conserua otros animales. Assí mismo adoran otra que llaman Machacuay á cuyo cargo están las Serpientes y Culebras, para que no les hagan mal, y generalmente todos los animales y aues que ay en la tierra, creyeron que ouiesse vn su semejante en el cielo, á cuyo cargo estaua su procreación y augmente. Y assí tenian cuento con diuersas estrellas, como la que llamauan, Chacana, y Topatorca, Mamana, y Mirco, y Miquiquiray, y otras assí" (Polo de Ondegardo 1916b:3–5 [1585: Ch. 1]).

3. "La adoración de las estrellas procedió de aquella opinión en que estaban de que para la conservación de cada especie de cosas había el Criador señalado, y como substituído, una causa segunda; en cuya conformidad cre-

yeron que de todos los animales y aves de la tierra había en el cielo un símil que atendía a la conservación y aumento dellos, atribuyendo este oficio y ministerio a varias constelaciones de estrellas. Y así, de aquella junta que se hace de estrellas pequeñas llamadas vulgarmente Las Cabrillas, y destos indios *Collca*, afirmaban que salieron todos los símiles, y que della manaba la virtud en que se conservaban; por lo cual la llamaban madre y tenían universalmente todos los *ayllos* y familias por *guaca* muy principal; conocíanla todos, y los que entre éstos algo entendían, tenían cuenta con su curso en todo el año más que con el de las otras estrellas; pero no se servían della de otra cosa, ni trataban de otra virtud que tuviese; y con todo eso, le hacían grandes sacrificios por todas las provincias. Las demás estrellas eran veneradas de solo aquellos que juzgaban tener dellas necesidad, conforme a los oficios que les atribuían, y ellos no más las conocían y tenían cuenta con ellas y les ofrecían sacrificios; y los otros no, ni lo tenían por precepto obligatorio. La veneración que a cada estrella hacían era por esta forma:

"Todos los pastores respetaban y hacían sacrificios a la llamada de los astrólogos Lira, que ellos nombraban *Urcuchillay*, la cual decían que era un carnero de muchos colores, que entendía en la conservación del ganado; y a otros dos pequeñas que tiene debajo a manera de T, decían ser los pies y la cabeza; y éstos también hacían veneración a otra que anda cerca désta y la llaman *Catachillay*, que también es algo grande, y a otra más pequeña que anda junto a ella; las cuales fingían que era un *llama* con su cordero que procedían del *Urcuchillay*.

"Los que viven en las montañas y tierras *yuncas*, hacían veneración y sacrificaban a otra estrella que llaman *Chuquichinchay*, que dicen ser un tigre y estar a su cargo los tigres, osos y leones: pedíanle en el sacrificio que no les hiciesen mal estas fieras. Encomendábanse también a ella los que habían de pasar por tierra fragosa y de boscaje, por la misma razón que los que vivían en ella.

"También tenían gran cuenta con venerar a otra llamada *Machacuay*, que pensaban entendía en la conservación de las culebras, serpientes y víboras; principalmente, porque, cuando truena el relámpago, parece de aquella figura; . . . Finalmente, veneraban a esta estrella, por la misma razón que a las otras, porque las serpientes y víboras no les hiciesen daño. Respetaban a otra estrella que llamaban *Ancochinchay*; la cual decían que miraba por la conservación de otros animales.

"En suma, de cada especie de animales conocían una estrella en el cielo, por donde son muchas las que adoraban y tenían puestos nombres y aplicados sacrificios, cuales son las que llaman *topatorca, chacana, mirco mamana, miquiquiray, quiantopa*, y otras; en cuyo número entraban todas las de primera magnitud, a ninguna de las cuales dejaron de poner nombre, el lucero de la mañana y tarde y los más notables signos y planetas" (Cobo 1956:159–160 [1653: Bk. 13, Ch. 6]).

4. This does not, however, imply that the stars of Urcuchillay were all the same stars used in the Western constellation of Lyra.

5. Catachillay is mentioned several times in this poem.

6. Lehmann-Nitsche (1928:134–142) and Bollaert (1865:275) also dis-

cuss the possible location of Urcuchillay and Catachillay in the area of Lyra.

7. Bertonio is unique among early writers in providing Catachillay with multiple identifications, which included a cross, the Pleiades, and a group of stars in a bright region of the Milky Way:

(1) "Cruzero estrellas. Vnuchilla catachilla" (Bertonio 1984: Pt. 1, 150 [1612]).

(2) "Cabrillas que llaman a vnas estrellas; Catachilla huara huara" (Bertonio 1984: Pt. 1, 107 [1612]).

(3) "Catachilla, Vna Estrella nebulosa en la via Lactea, o las estrellas sobre la nebulosa" (Bertonio 1984: Pt. 2, 38 [1612]).

8. Cusihuamán (1976:115) translates the word *Qolqa* as "morning star" or "bright star."

9. Another short reference to the Cabrillas (Pleiades) is found in Polo de Ondegardo (1916c:189 [1571]).

10. The *Arte y vocabulario* . . . (1951:97 [1586]) and Gonçález Holguín (1989:454 [1608]) also associate the terms "Cho'qechinchay" and "Chuqui chinchay" as well as "A'qochinchay" and "Acochincay" with comets. Pachacuti Yamqui Salcamayhua (1950:226 [1613]) uses the term "Chuquechinchay" to describe jaguars and includes it on a drawing of the Coricancha.

11. The star Quiantopa is found only in Cobo's list.

12. Cobo (1990:32 [1653: Bk. 13, Ch. 7]) also writes, apparently using information provided by Polo de Ondegardo (1965b:6–8 [1585: Ch. 1]), that "the Thunder was represented by a man made of stars who lived in the sky."

13. "No hablo sólo de las partes lúcidas y resplandecientes, . . . sino mucho más digo esto por otras partes oscuras y negras que hay en el cielo. Porque realmente vemos en él unas como manchas, que son muy notables, las cuales jamás me acuerdo haber echado de ver en el cielo cuando estaba en Europa, y acá, en este otro hemisferio, las he visto muy manifiestas. Son estas manchas de color y forma que la parte de la luna eclipsada, y parécensele en aquella negrura y sombrío. Andan pegadas a las mismas estrellas y siempre de un mismo tenor y tamaño" (Acosta 1954:7–8 [1590: Bk. 1, Ch. 2]).

14. "Eruditus quidam vir & religiosus vitam degens in provincia Peru . . . altera experientia consistit in partibus coeli rarioribus, cuiusmodi non paucae cernuntur . . . prope polum antarcticum, ita ut nigror quidam plerisque in locis coeli appareat, ac si coelum quodammodo esset perforatum" (Clavius 1612:47).

15. "En la vía que los astrólogos llaman láctea, en unas manchas negras que van por ella a la larga, quisieron imaginar que havía una figura de oveja con su cuerpo entero, que estava amamantando un cordero. A mí me la querían mostrar, diziendo: 'Ves allí la cabeça de la oveja, ves acullá la del cordero mamando, ves el cuerpo, braços y piernas del uno y de el otro.' Mas yo no veía las figuras, sino las manchas, y devía de ser por no saberlas imaginar" (Garcilaso de la Vega 1945:114 [1609: Vol. 1, Bk. 2, Ch. 23]).

16. These birds are originally written as "Condormi," "Suyuntuytapas," and "Guamantapas."

17. The "Pleiades" is originally written as "Cabrillas."

18. See Ziólkowski and Sadowski (1992:145–147) for an alternative interpretation of this passage.

19. ". . . llamado Orcorara, quiere decir tres estrellas todas yquales" (Pachacuti Yamqui Salcamayhua 1950:226 [1613]).

20. Lehmann-Nitsche (1928:108) suggests that this should read as "Saramanca" (maize jar).

21. A note in Spanish below this star states that it is the evening star, "este de la tarde," and a note in Aymará identifies it as *apachi* (grandmother).

22. Gonçález Holguín (1989:117 [1608]) suggests that Chhoque chinchay was a llama.

23. A note below this star indicates that it is the morning star, "este es el luzero de la mañana," and a note in Aymará identifies it as *achachi* (grandfather).

24. "Estas bozes decía las yndias y decían los filósofos que conosen en las estrellas que ay hombres y mugeres y carneros con su cría y perdises y casador y pastor, batán, león, uenado. Y de las cometas sauen lo que a de suseder, bueno y mala señal: *cuyllorcona, Chasca Cuyllor, Oncoy Cuyllor, Caza Cuyllor, Pacari Cuyllor, Uara Uara*" (Guaman Poma de Ayala 1980:831 [1615:885 (899)]). Translations for the star names are provided in the 1980 text of Guaman Poma de Ayala (1980:831 [1615: 885 (899)]). Since we are not in full agreement with these translations, they have not been reproduced here.

25. Both Spanish and Quechua are used in naming this star.

26. "Acabadas las confesiones en las fiestas solemnes, que suelen ser tres cada año, la principal cerca de la fiesta del Corpus, o en ella misma, que llaman Oncoy mitta, que es cuando aparecen las siete cabrillas que llaman Oncoy las cuales adoran porque no se les sequen los maíces" (Arriaga 1968a:213 [1621: Ch. 5]).

27. For additional references to Oncoy as the Pleiades, and their relation to Corpus Christi, see Arriaga (1968a:201, 223 [1621: Chs. 2 and 8]).

28. The author of the Huarochirí manuscript (1991:84 [ca. 1608: Ch. 13]) mentions a five-day period, determined by solar observations, as taking place in June near the time of Corpus Christi:

> We know people schedule Chaupi ñamca's rites during the month of June, in such a way that they almost coincide with Corpus Christi. When the *yanca* (margin, in Quechua:)[yanca] had made calculations from his solar observatory, people said, 'They'll take place in so many days'" (*Huarochirí Manuscript* 1991:78 [ca. 1608: Ch. 10]).

29. "Si saben que alguna o algunas personas hayan adorado al Sol, Luna y a las estrellas que llaman Oncoy, que son las siete cabrillas, y a las estrellas

que llaman Charca, que son las tres Marías, y al Lucero, que llaman Pacha-huarac o Coyahuarac" (Arriaga 1968a:273 [1621]).

30. Also see Arriaga (1968a:277; 1968b:172–173 [1621]).

31. "Al Sol llamaron *Inti*, a la luna *Quilla* y al luzero Venus *Chasca*, que es crinita o crespa, por sus muchos rayos. Miraron en las siete cabrillas por verlas tan juntas y por la diferencia que hay dellas a las otras estrellas, que les causava admiración, mas no por otro respecto. Y no miraron en más estrellas porque, no teniendo necesidad forçosa, no sabían a qué propósito mirar en ellas, ni tuvieron más nombres de estrellas en particular que los dos que hemos dicho. En común las llamaron *cóillur*, que quiere dezir estrella" (Garcilaso de la Vega 1945:110 [1609: Vol. 1, Bk. 2, Ch. 21]).

32. Guaman Poma de Ayala (1980: 63, 161, 236, 239, 272 [1615:80 (80), 185 (187), 263 (265), 265 (267), 299 (301)]) indicates several times that the Inca worshiped the star Chasca Cuyllor, and that the Spaniards called this star "luzero." The term "luzero" (or "lucero") can be used for any bright star, but it is most frequently applied to Venus.

33. "Acerca de la estrella Venus, que unas vezes la veían al anochecer y otras al amanecer, dezían que el Sol, como señor de todas las estrellas, mandava que aquélla, por ser más hermosa que todas las demás, anduviesse cerca dél, unas vezes delante y otras atrás" (Garcilaso de la Vega 1945:114 [1609: Vol. 1, Bk. 2, Ch. 23]).

34. The astronomical information provided by an anonymous writer, frequently attributed to Blas Valera (1950 [ca 1585]), has not been included in this report. His identifications of Mars as Aucayoc (the warrior), Mercury as Catuilla (the messenger), and others are Eurocentric. It should be noted, however, that he does identify Venus as Chasca and mentions that there was a host of animals in the sky, including sheep, lions, and snakes.

35. "Y que por mandado de los Ingas adoraban al sol y á la luna y á las estrellas y en particular al lucero de la mañana, que en su lengua le dicen *auquilla*, y á las Cabrillas, que en su lengua se llaman *larilla*, y á otras estrellas grandes" (Monzón 1881:204–205 [1586]).

36. Also see *Misión de las provincias de los Huachos y Yauyos* (1919:188 [1613]).

37. ". . . uno era cuando la primera vez aparecían, y se descubrían en su hemisferio el Oncoy, que son las 'siete cabrillas'" (*Misión de las provincias de los Huachos y Yauyos* 1919:183 [1613]).

38. A transcription of this document can also be found in Duviols (1986).

39. "Adoran los indios dos géneros de ídolos, unos fijos, como son cerros y peñascos y cumbres altas de la sierra nevada, y al sol, luna y las estrellas, las siete Cabrillas y las tres Marías, y al trueno y rayo, y á la mar y á los manantiales; otros son móviles, de los cuales unos tienen en sus chaccras" (Avendaño 1904:380 [1617]).

40. "Y la [fiesta] mayor del año era por Pascua de Espíritu Sancto ó Corpus Cristi, que era cuando se descubrían mejor las siete Cabrillas y la llaman oncoimita, y tenían particularmente dedicado este tiempo, porque es en el que se les hiela el maíz y se les pierden las sementeras" (Avendaño 1904:381 [1617]).

41. "Adoraron . . . a las estrellas, al luzero de la mañana i la estrella Venus de la tarde; las cabrillas que ellos llamavan Collca" (Calancha 1981: 835 [1638: Bk. 2, Ch. 11]).

42. "No contavan el año por Lunas, ni por el curso del Sol, sino desde que salían las estrellas que nosotros llamamos las Cabrillas, i ellos llaman Fur. La causa se funda en una larga fábula, que no es para mi asunto. Era ley que así le contasen, porque aquellas estrellas les davan de comer, i criavan sus senbrados, i tenían por cosa de vida començar los años desde que vían la cara a quien les dava el sustento" (Calancha 1981:1244–1245 [1638: Bk. 3, Ch. 2]).

43. "Tenían por deidad dos estrellas que llamavan Patá, que son las que llamamos las Marías, i muchos destos Indios cuentan oy (i muchos quiçá lo creen) que la estrella de en medio es un ladrón, i malechor i facinoroso, que la Luna quiso castigar, i enbió las dos estrellas que lo llevasen asido (que eso quiere decir Patá) i lo entregaron a que se lo comiesen buytres, que son éstos gallinaços figurados en quatro estrellas que están más abajo de las Marías, i que en memoria deste castigo egenplar están aquellas siete estre- llas en el cielo acordando la culpa i el castigo" (Calancha 1981:1243 [1638: Bk. 3, Ch. 2]).

44. "Y asi mesmo asi adorar el lusero de la mañana que llaman atungara como criador de los mayores y prinsipales y asi mesmo dos estrellas pe- queñas que andan junto a las siete cabrillas que las llaman chuchucollor por criadoras de los chuchus y chacpas que son los que nasen de pies y los que nasen dos de vn bientre que disen son hijos de los ydolos y guacas.

"Y asi mesmo asia adorar las siete estrellas que llaman las siete cabrillas que ellos llaman en su lengua oncoicoillur las quales estrellas se aparesen quando enpiesan las eladas que son por corpus y san Juan para que no se ye- len sus chacras y ya no aya emfermedades y pestes y les desia esta orasion: *pacoc yaya oncoiyaya ama micuita cagachum ama micuita rachachum* señor poderoso que tienes muchas comidas y asienda no permitas que se ye- len y se echen a perder las chacras" (Hernando Hacaspoma 1656: fol. 14– 14v, in Duviols 1986:151).

45. The constellation of Chuchucoyllor is mentioned over twenty times in the Cajatambo testimonies.

46. It is tempting to suggest an identification among the stars of the nearby Hyades cluster, but there is no specific mention of the bright star Aldebaran, the sixteenth brightest star in the sky, which appears in that direction.

47. Also see Ziólkowski and Sadowski (1992:167–233).

48. Precession does cause a slow shift in the rise and set position of stars. The azimuth at which the Pleiades rise shifts by approximately ten min- utes of arc in fifty years.

49. Bauer's survey work in the Chinchaysuyu region of Cuzco has found a possible candidate for this shrine, a small spring called the Llama's Eye. It is located near the Inca road to Chinchaysuyu, on the first flat area after leaving the Cuzco Valley.

50. In an earlier article, Zuidema (1977b) misidentified the location of Susumarca, an error that he later corrects (Zuidema 1982b:228 n. 20).

51. All of our candidates lie in or near the Milky Way, consistent with the focus found by Urton (1981a) in his ethnographic work. It must be noted, however, that since sixteen of the twenty brightest stars fall within 25 degrees of the Milky Way, it is not surprising that the tentative identifications lie along it.

52. As an alternative, Urton (1981a:103) suggests that the dark lane that tends from Centaurus to Scorpio could also be the Machacuay.

6. Other Celestial Phenomena

1. A sun dog (sometimes called a mock sun) is a bright area that can occur on either side of the sun. They are slightly larger than the sun and separated from it by 22 degrees. Sun dogs are caused by refraction through systematically oriented ice crystals in thin cirrus clouds, and can appear in a nearly clear sky. They are not uncommon sights to people who look for them. A highly speculative reference to a sun dog observation can be found in Cobo (1990:26 [1653: Bk. 13, Ch. 5]) when he says that three suns were seen in the same sky.

2. Aurorae are dramatic nighttime phenomena, but their appearances in Peru would be exceedingly rare.

3. Cieza de León (1976:316 [1553: Bk. 1, Ch. 15]) and Cobo (1990:175 [1653: Bk. 13, Ch. 38]) mention meteors (falling stars). Like star watching, meteor watching for purposes of divination continues to be practiced in Andean villages (Urton 1981a:88–94).

4. Sir Edmond Halley discovered in 1682 that some comets are periodic. Most comets, however, have periods so long that they are meaningless on historic time scales. Eclipses are predictable, and the saros cycle of eclipses was known by the neo-Babylonians.

5. Information on these subjects can also be found in Ziólkowski and Sadowski (1992).

6. If annular and partial eclipses in which a substantial fraction of the sun is occulted were included, the frequency with which eclipses are experienced increases to once every few decades. Some locations have experienced eclipses much more frequently. Liller (1986) discusses a ten-year period in which four total eclipses occurred over Easter Island.

7. There is brief reference to eclipses in Guaman Poma de Ayala (1980: 831 [1615:885 (899)]).

8. "Con el cual también han cobrado para con ellos muy grande opinión de sabios los españoles, porque es notable la admiración que les causa ver que podemos nosotros alcanzar a saber los eclipses antes que vengan, con tanta puntualidad que les avisamos antes no sólo de la noche en que suceden, sino hasta de la hora, en que han de comenzar, la cantidad de luna que se escurecerá, y el tiempo que durarán. Y la verdad, no comprendiendo ellos las causas de un efecto tan admirable, quedan como fuera de sí de ver

que nosotros lo podamos saber antes que suceda" (Cobo 1956:159 [1653: Bk. 13, Ch. 6]).

9. Watching a partially eclipsed sun can cause damage to the eye. However, the believed ease with which damage can occur has reached almost mythical proportions in modern American society.

10. Calancha (1981 [1638]) also provides information on solar eclipses, and Gutiérrez de Santa Clara (1963:231 [ca. 1600: Bk. 3, Ch. 56]) mentions lunar eclipses.

11. "Quando se eclipsa el sol, ó la luna, ó parece algún cometa, ó resplandor en el ayre suelen gritar y llorar, y hazer que otros griten y lloren, y que ladren los perros, ó aullen y para esto los aporrean. Suelen cercar sus casas en procession de noche con hazes de fuego y hazer otras cerimonias para que no les venga el mal que temen y que tienen por aguero malo" (Polo de Ondegardo 1916d:198 [1567: Ch. 4]).

12. "Tenían por cosa grave el eclipse del sol, y cuando sucedía consultaban a los agoreros sobre la significación dél; y certificados de los efectos que denotaban, hacían grandes y costosos sacrificios, ofreciendo en ellos varias figuras de plata y oro y matando cantidad de ganado y de muchachos y muchachas. Fingían comúnmente los hechiceros que el eclipse pronosticaba la muerte de algún príncipe, y que el sol se ponía luto por la falta que había de hacer en el mundo; y cuando esto sucedía, todas las mujeres dedicadas al sol hacían grandes ayunos, vestían ropas de tristeza y ofrecían frecuentes sacrificios. . . .

"Acerca del eclipse de la luna tenían tantas boberías como del sol: decían, cuando se eclipsaba, que un león o serpiente la embestía para despedazarla; y por esto, cuando comenzaba a eclipsarse, daban grandes voces y gritos y azotaban los perros para que ladrasen y aullasen. Poníanse los varones a punto de guerra, tañendo sus bocinas, tocando atambores, y dando grandes alaridos, tiraban flechas y varas hacia la luna, y hacían grandes ademanes con las lanzas, como si hubiesen de herir al león y sierpe; porque decían que desta manera los asombradan y ponían espanto para que no despedazasen la luna.

"Lo cual hacían, porque tenían aprehendido que si el león hiciese su efecto, quedaría en oscuridad y tinieblas; y estaba esta costumbre tan arraigada en sus ánimos, que con haber tantos años que son cristianos y predicarles siempre contra ella, aún no la han dejado del todo, sino que todavía gritan y vocean cuando se eclipse la luna; si bien hacen hoy esto sólo por la costumbre que tienen tan de antiguo y no por el rito e imaginación en que ella se fundó" (Cobo 1956:158–159 [1653: Bk. 13, Chs. 5 and 6]).

13. "Tuvieron cuenta con los eclipses del Sol y de la luna, mas no alcançaron las causas. Dezían al eclipse solar que el Sol estava enojado por algún delicto que havían hecho contra él, pues mostrava su cara turbada como hombre airado, y pronosticavan (a semejança de los astrólogos) que les havía de venir algún grave castigo. Al eclipse de la luna, viéndola ir negreciendo dezían que enfermava la luna, y que si acabava de escurecerse havía de morir y caerse del cielo y cogerlos a todos debaxo y matarlos, y que se havía de acabar el mundo. Por este miedo, en empeçando a eclipsarse la

luna, tocavan trompetas, cornetas, caracoles, atabales y atambores y cuan-
tos instrumentos podían haver que hiziessen ruido; atavan los perros
grandes y chicos, dávanles muchos palos para que aullassen y llamassen la
luna, que, por cierta fábula que ellos contavan, dezían que la luna era afi-
cionada a los perros, por cierto servicio que le havían hecho, y que, oyéndo-
los llorar, havría lástima dellos y recordaría del sueño que la enfermedad le
causava. . . .

"Conforme al eclipse grande o pequeño, juzgavan que havía sido la enfermedad de la luna. Pero si llegava a ser total, ya no havía que juzgar sino que
estava muerta, y por momentos temían el caer la luna y el perecer dellos;
entonces era más de veras el llorar y plañir, como gente que veía al ojo la
muerte de todos y acabarse el mundo. Cuando veían que la luna iva poco a
poco bolviendo a cobrar su luz, dezían que convalecía de su enfermedad,
porque el Pachacámac, que era el sustentador del universo, le havía dado salud y mandádole que no muriese, por que no pereciesse el mundo. Y cuando
acabava de estar de todo clara, le davan la norabuena de su salud y muchas
gracias porque no se havía caído. Todo esto de la luna vi por mis ojos" (Garcilaso de la Vega 1945:113–114 [1609: Vol. 1, Bk. 2, Ch. 23]).

14. "Lo que usaban antiguamente en los eclipses de la luna, que llaman
Quillamhuañun, la luna se muere, o Quillatutayan, la luna se escurece, usan
también ahora azotando los perros, tocando tambores y dando gritos por
todo el pueblo para que resucite la luna" (Arriaga 1968a:218 [1621: Ch. 6]).

15. Ziólkowski and Lebeuf (1993) suggest a method by which lunar
eclipses could have been predicted by the Inca using the pillars of Picchu.
We noted, however, that there are no colonial documents that indicate that
the Inca could predict lunar eclipses.

16. For additional references to possible pre-Hispanic comet sightings recorded by Montesinos (1920 [1630]) see Ziólkowski and Sadowski (1980:
22–26; 1992:130–137).

17. "En este tiempo dizen que llegó la nueva como en el Cuzco obo vn
milagro, que cómo un *yauirca* ó *amaro* abia salido del serro de Pachatusan,
muy fiera bestia, media legua de largo y gruesso, de dos braças y medio de
ancho, y con orejas y colmillos y barbas; y viene por Yuncaypampa y Sinca,
y de alli entra á la laguna de Quibipay; entonçes salen de Asoncata, dos
sacacas de fuego, y passa á Potina de Arequipa, y otro viene para mas abaxo
de Guamanca, que esta y tres ó quatro serros muy altos cubiertos de niebes,
los quales dizen que eran animales con alas y orejas y colas y quatro pies,
y encima de las espaldas muchas espinas como de pescado; y desde lejos
dizen que les parecia todo fuego" (Pachacuti Yamqui Salcamayhua 1950:
242 [1613]).

18. "Agora quiero decir una cosa admirable, y es, que veinte días antes
que esto acaesciese, . . . estando Atabaliba una noche muy alegre con algunos españoles, hablando con ellos, pareció a deshora una señal en el cielo,
a la parte del Cuzco, como cometa de fuego, que duró mucha parte de la
noche; y vista esta señal por Atabaliba, dijo que muy presto había de morir
en aquella tierra un gran señor" (Xérez 1985:156 [1534]).

19. Huayna Capac was Topa Inca Yupanqui's son.

20. Garcilaso de la Vega (1966:707–708 [1609: Vol. 2, Bk. 1, Ch. 34; also see 1609: Vol. 1, Bk. 9, Ch. 14; Vol. 1, Bk. 5, Ch. 28]) also writes that the deaths of Huayna Capac and Atahualpa were foretold by comets; however, this information was most likely copied from Cieza de León.

21. "Quando se prendió Atabalipa en la prouincia de Caxamalca, ay viuos algunos christianos que se hallaron con el marqués don Francisco Piçarro que lo prendió, que vieron en el cielo de medianoche abaxo vna señal verde tan gruessa como vn braço, y tan larga como una lança gineta. Y como los Españoles anduuiessen mirando en ello, y Atabalipa lo entendiesse: dizen que les pidió que lo sacassen para la ver: y como la vió, se paró triste, y lo estuuo el día siguiente. Y el gouernador don Francisco Piçarro le preguntó, que porqué se auía parado tan triste: respondió él he mirado la señal del cielo: y dígote, que quando mi padre Guaynacapa murió, se vió otra señal semejante a aquella. Y dentro de quinze días murió Atabalipa" (Cieza de León 1984:201 [1553: Pt. 1, Bk. 1, Ch. 65]).

7. An Overview of Inca Astronomy and Calendrics

1. When only one solstice is observed, an intercalation month must be inserted just before that solstice approximately every third year. The temporal occurrence of two new moons in a single solar month is more random. However, the average frequency is the same.

Glossary

The glossary includes Aymará [A], English [E], Spanish [S], and Quechua [Q] terms used in this work. For more extensive definitions of the Quechua terms, see the early colonial dictionaries of Domingo de Santo Tomás (1951 [1560]), the *Arte y vocabulario* . . . (1951 [1586]), Goncález Holguín (1989 [1608]), as well as the modern dictionaries of Middendorf (1890), Lira (1944), and Cusihuamán (1976). For expanded definitions of the Aymará terms, see Bertonio (1984 [1612]).

Amaru [Q].   Large snake, serpent.

Amaru Topa Inca [Q].   The older brother of Topa Inca and the eldest son of Pachacuti Inca Yupanqui. It is said that Pachacuti Inca Yupanqui selected Topa Inca as his successor rather than Amaru Topa Inca.

Ancochinchay [Q].   A star that protects other animals (Polo de Ondegardo 1965a:2–5 [1585: Ch. 1]).

Annular eclipse [E].   An eclipse in which the apparent size of the moon is smaller than the sun, so that the outer edge of the sun remains visible as a thin ring.

Antarctic Hemisphere [E].   Southern Hemisphere.

Antisuyu [Q].   The northeast quadrant of Cuzco and, by extension, of the Inca Empire.

Antizenith [E].   Zuidema (1981b, 1988b) refers to the date when the sun sets 180 degrees from the position where it rises on the zenith passage day as the "antizenith passage date."

Apachita [Q].   Sacred cairn.

Atahualpa (Atawallpa) [Q].   The Inca ruler captured and killed by the Spaniards at Cajamarca.

Aucaypata [Q].   *See* Haucaypata.

Auquilla [Q].   A name for the morning star (Venus) from the Guamanga area provided by Luis de Monzón (1881:204–205 [1586]).

Ayllu (Ayllo) [Q].   Kin group, clan, lineage, community.

Aymará [A].   Indigenous language of much of Bolivia.

Batán [S]. Grinding stone.

Braza [S]. Fathom; the length of two outstretched arms.

Cabrillas [S]. Kids (young goats). The Spaniards call the Pleiades the "siete cabrillas" (seven kids).

Cancha [Q]. An enclosure that may contain several rooms.

Cancho Huarac [Q]. A bright star named in the Huarochirí manuscript (1991:132–133 [ca. 1608: Ch. 29]).

Capac [Q]. Royal.

Capac Raymi [Q]. A festival month associated by most authors with the December solstice and the beginning of a new year. During this month the Waracikcoy ritual took place.

Carmenca (Carmenga, Karminka) [Q]. A section of ancient Cuzco now called Santa Ana.

Carnero con su cría [S]. Sheep and its young. The Spaniards often referred to llamas and alpacas as *carneros*.

Casador [S]. Hunter.

Catachillay [Q]. The name of a constellation near Lyra that represented a llama and its lamb.

Caza [S?]. Game or hunt. Used by Guaman Poma de Ayala (1980:831 [1615:885 (899)]) to name a star.

Celestial equator [E]. A line marking the part of the sky directly above the earth's equator.

Ceque [Q]. Line, border. In Cuzco it was used to designate a group of shrines.

Chacana (Chaccana) [Q]. Crossed lines, a name associated with the belt of Orion.

Chacara (chacra) [Q]. Agricultural field.

Chacra (chacara, chakra) [Q]. *See* Chacara.

Chasca (Chaska, Chhasca, chhascca) [Q]. Shaggy hair; day; bright star.

Chicha [S (Carib)]. The Carib name for a fermented drink generally made of corn. This name was introduced into the Andean region by the Spaniards. The Quechua term for corn beer is *aka*.

Chinchaysuyu [Q]. The northwest quadrant of Cuzco and, by extension, of the Inca Empire.

Chinchero canal [E]. A major canal that brought water to colonial Cuzco.

Chinchincalla [Q]. A hill with twin pillars that represented the third shrine of the thirteenth ceque of Cuntisuyu (Cu. 13:3). The approximate positions of these pillars include the locations where the sun is seen to set on the December solstice as viewed from the Coricancha and from the central plaza of Cuzco.

Chirao [Q]. Clear or burning.

Chiraopacha [Q]. Dry season.

Chirao Sucanca [Q]. Solar pillars in the Cuzco area marking the June solstice, the beginning of the dry season.

Chuquechinchay (Chhoquechinchay, Chuquichinchay) [Q]. Frequently translated as "Golden Cat." The name of a star or constellation representing large cats.

Citua Raymi [Q].   The Inca celebration of expelling evils from Cuzco, held in the ninth month of the year corresponding most closely with September. (*See also* Coya Raymi).

Collas [Q].   People who inhabited the Lake Titicaca region.

Collasuyu [Q].   The southeast quadrant of Cuzco and, by extension, of the Inca Empire.

Collca (collcca, qollqa) [Q].   Storehouse; a name also used for the Pleiades.

Collcampata [Q].   A terraced area of Cuzco on the slope of Sacsahuaman.

Condor [Q].   Condor.

Coricancha [Q].   An enclosure containing the principle sun temple in Cuzco, called the Templo del Sol (Temple of the Sun) by the Spaniards.

Corregidor [S].   Chief Magistrate.

Coya [Q].   Queen, sister/wife of an Inca.

Coya Raymi [Q].   The ninth month of the year; September festival during which Cuzco was ritually cleaned. This festival was also called Citua Raymi.

Coyllor (ccoyllur, cuyllur, cuylluy) [Q].   Star.

Cullor [Q].   *See* Coyllor.

Cuntisuyu [Q].   The southwest quadrant of Cuzco and, by extension, of the Inca Empire.

Cuyllorcona (coyllorcona) [Q].   Stars.

Cygnus [E].   A constellation of Greek origin that was commonly called the cross in medieval and renaissance Europe.

December solstice [E].   The date (near 22 December) on which the apparent solar motion reaches its farthest southerly extension, and the sun begins moving northward. As the north/south motion is very slow at this time, the sun appears to rise and set in the same position for a few days. On this date the sun passes directly above the Tropic of Capricorn.

Declination [E].   The coordinate of a celestial object measured in degrees north or south of the celestial equator.

Encomienda [S].   A land grant by the Spanish crown that included the indigenous inhabitants.

Equinox [E].   Dates near 21 March and 22 September when the sun crosses the equator and the days and the nights are of equal length. The dates of the equinoxes are not exactly midway between the solstices, but shifted by a few days from the halfway point.

Estado [S].   The height of an average man, about 1.5 meters.

Fathom [E].   The length of outstretched arms, usually taken to be six feet, or a little short of two meters.

Fiducial [E].   A reference point or mark.

Gnomon [E].   An object that, by its position or the length of its shadow, serves as an indicator of the hour of the day.

Gregorian calendar [E].   The calendar in common usage today. It was established in 1582 to correct the Julian calendar.

Guaca [Q].   *See* Huaca.

Guaman (Huaman) [Q].   Falcon.

Hanan Cuzco [Q].   The upper part of Cuzco.

Hanansaya [Q]. Upper part.

Haucaypata (Aucaypata) [Q]. The central plaza of Cuzco.

Heliacal rise [E]. The first morning of the year that the star can be seen rising before the dawn.

Heliacal set [E]. The last evening of the year on which the star can still be seen after sunset.

Hombres [S]. Men.

Huaca (guaca) [Q]. A sacred location or object; shrine.

Huara (huara huara) [A]. Star.

Huascar [Q]. A son of Huayna Capac, and half brother of Atahualpa.

Huata [Q]. Year.

Huayna Capac [Q]. The last undisputed Inca ruler. He is believed to have died of a plague that swept the Inca Empire, leading to a civil war between the half brothers Atahualpa and Huascar.

Hurin Cuzco [Q]. The lower part of Cuzco.

Hurinsaya [Q]. Lower part.

Illaris [Q]. An object that shines or radiates light.

Inca Yupanqui [Q]. *See* Pachacuti Inca Yupanqui.

Intercalation month [E]. A month that is inserted into a lunar calendar to maintain the phase with the solar year.

Intercalation period [E]. A set of days that are inserted into a calendar to maintain the phase with the year.

Inti [Q]. Sun.

Intipata [Q]. Terrace of the sun. An open area immediately north of the Coricancha.

Inti Raymi [Q]. A festival associated with the June solstice.

Julian calendar [E]. A calendar established by Julius Caesar in 46 B.C. It was in common usage in Europe until its replacement in 1582 by the Gregorian calendar.

June solstice [E]. The date (near 21 June) on which the apparent solar motion reaches its farthest northern extent, and the sun begins to move south. As the north/south motion is very slow at this time, the sun appears to rise and set in the same position for a few days. On this date the sun passes directly above the Tropic of Cancer.

Larilla [Q]. A name for the Pleiades from the Guamanga area provided by Luis de Monzón (1881:204–205 [1586]).

League [E]. The average distance traveled by a man on a horse in an hour, a distance equal to about 5.50 kilometers.

León [S]. Lion; used in Peru to refer to the puma.

Light casting [E]. A method of astronomical observation in which the position of a ray of light cast into a shaded area is measured. (*See also* Shadow casting.)

Limacpampa (Rimacpampa) [Q]. A large flat area on the eastern edge of ancient Cuzco at which a number of important festivals were held.

Locero [S]. *See* Luzero.

Lunar calendar [E]. A calendar based on the phases of the moon. The fundamental period in this calendar is 29.5 days.

Lunar eclipse [E].   When the earth passes directly between the sun and a full moon, the earth's shadow can be seen crossing the lunar surface. The eclipse lasts approximately two hours, and is visible from the entire hemisphere facing the moon at that time.

Luzero [S].   A bright star; Venus. ["Lucero" in modern Spanish.]

Lyra (Lira) [E].   An ancient constellation of Greek and Roman origin that was widely accepted across sixteenth-century Europe.

Machacuay [Q].   Snake.

Mamacona [Q].   Holy women, chosen women.

Maman Mirco (Mamana Mirco, Maman Mirccuc) [Q].   Mother eater.

Manco Capac [Q].   The first mythical Inca.

Mara [A].   Year.

masl [E].   Abbreviation for "meters above sea level."

Mayu (mayo) [Q].   River; a term also used for the Milky Way.

Miquiquiray [Q].   A star named by Polo de Ondegardo (1965a:2–5 [1585: Ch. 1]) and said to be the patron of some animal.

Mitta (mita) [Q].   Turn, rotation; used for public labor.

Moiety [E].   One of two equal parts. Andean communities were commonly divided into two sectors called the "upper part" and the "lower part."

Mojón [S].   Boundary marker.

Mugeres [S].   Women. ["Mujeres" in modern Spanish.]

Nadir [E].   The direction opposite the zenith. In tropical regions (between the Tropics of Capricorn and Cancer), the sun will pass through the nadir on two days of the year.

Noctilucent clouds [E].   Thin, luminous clouds seen at night, usually near sunrise or sunset. Caused by clouds with a high enough altitude (above 50 miles) that they are illuminated by sunlight. Because the sunlight illuminating them often travels through a great deal of atmosphere, they are frequently orange or pink.

Northern Sea [E].   The Atlantic Ocean.

Obliquity of the ecliptic [E].   The 23.45-degree angle between the earth's rotational axis and the axis of the earth's orbit. Over the course of a year this tilt causes the sun to appear to move north and south in the sky. This angle currently changes by about 1 minute of arc per century.

Oncoy (oncoi) [Q].   Sickness; a name also used for the Pleiades.

Orcorara [A].   Flock or group.

Orejones [S].   Spanish term for Incas of high rank.

Pacari (Paccarik) [Q].   Morning.

Pacha [Q].   Time; earth.

Pachacuti Inca Yupanqui [Q].   The ninth king of Cuzco, traditionally believed to be responsible for the initial expansion of the empire.

Pacsi [A].   Moon or month.

Paqarina (pacarina) [Q].   Origin place; location from which mythical ancestors emerged from the earth.

Pasos [S].   Paces.

Pastor [S].   Pastor, shepherd.

Paullu Inca [Q].   An Inca who ruled the empire under Spanish direction.

Perdices (Perdiz) [S]. Partridges.

Picchu [Q]. Mountain; a hill northwest of Cuzco.

Pihca Conqui [Q]. A constellation named in the Huarochirí manuscript (1991:132–133 [ca. 1608: Ch. 29]) and said to consist of a perfect ring of stars.

Plaza de Armas [S]. Central square of a town.

Poco Huarac [Q]. A bright star named in the Huarochirí manuscript (1991:132–133 [ca. 1608: Ch. 29]).

Precession [E]. The sun and moon apply a torque on the earth, resulting in a change in the orientation of its axis of rotation. As a result, the declination of stars shifts by as much as 47 degrees over a period of 25,800 years, shifting in the location at which stars rise and set. The path followed by the earth's rotational axis is a small circle in the sky that maintains the obliquity of the ecliptic at about 23.5 degrees, so precession does not change the rise and set position of the sun.

Pucuypacha [Q]. Wet season.

Pucuy Sucanca [Q]. Solar pillars in the Cuzco area marking the December solstice, the beginning of the rainy season.

Punchao (punchau) [Q]. Dawn, the day, the sun; a gold idol held in the Coricancha.

Puquín [Q]. A hill south of Cuzco.

Puquín Cancha [Q]. A temple of the sun on the hill of Puquín where a portion of the December Capac Raymi celebrations took place.

Quechua [Q]. Native language of the Inca. It is still spoken in parts of Peru, Ecuador, Bolivia, Chile, and Argentina.

Quiancalla (quiangalla) [Q]. A hill with two pillars that were the ninth shrine of the sixth ceque of Chinchaysuyu (Ch. 6:9). Cobo states that they marked the beginning of summer, though substantial arguments can be made that they marked the June solstice.

Quiantopa [Q]. The name of a star mentioned by Cobo (1990:30–31 [1653: Bk. 13, Ch. 6]).

Quilla [Q]. Moon or month.

Quipu (khipu) [Q]. A knotted cord for encoding information.

Quipucamayocs [Q]. People who kept and read quipus.

Raymi (raimi) [Q]. Festival.

Riti [Q]. Snow.

Sacaca [Q]. An unusual thing; a comet.

Sacsahuaman (Sacsayhuaman) [Q]. A large fort/temple above Cuzco.

Sayba [Q]. *See* Sayhua.

Sayhua (sayba) [Q]. Marker.

Shadow casting [E]. A method of astronomical observation in which the position of a shadow is measured.

Sidereal calendar [E]. A calendar based on the orbital period of a celestial object in a reference frame fixed to the stars. The sidereal lunar period is the time required for the moon to complete one orbit and appear against the same background of stars. It is over two days less than the lunar month defined by phases of the moon.

Solar eclipse [E]. On new moon days when the moon aligns well enough with the sun to occult it, the shadow of the moon touches the earth. The solar eclipse is total when there is a location at which the disk of the sun appears entirely covered. The partial phases of a solar eclipse last hours, but totality averages only three to four minutes.

Solstice [E]. The most northerly and southerly points along the path that the sun appears to follow in the sky. The arrival of the sun at these locations defines the beginning of summer and winter.

Sucanca [Q]. Exact meaning unknown. Cobo (1979:252 [1653: Bk. 12, Ch. 37]) and Polo de Ondegardo (1965b:20–22 [1585: Ch. 7]) used this name for solar pillars on the Cuzco horizon.

Sun dog [E]. A bright spot flanking either side of the sun. Sometimes called mock suns, they are slightly larger than the sun and separated from it by 22 degrees. Sun dogs are caused by refraction through systematically oriented ice crystals in thin cirrus clouds, and they can appear in a nearly clear sky.

Suyu [Q]. Division, region of the empire.

Suyuntuy [Q]. Vulture.

Synodic calendar [E]. The synodic period of a celestial object is the period that it appears to have in the earth-sun reference frame. For planets this is the time between oppositions or conjunctions, and for the moon this is the time between new moons. The synodic period of the moon was commonly used to make a lunar calendar.

Tahuantinsuyu (Tawantinsuyu) [Q]. Name of the Inca Empire (the four parts).

Tarpuntaes [Q]. Kin group of Cuzco that held certain ritual responsibilities.

Tinamou [S (Carib)]. The Carib name for a partridgelike bird called Yutu in Quechua.

Topa (tupa) [Q]. Royal.

Topa Amaru [Q]. The last legitimate heir to the Inca crown. He was captured and executed in Cuzco under the orders of Viceroy Toledo in 1572.

Topa Inca [Q]. Younger son of Pachacuti Inca Yupanqui; said to have ruled as the tenth king of Cuzco.

Topatoraca [Q]. The name of a star mentioned by Cobo (1990:30–31 [1653: Bk. 13, Ch. 6]).

Tropic of Cancer [E]. Approximately 23.5 degrees south of the equator. When the sun reaches (is directly above) the Tropic of Cancer, it is the June solstice.

Tropic of Capricorn [E]. Approximately 23.5 degrees north of the equator. The sun reaches the Tropic of Capricorn on the December solstice.

Tupa [Q]. *See* Topa.

Uara Uara [A]. Star.

Uenado (Venado) [S]. Deer.

Urcuchillay (Urcuchilla, Orcochillay) [Q]. The name of a star constellation that includes stars of Lyra. It represents a male llama.

Usno (Usnu, Osno) [Q].   A centrally located dais of ritual importance in Inca settlements; a seat.

Vara [S].   A Castilian yard, equal to about 85 centimeters.

Villca [Q].   Sacred.

Villca Huarac [Q].   A bright star named in the Huarochirí manuscript (1991:132–133 [ca. 1608: Ch. 29]).

Vrcuchillay [Q].   *See* Urcuchillay.

Yacana [Q].   A dark lane in the Milky Way thought to resemble a llama.

Yanca (or Yañac) [Q].   A priest who, among other things, makes astronomical observations.

Yañac [Q].   *See* Yanca.

Yauirca [Q].   Rope.

Yunga [Q].   Lowland, lowlander; applied to both the coast and tropical forest areas of Peru and Bolivia.

Yutu [Q].   A partridgelike bird.

Waracikoy [Q].   A ritual in which the elite young men of Cuzco were recognized as adults.

Zenith [E].   The point in the sky directly overhead. In tropical regions (between the Tropics of Capricorn and Cancer) the sun will pass through the zenith on two days of the year.

Bibliography

Acosta, José de. 1954. *Historia natural y moral de las Indias* [1590]. In *Obras del P. José de Acosta de la Compañía de Jesús*. Edited by P. Francisco Mateos. Biblioteca de Autores Españoles (continuación), vol. 73, pp. 3–247. Madrid: Ediciones Atlas.

Albornoz, Cristóbal de. 1984. Instrucción para descubrir todas las guacas del Pirú y sus camayos y haziendas [ca. 1582]. In "Albornoz y el espacio ritual andino prehispánico." Edited by Pierre Duviols. *Revista Andina* 2 (1): 169–222.

Allen, Richard H. 1963. *Star names, their lore and meaning*. New York: Dover Publications.

Anders, Martha B. 1986a. *Dual organization and calendars inferred from the planned site of Azángaro*. Ann Arbor, Mich.: University Microfilms.

———. 1986b. Wari experiments in statecraft: A view from Azángaro. In *Andean archaeology: Papers in memory of Clifford Evans*. Edited by Ramiro Matos M., Solveig A. Turpin, and Herbert H. Eling, Jr., pp. 201–224. Monograph 27, Institute of Archaeology, University of California at Los Angeles.

Anonymous Chronicler. 1906. Discurso de la sucesión y gobierno de los Yngas [ca. 1570]. *Juicio de límites entre el Perú y Bolivia; Prueba peruana presentada al gobierno de la República Argentina*. Edited by Víctor M. Maúrtua, vol. 8, pp. 149–165. Madrid: Tipografía de los Hijos de M. G. Hernández.

Archivo Departamental del Cuzco. 1851. Judicial Civil: Leg. 73, "Instrumento del Señor Campero. Archivado el 26 de Mayo de 1852."

Ardiles Nieves, Percy E. 1986. Sistema de drenaje subterráneo prehispánico. *Allpanchis* 18 (27): 75–97.

Arriaga, Pablo Joseph de. 1968a. *La extirpación de la idolatría del Pirú* [1621]. In *Crónicas peruanas de interés indígena*. Edited by Francisco Esteve Barba. Biblioteca de Autores Españoles (continuación), vol. 209, pp. 191–277. Madrid: Ediciones Atlas.

———. 1968b. *The extirpation of idolatry in Peru* [1621]. Translated and edited by L. Clark Keating. Lexington: University of Kentucky Press.

Arte y vocabulario en la lengua general del Peru llamada Quichua y en la lengua Española [1586]. 1951. Lima: Antonio Ricardo. Facsimile edition, Publicaciones del Cuarto Centenario. Lima: Facultad de Letras, Instituto de Historia, Universidad Nacional Mayor de San Marcos.

Avendaño, Fernando de. 1904. Letter written in Lima (Los Reyes) on 3 April, 1617. In *La imprenta en Lima* (1584–1824). Edited by José Toribio Medina, vol. 1, pp. 380–383. Santiago de Chile: Impreso del autor.

Aveni, Anthony F. 1980. *Skywatchers of ancient Mexico*. Austin: University of Texas Press.

———. 1981. Horizon astronomy in Incaic Cuzco. In *Archaeoastronomy in the Americas*. Edited by R. A. Williamson, pp. 305–318. Los Altos, Calif.: Ballena Press.

———. 1987. On seeing the light (a reply to "Here comes the sun" by D. Dearborn and K. Schreiber). *Archaeoastronomy* 10:22–24.

———. 1989. Introduction: Whither archaeoastronomy. In *World archaeoastronomy*. Edited by Anthony F. Aveni, pp. 3–12. Cambridge: Cambridge University Press.

———, ed. 1990. *The lines of Nazca*. Philadelphia: The American Philosophical Society.

Aveni, Anthony F., and David S. Dearborn. 1993. The Colgate Cuzco ceque symposium. In *Archaeoastronomy and Ethnoastronomy News* 8:2.

Avila, Francisco de. See *Huarochirí Manuscript*.

Bandelier, Adolph F. A. 1910. *The islands of Titicaca and Koati*. New York: The Hispanic Society of America.

Bauer, Brian S. 1991. Pacariqtambo and the mythical origins of the Inca. *Latin American Antiquity* 2 (1): 7–26.

———. 1992a. Ritual pathways of the Inca: An analysis of the Collasuyu ceques in Cuzco. *Latin American Antiquity* 3 (3): 183–205.

———. 1992b. *The development of the Inca state*. Austin: University of Texas Press.

———. 1992c. Caminos rituales de los Incas: Un análisis de los ceques del Collasuyu (Cuzco). In *Avances en Arqueología Andina*, pp. 15–40. Cuzco: Centro de Estudios Rurales Andinos "Bartolomé de las Casas."

———. 1994. Recent archaeological investigations in the sites of Maukallaqta and Puma Orco, Department of Cuzco, Peru. *Ñawpa Pacha* 25. Forthcoming.

———. n.d.a. The original ceque system. Manuscript.

———. n.d.b. The Cuzco ceque system: An introduction to the sacred geography of the Inca heartland.

Bayer, Johann. 1603. *Uranometria, omnium asterismorum continens schemata, nova methodo delineata, aereis laminis expressa*. Augustae Uindelicorum: C. Mangus.

Bertonio, Ludovico. 1984. *Vocabulario de la lengua Aymará* [1612]. Facsimile edition. Cochabamba, Bolivia: Centro de Estudios de la Realidad Económica y Social.

Betanzos, Juan de. 1987. *Suma y narración de los Incas* [1551]. Edited by María del Carmen Martín Rubio. Madrid: Ediciones Atlas.

Bocanegra, Juan Pérez. *See* Pérez Bocanegra, Juan de.

Bollaert, William. 1860. *Antiquarian, ethnological, and other researches in New Granada, Equador, Peru and Chile, with observations on the pre-Incarial, Incarial, and other monuments of Peruvian nations.* London: Trübner & Co.

————. 1861. An account of a zodiac of the Incas, and also of some antiquities recently found at Cuzco, now in the possession of General Echenique, late president of Peru. *Proceedings of the Society of Antiquarians of London*, 2d ser., 1:78–81.

————. 1865. Some account of the astronomy of the Red Man of the New World . . . *Memoirs read before the Anthropological Society of London* 1:210–280.

Cabello Balboa, Miguel. 1951. *Miscelánea antártica, una historia del Perú antiguo* [1586]. Edited by L. E. Valcárcel. Lima: Universidad Nacional Mayor de San Marcos, Instituto de Etnología.

Calancha, Antonio de la. 1981. *Corónica moralizada del Orden de San Augustín en el Perú* [1638]. Edited by Ignacio Prado Pastor. Lima: Universidad Nacional Mayor de San Marcos, Editorial de la Universidad.

Callapiña, Supno, y otros Quipucamayos. 1974. *Relación de la descendencia, gobierno y conquista de los Incas* [1542/1608]. Edited by Juan José Vega. Lima: Ediciones de la Biblioteca Universitaria.

Callegari, G. V. 1914. Conoscenze astronomiche degli antichi Peruviani. *Revista Abruzzesi* 29 (3): 113–126.

Chávez Ballón, Manuel. 1970. Ciudades Incas: Cuzco, capital del imperio. *Wayka* 3:1–15.

Cieza de León, Pedro de. 1976. *The Incas of Pedro Cieza de León* [Part 1, 1553 and Part 2, 1554]. Translated by Harriet de Onís and edited by Victor W. von Hagen. Norman: University of Oklahoma Press.

————. 1984. *Crónica del Perú: Primera parte* [1553]. Introduction by Franklin Pease G. Y. and notes by Miguel Maticorena E. Pontífica Universidad Católica del Perú. Lima: Academia Nacional de la Historia.

————. 1985. *Crónica del Perú: Segunda parte* [1554]. Introduction by Franklin Pease G. Y. and notes by Miguel Maticorena E. Pontífica Universidad Católica del Perú. Lima: Academia Nacional de la Historia.

Clavius, Christoph. 1612. *Commentarium in Sphaeram Ioannis de Sacro Bosco* [1596/1611]. In *Opera Mathematica*, vol. 3. Mainz: Reinhardus Eltz.

Cobo, Bernabé. 1956. *Historia del Nuevo Mundo* [1653]. In *Obras del P. Bernabé Cobo de la Compañía de Jesús.* Edited by P. Francisco Mateos. Biblioteca de Autores Españoles (continuación), vols. 91 and 92. Madrid: Ediciones Atlas.

————. 1979. *History of the Inca Empire: An account of the Indians' customs and their origin together with a treatise on Inca legends, history, and social institutions* [1653]. Translated and edited by Roland Hamilton. Austin: University of Texas Press.

————. 1980. Relación de las guacas del Cuzco [1653]. In "An account of the shrines of ancient Cuzco." Translated and edited by John H. Rowe. *Ñawpa Pacha* 17 (1979): 2–80.

————. 1981. Relación de las guacas del Cuzco [1653]. In "Una relación de los adoratorios del antiguo Cuzco." Introducción por John H. Rowe. *Histórica* 5 (2): 209–261.

————. 1990. *Inca religion and customs* [1653]. Translated and edited by Roland Hamilton. Austin: University of Texas Press.

Cusihuamán Gutiérrez, Antonio. 1976. *Diccionario Quechua: Cuzco-Collao*. Lima: Ministerio de Educación, Instituto de Estudios Peruanos.

D'Altroy, Terence N. 1992. *Provincial power in the Inka Empire*. Washington, D.C.: Smithsonian Institution Press.

Dearborn, David S. P. 1986. The death of an Inka. *Griffith Observer* 50 (8): 17–20.

————. 1987. Blinded by the light (a reply to "On seeing the light" by A. Aveni). *Archaeoastronomy* 10:24–27.

Dearborn, David S. P., and Katharina J. Schreiber. 1986. Here comes the sun: The Cuzco-Machu Picchu connection. *Archaeoastronomy* 9:15–37.

————. 1989. Houses of the rising sun. In *Time and calendars in the Inca Empire*. Edited by M. S. Ziólkowski and R. M. Sadowski, pp. 49–75. BAR International Series 454. Oxford: British Archaeological Reports.

Dearborn, David S. P., and Raymond E. White. 1983. The "torreón" at Machu Picchu as an observatory. *Archaeoastronomy* 5:S37–S49.

Dearborn, David S. P., Katharina J. Schreiber, and Raymond E. White. 1987. Intimachay, a December solstice observatory. *American Antiquity* 52: 346–352.

Dillehay, Tom D. 1990. Mapuche ceremonial landscape, social recruitment and resource rights. *World Archaeology* 2 (2): 223–241.

Discurso de la sucesión y gobierno de los Yngas [ca. 1570]. *See* Anonymous Chronicler.

Domingo de Santo Tomás. 1951. *Lexicón, o vocabulario de la lengua general del Perú* [1560]. Facsimile edition. Lima: Instituto de Historia, Universidad Nacional Mayor de San Marcos.

Donnan, Christopher B. 1978. Moche art of Peru: Pre-Columbian symbolic communication. Revised edition. Los Angeles: Museum of Cultural History, University of California.

DuGourcq, Jean. 1893. L'Astronomie chez les Incas. *Revue Scientifique* 52: 265–272.

Duviols, Pierre. 1979. Datation, paternité et ideologie de la "Declaracion de los Quipucamayocs a Vaca de Castro." In *Discurso de la descendencia y gobierno de los Ingas*, pp. 583–591. Les Cultures Iberiques en Devenir. Paris: Fondation Singer-Polignac.

————. 1986. *Cultura andina y represión: Procesos y visitas de idolatrías y hechicerías Cajatambo, siglo XVII*. Archivos de Historia Andina Rural 5. Cuzco: Centro de Estudios Rurales Andinos "Bartolomé de las Casas."

Esquivel y Navia, Diego de. 1980. *Noticias cronológicas de la gran ciudad del Cuzco* [1749]. Edición, prólogo y notas de Félix Denegri Luna con la colaboración de Horacio Villanueva Urteaga y César Gutiérrez Muñoz, Tomos I y II. Lima: Fundación Augusto N. Wiese, Banco Wiese Ltdo.

Farrington, Ian S. 1992. Ritual geography, settlement patterns and the characterization of the provinces of the Inka heartland. *World Archaeology* 23 (3): 368–385.

Fernández, Diego ("El Palentino"). 1963. *Primera y segunda parte de la historia del Perú* [1571]. In *Crónicas del Perú*. Edited by Juan Pérez de Tudela Bueso. Biblioteca de Autores Españoles (continuación), vols. 164 and 165. Madrid: Ediciones Atlas.

Garcilaso de la Vega, Inca. 1945. *Comentarios reales de los Incas* [1609]. 2d edition. Notes by Ricardo Rojas. Buenos Aires: Emecé Editores S.A.

———. 1966. *Royal commentaries of the Incas and general history of Peru*, parts 1 and 2 [1609]. Translated by H. V. Livermore. Austin: University of Texas Press.

Gasparini, Graziano, and Luise Margolies. 1980. *Inca architecture*. Translated by P. J. Lyon. Bloomington: Indiana University Press.

Gonçález Holguín, Diego. 1989. *Vocabulario de la lengua general de todo el Perú llamada lengua Qquichua o del Inca* [1608]. Presentación Ramiro Matos Mendieta. Prólogo de Raúl Porras Barrenechea. Lima: Universidad Nacional Mayor de San Marcos, Editorial de la Universidad.

Gregory of Tours. 1885. *De Cursu Stellarum Ratio* [ca 575]. In *Monument Germaniae Historica, scriptorum rarum merouingicarum*, vol. 2, pt. 2. Hanover: Hahn.

Guaman Poma de Ayala, Felipe. 1980. *El primer nueva corónica y buen gobierno* [1615]. Edited by J. V. Murra and R. Adorno and translated by Jorge I. Urioste. 3 vols. Mexico City: Siglo Veintiuno.

Gutiérrez de Santa Clara, Pedro. 1963. *Quinquenarios* [ca. 1600]. Edited by Juan Pérez de Tudela Bueso. Biblioteca de Autores Españoles (continuación), vols. 165 and 166. Madrid: Ediciones Atlas.

Hadingham, Evan. 1984. *Early man and the cosmos*. Norman: University of Oklahoma Press.

Hagar, Stansbury. 1902. The Peruvian star-chart of Salcamayhua. *Congrés International des Américanistes* 12:272–284.

———. 1904. The Peruvian asterisms and their relation to the ritual. *American Antiquarian and Oriental Journal* 26:329–337.

———. 1905. Cuzco, the celestial city. *Acts of the International Congress of Americanists* 13:217–225.

Hemming, John. 1970. *The conquest of the Incas*. New York: Harcourt Brace Jovanovich.

Hocquenghem, Anne Marie. 1987. *Iconografía mochica*. 2d edition. Lima: Pontífica Universidad Católica del Perú, Fondo Editorial.

Huaman Poma de Ayala, Felipe. *See* Guaman Poma de Ayala, Felipe.

The Huarochirí Manuscript: A testament of ancient and colonial Andean religion [ca. 1608]. 1991. Translated from the Quechua by Frank Salomon and George L. Urioste. Austin: University of Texas Press.

Hyslop, John, Jr. 1985. *Inkawasi: The new Cusco, Cañate, Lunahuaná, Peru*. BAR International Series 234. Oxford: British Archaeological Reports.

———. 1990. *Inka settlement planning*. Austin: University of Texas Press.

Isbell, Billie Jean. 1978. *To defend ourselves: Ecology and ritual in an Andean village*. Austin: University of Texas Press.

Kirchhoff, Paul. 1949. The social and political organization of the Andean peoples. In *The Handbook of South American Indians*, vol. 5, *The Comparative Ethnology of South American Indians*. Edited by Julian Steward. Bulletin of the Bureau of American Ethnology, no. 143, pp. 293–311. Washington, D.C.: U.S. Government Printing Office.

Krupp, Edwin C. 1983. *Echoes of the ancient skies: The astronomy of lost civilizations*. New York: Harper & Row.

———. 1991. *Beyond the blue horizon: Myths and legends of the sun, moon, stars, and planets*. New York: Harper Collins.

Larco Hoyle, Rafael. 1938–1939. *Los mochicas*. Lima: Casa Editora "La Crónica" y "Variedades," S.A. Ltda.

Lattis, James. 1994. *Between Copernicus and Galileo: Christoph Clavius and collapse of the Ptolemaic system*. Forthcoming from University of Chicago Press.

Lehmann-Nitsche, Robert. 1928. Coricancha: El Templo del Sol en el Cuzco y las imágenes de su altar mayor. *Revista del Museo de La Plata* 31:1–256.

Liller, William. 1986. Celestial happenings on Easter Island: A.D. 760–837. *Archaeoastronomy* 9:52–59.

Lira, Jorge A. 1944. *Diccionario Kkéchuwa-Español*. Tucumán, Argentina: Universidad Nacional de Tucumán.

MacCormack, Sabine. 1991. *Religion in the Andes: Vision and imagination in early colonial Peru*. Princeton: Princeton University Press.

Markham, Clements Robert. 1856. *Cuzco: A journey to the ancient capital of Peru; with an account of the history, language, literature, and antiquities of the Incas. And Lima: A visit to the capital and provinces of modern Peru; with a sketch of the viceregal government, history of the republic, and a review of the literature and society of Peru*. London: Chapman and Hall.

Marsden, Brian G. 1975. *Catalogue of Cometary Orbits*. 2d edition. Cambridge, Mass.: Smithsonian Astrophysical Observatory.

McEwan, Gordon F. 1987. *The middle horizon in the Valley of Cuzco, Peru: The impact of the Wari occupation of the Lucre Basin*. BAR International Series 372. Oxford: British Archaeological Reports.

———. 1991. Investigations at the Pikillacta site: A provincial Huari center in the Valley of Cuzco. In *Huari administrative structure: Prehistoric monumental architecture and state government*. Edited by William H. Isbell and Gordon F. McEwan, pp. 93–119. Washington, D.C.: Dumbarton Oaks.

Middendorf, Ernest W. 1890. *Das Runa Simi oder die Keshua Sprache wie sie gegenwärtig in der Provinz von Cusco gesprochen wird*. Leipzig: F. A. Brockhaus. [Spanish translation by E. More 1970. *Gramática keshua*. Madrid: Aguilar.]

Misión de las provincias de los Huachos y Yauyos [1613]. 1919. [Attributed to an anonymous Jesuit priest.] In "Idolatrías de los Indios Huachos y Yauyos." *Revista Histórica* 6:180–197.

Molina (el Cusqueño), Cristóbal de. 1989. Relación de las fábulas i ritos de los Ingas . . . [ca. 1575]. In *Fábulas y mitos de los incas*. Edited by Henrique Urbano and Pierre Duviols, pp. 47–134. Crónicas de América series. Madrid: Historia 16.

Molina (el Almagrista), Cristóbal de. *See* Segovia, Bartolomé de.

Montesinos, Fernando de. 1882. *Memorias antiguas historiales y políticas del Perú* [1630]. Colección de libros españoles raros o curiosos. Edited by Marcos Jiménez de la Espada. Vol. 16. Madrid: Imprenta de Miguel Ginesta.

————. 1920. *Memorias antiguas historiales del Perú* [1630]. Translated and edited by Philip Ainsworth Means. Introduction by Clements R. Markham. London: The Hakluyt Society.

Monzón, Luis de. 1881. Descripción de la tierra del repartimiento de los Rucanas Antamarcas de la Corona Real, jurisdicción de la ciudad de Guamanga, año de 1586. In *Relaciones geográficas de Indias, Perú*, vol. 1, pp. 197–216. Edited by Marcos Jiménez de la Espada. Ministerio de Fomento. Madrid: Tipografía de Manuel G. Hernández.

Morúa, Martín dê. *See* Murúa, Martín de.

Müller, Rolf. 1972. *Sonne, Mond und Sterne über dem Reich der Inka*. Verstänliche Wissenschaft Bd. 110, Naturwissenschaftliche Alteilung. Berlin: Springer Press.

Murúa, Martín de. 1946. *Historia del origen y genealogía real de los reyes Incas del Perú* [ca. 1615]. Introduction and notes by Constantino Bayle. Biblioteca "Missionalia Hispánica," vol. 2. Madrid: Instituto Santo Toribio de Mogrovego.

Niles, Susan A. 1987. *Callachaca: Style and status in an Inca community*. Iowa City: University of Iowa Press.

Nordenskiöld, Erland. 1925. *Calculations with years and months in the Peruvian quipus*. Comparative Ethnographical Studies, vol. 6, pt. 2. Göteborg: Elanders Boktryckeri Akjebolag.

Oppolzer, Theodor Ritter von. 1962. *Canon of eclipses*. Translated by Owen Gingerich, with a preface by Donald H. Menzel and Owen Gingerich. New York: Dover Publications.

Pachacuti Yamqui Salcamayhua, Juan de Santa Cruz. 1950. Relación de antigüedades deste Reyno del Perú [1613]. In *Tres relaciones de antigüedades peruanas*. Edited by M. Jiménez de la Espada, pp. 207–281. Asunción del Paraguay: Editora Guaranía.

Pérez Bocanegra, Juan. 1631. *Ritual formulario e institución de curas para administrar a los naturales de este Reyno los santos sacramentos . . .* Lima: Geronymo de Contreras.

Pingré, Alexandre Guy. 1783. *Cometographie. ou, traité historique et théorique des comètes*. Paris: Imprimerie royale.

Pizarro, Pedro. 1921. *Relation of the discovery and conquest of the kingdoms of Peru* [1571]. Translated and edited by Philip Ainsworth Means. New York: The Cortes Society.

Polo de Ondegardo, Juan. 1872. Relación de los fundamentos acerca del notable daño que resulta de no guardar a los Indios sus fueros [1571]. Edited by Horacio H. Urteaga. *Colección de Documentos Inéditos . . .*

de América y Oceanía, vol. 16, pp. 5–177. Madrid: Imprenta del Hospicio.

———. 1916a. Relación de los fundamentos acerca del notable daño que resulta de no guardar a los Indios sus fueros. Edited by Horacio H. Urteaga and Carlos Romero. *Colección de Libros y Documentos Referentes a la Historia del Perú*, ser. 1, vol. 3. Lima: Sanmartí.

———. 1916b. De los errores y supersticiones de los indios, sacados del tratado y averiguación que hizo el Licenciado Polo [first published in 1585, researched ca. 1559]. Edited by Horacio H. Urteaga and Carlos Romero. *Colección de Libros y Documentos Referentes a la Historia del Perú*, ser. 1, vol. 3, pp. 3–43. Lima: Sanmartí.

———. 1916c. Relación de los fundamentos acerca del notable daño que resulta de no guardar a los Indios sus fueros [1571]. Edited by Horacio H. Urteaga and Carlos Romero. *Colección de Libros y Documentos Referentes a la Historia del Perú*, ser. 1, vol. 3, pp. 45–189. Lima: Sanmartí.

———. 1916d. Instrucción contra las ceremonias y ritos que usan los indios conforme al tiempo de su infidelidad [1567]. Edited by Horacio H. Urteaga and Carlos Romero. *Colección de Libros y Documentos Referentes a la Historia del Perú*, ser. 1, vol. 3 (Apéndice A), pp. 189–204. Lima: Sanmartí.

———. 1916e. Supersticiones de los indios, sacadas del segundo Concilio Provincial de Lima [first published in 1567, researched ca. 1559]. Edited by Horacio H. Urteaga and Carlos Romero. *Colección de Libros y Documentos Referentes a la Historia del Perú*, ser. 1, vol. 3 (Apéndice B), pp. 205–208. Lima: Sanmartí.

———. 1917. Del linaje de los Ingas y como conquistaron. Edited by H. Urteaga. *Colección de Libros y Documentos Referentes a la Historia del Perú*, ser. 1, vol. 4, pp. 45–94. Lima: Sanmartí.

———. 1940. Informe del Licenciado Juan Polo de Ondegardo al Licenciado Briviesca de Muñatones sobre la perpetuidad de las encomiendas en el Perú [1561]. *Revista Histórica* 13:125–196.

———. 1965a. On the errors and superstitions of the Indians, taken from the treatise and investigation done by Licentiate Polo. Translated by A. Brunel, John Murra, and Sidney Muirden. New Haven, Conn.: Human Relations Area Files.

———. 1965b. On the errors and superstitions of the Indians, taken from the treatise and investigation done by Licentiate Polo [first published in 1585, researched ca. 1559]. Translated by A. Brunel, John Murra and Sidney Muirden, pp. 1–53. New Haven, Conn.: Human Relations Area Files.

———. 1965c. A report on the basic principles explaining the serious harm which follows when the traditional rights of the Indians are not respected [1571]. Translated by A. Brunel, John Murra, and Sidney Muirden, pp. 53–196. New Haven, Conn.: Human Relations Area Files.

———. 1965d. Instruction against the ceremonies and rites that the Indians practice in conformance with the stage of their infidelity [1567]. Translated by A. Brunel, John Murra, and Sidney Muirden, (Appendix A), pp. 196–208. New Haven, Conn.: Human Relations Area Files.

———. 1965e. Superstitions of the Indians, taken from the Second Provincial Council of Lima [first published in 1567, researched ca. 1559]. Translated by A. Brunel, John Murra, and Sidney Muirden, (Appendix B), pp. 209–211. New Haven, Conn.: Human Relations Area Files.

Posnansky, Arthur. 1942. Los conocimientos astronómicos de los constructores de Tihuanacu y su aplicación en el templo del sol para la determinación exacta de las fechas agrícolas. Boletín de la Sociedad Geográfica de La Paz 64:40–49.

———. 1945. Tihuanacu: The cradle of American man (Tihuanacu: La cuna del hombre americano). 2 vols. New York and La Paz: J. J. Augustín and Ministerio de Educación de Bolivia.

Randall, Robert. 1982. Qoyllur Rit'i, an Inca fiesta of the Pleiades: Reflections on time and space in the Andean world. Bulletin de l'Institut Français d'Études Andines 11 (1–2): 37–81.

Ricardo, Antonio. See Arte y vocabulario en la lengua general del Peru llamada Quichua y en la lengua Española [1586].

Rivera Sundt, Oswaldo. 1984. La horca del Inka. Arqueología Boliviana 1:91–101.

Rowe, John H. 1944. An introduction to the archaeology of Cuzco. In Papers of the Peabody Museum of American Archaeology and Ethnology, vol. 27, no. 2. Cambridge, Mass.: Harvard University.

———. 1946. Inca culture at the time of the Spanish Conquest. In Handbook of South American Indians, vol. 2, The Andean civilizations. Edited by Julian Steward. Bulletin of the Bureau of American Ethnology, no. 143, pp. 183–330. Washington, D.C.: U.S. Government Printing Office.

———. 1978. La fecha de la muerte de Wayna Qhapaq. Histórica 2 (1): 83–88.

———. 1980. Relación de las guacas del Cuzco [1653]. In "An account of the shrines of ancient Cuzco." Translated and edited by John H. Rowe. Ñawpa Pacha 17 (1979): 2–80.

———. 1981. Relación de las guacas del Cuzco [1653]. In "Una relación de los adoratorios del antiguo Cuzco." Introduction by John H. Rowe. Histórica 5 (2): 209–261.

———. 1985. La constitución inca del Cuzco. Histórica 9 (1): 35–73.

———. 1991. Los monumentos perdidos de la plaza mayor del Cuzco incaico. Saqsaywaman 3:81–109.

Sadowski, Robert M. 1989a. A few remarks on the astronomy of R. T. Zuidema's "quipu-calendar." In Time and calendars in the Inca Empire. Edited by M. S. Ziólkowski and R. M. Sadowski. BAR International Series 454, pp. 209–213. Oxford: British Archaeological Reports.

———. 1989b. The sky above the Incas: An abridged astronomical calendar for the 16th century. In Time and calendars in the Inca Empire. Edited by M. S. Ziólkowski and R. M. Sadowski. BAR International Series 479, pp. 75–106. Oxford: British Archaeological Reports.

Salazar, Antonio. 1867. Relación sobre el período de gobierno de los virreyes Don Francisco de Toledo y Don García Hurtado de Mendoza [1596]. In Colección de documentos inéditos relativos al descubrimiento, conquista y organización de las antiguas posesiones españolas de América *y Oceanía*, vol. 8, pp. 212–421. Madrid: Imprenta de Frias y Compañía.

Santa Cruz Pachacuti Yamqui Salcamayhua, Juan de. *See* Pachacuti Yamqui Salcamayhua, Juan de Santa Cruz.

Santo Tomás, Domingo de. *See* Domingo de Santo Tomás.

Sarmiento de Gamboa, Pedro. 1906. Segunda parte de la historia general llamada Indica . . . [1572]. In *Geschichte des Inkareiches von Pedro Sarmiento de Gamboa*. Edited by Richard Pietschmann. Abhandlungen der Königlichen Gesellschaft der Wissenschaften zu Göttingen, Philologisch-Historische Klasse, Neue Folge, vol. 6, no. 4. Berlin: Weidmannsche Buchhandlung.

Segovia, Bartolomé de. 1943. Relación de las muchas cosas acaecidas en el Perú . . . [1553]. In *Las crónicas de los Molinas*. Los Pequeños Grandes Libros de Historia Americana, series 1, vol. 4, first document, pp. 1–88. Lima: Librería e Imprenta D. Miranda. [Incorrectly attributed to Cristóbal de Molina (el Almagrista).]

Sherbondy, Jeanette. 1982. The canal systems of Hanan Cuzco. Ann Arbor, Mich.: University Microfilms.

———. 1986. Los ceques: Código de canales en el Cusco incaico. *Allpanchis Phuturinqa* 27:39–73.

———. 1987. Organización hidráulica y poder en el Cuzco de los incas. *Revista Española de Antropología Americana* 17:117–153.

Taylor, Gerald. 1987. Cultos y fiestas de la comunidad de San Damián (Huarochirí) según la Carta Annua de 1609. *Bulletin de l'Institut Francais d'Études Andines* 16 (3–4): 85–96.

Toledo, Francisco de. 1924. Carta de D. Francisco de Toledo, virrey del Perú, sobre lavictoria obtenida en Vilcabamba contra los indios, y la prisión de los incas, ejecución de Tupac Amarú y descubrimiento del ídolo Punchau [1572]. In *Gobernantes del Perú: Cartas y papeles, siglo XVI*, vol. 4, pp. 268–288. Documentos del Archivo de Indias. Publicación dirigida por D. Roberto Levillier. Madrid: Colección de Publicaciones Históricas de la Biblioteca del Congreso Argentino, Imprenta de Juan Pueyo.

Trimborn, Hermann. 1959. Archäologische Studien in den Kordilleren Boliviens. *Baessler-Archiv, zur Völkerkunde*, Neue Folge. Berlin: Beiheft 2.

Urbano, Henrique. 1981. *Wiracocha y Ayar: Héroes y funciones en las sociedades andinas*. Cuzco: Centro de Estudios Rurales Andinos "Bartolomé de las Casas."

Urteaga, Horacio H. 1913. Informe sobre los observatorios astronómicos o piedras del sol de los Incas. *Boletín de la Sociedad Geográfica de Lima* 29:40–46.

Urton, Gary D. 1980. Celestial crosses: The cruciform in Quechua astronomy. *Journal of Latin American Lore* 6 (1): 87–110.

———. 1981a. *At the crossroads of the earth and the sky: An Andean cosmology*. Austin: University of Texas Press.

———. 1981b. Animals and astronomy in the Quechua universe. *Proceedings of the American Philosophical Society* 125 (2): 110–127.

———. 1982. Astronomy and calendrics on the coast of Peru. In *Ethnoas-*

tronomy and archaeoastronomy in the American Tropics. Edited by A. F. Aveni and G. Urton, pp. 231–259. New York: Annals of the New York Academy of Sciences, vol. 385.

———. 1984. Chuta: El espacio de la práctica social en Pacariqtambo, Perú. *Revista Andina* 2 (1): 7–56.

———. 1990. *The history of a myth: Pacariqtambo and the origin of the Inkas*. Austin: University of Texas Press.

Urton, Gary, and Anthony Aveni. 1983. Archaeoastronomical fieldwork on the coast of Peru. In *Calendars in Mesoamerica and Peru: Native American computations of time*. Edited by A. Aveni and G. Brotherston, pp. 221–234. BAR International Series 174. Oxford: British Archaeological Reports.

Valcárcel Vizquerra, Luis E. 1946. The Andean calendar. In *Handbook of South American Indians*, vol. 2, *The Andean civilizations*. Edited by Julian Steward. Bulletin of the Bureau of American Ethnology, no. 143, pp. 471–476. Washington, D.C.: U.S. Government Printing Office.

Valera, Blas. 1950. De las costumbres antiguas de los naturales del Pirú [ca. 1585]. In *Tres relaciones de antigüedades peruanas*. Edited by M. Jiménez de la Espada, pp. 135–203. Asunción del Paraguay: Editorial Guaranía.

Van der Guchte, Maarten. 1984. El ciclo mítico andino de la Piedra Cansada. *Revista Andina* 2 (2): 539–556.

———. 1990. Carving the world: Inca monumental sculpture and landscape. Ann Arbor, Mich.: University Microfilms.

Vázquez de Espinosa, Antonio. 1948. *Compendio y descripción de las Indias Occidentales* [1628]. Transcribed from the original manuscript by Charles Upson Clark. Smithsonian Miscellaneous Collections, vol. 108. Washington, D.C.: Smithsonian Institution.

Villarreal, Federico. 1894. Los cometas en tiempo de Huayna Capac. *Boletín de la Sociedad Geográfica de Lima* 4:268–281.

von Arnim, B. 1942. Slavische Sternsagen und Sternnamen. *Zeitschrift fur Salvische Philologie* 18:86–103.

Wachtel, Nathan. 1973. Estructuralismo e historia: A propósito de la organización social del Cuzco. In *Sociedad e ideología: Ensayos de historia y antropología*, pp. 23–58. Lima: Instituto de Estudios Peruanos.

Williams León, Carlos. 1992. Sukankas y ceques: La medición del tiempo en el Tahuantinsuyu. *Pachacámac* (Revista del Museo de la Nación, Lima) 1, no. 1 (Agosto): 101–113

Xérez, Francisco de. 1985. *Verdadera relación de la conquista del Perú* [1534]. Edited by Concepción Bravo. Crónicas de América 14. Madrid: Historia 16.

Zamorano, Rodrigo. 1585. *Cronología y reportorio de la razón de los tiempos*. Sevilla: Imprenta de Andrea Pescioni y Iván de León.

Ziólkowski, Marius S. 1985. Hanan pachap unanchan: Las "señales del cielo" y su papel en la etno-historia andina. *Revista Española de Antropología Americana* 15:147–182.

———. 1989a. Knots and oddities: The quipu-calendar or supposed Cuzco luni-sidereal calendar. In *Time and calendars in the Inca Empire*. Edited by M. S. Ziólkowski and R. M. Sadowski. BAR International Series 479, pp. 197–208. Oxford: British Archaeological Reports.

———. 1989b. El calendario metropolitano del Estado Inka. In *Time and calendars in the Inca Empire*. Edited by M. S. Ziólkowski and R. M. Sadowski. BAR International Series 479, pp. 129–166. Oxford: British Archaeological Reports.

Ziólkowski, Marius S., and Arnold Lebeuf. 1993. Were the Incas able to predict lunar eclipses. In *Archaeoastronomy in the 1990's*. Edited by Clive Ruggles. Loughborough, Leicestershire, U.K.: Group D Publications.

Ziólkowski, Marius S., and Robert M. Sadowski. 1980. The astronomical data in Fernando Montesinos' Peruvian chronicle: The comets of Qhapaq Yupanqui. *Archaeoastronomy* 3 (2): 22–26.

———. 1985. Informe de la segunda temporada de investigaciones arqueoastronómicas en Ingapirca (Ecuador). In *Memorias del Primer Simposio Europeo sobre Antropología del Ecuador*. Compilador S. E. Moreno Yáñez con la colaboración de Sophia Thyssen, pp. 91–116. Instituto de Antropología Cultural de la Universidad de Bonn. Quito: Ediciones Abya-Yala.

———. 1992. *La arqueoastronomía en la investigación de las culturas andinas*. Quito, Ecuador: Instituto Otavaleño de Antropología, Banco Central del Ecuador.

———, eds. 1989. *Time and calendars in the Inca Empire*. BAR International Series 479. Oxford: British Archaeological Reports.

Zuidema, R. Tom. 1964. *The ceque system of Cuzco: The social organization of the capital of the Inca*. Translated by Eva M. Hooykaas. International Archives of Ethnography, supplement to vol. 50. Leiden: E. J. Brill.

———. 1977a. The Inca calendar. In *Native American astronomy*. Edited by Anthony F. Aveni, pp. 219–259. Austin: University of Texas Press.

———. 1977b. La imagen del sol y la huaca de Susurpuquio en el sistema astronómico de los Incas en el Cuzco. *Journal de la Société des Américanistes*, n. s., 63:199–230.

———. 1977c. The Inca kinship system: A new theoretical view. In *Andean kinship and marriage*. Edited by R. Bolton and E. Mayer, pp. 240–281. Washington, D.C.: American Anthropological Association, Special Publication No. 7.

———. 1980. El Ushnu. *Revista de La Universidad Complutense, Madrid*. 28 (117): 317–362.

———. 1981a. Anthropology and archaeoastronomy. In *Archaeoastronomy in the Americas*. Edited by Ray A. Williamson, pp. 29–31. Los Altos, Calif.: Ballena Press.

———. 1981b. Inca observations of the solar and lunar passages through zenith and anti-zenith at Cuzco. *Archaeoastronomy in the New World*. Edited by Ray A. Williamson, pp. 319–342. Los Altos, Calif.: Ballena Press.

———. 1981c. Comment. *Latin American Research Review* 16 (3): 167–170.

———. 1982a. Bureaucracy and systematic knowledge in Andean civilization. In *The Inca and Aztec states, 1400–1800: Anthropology and history*. Edited by G. A. Collier, R. I. Rosaldo, and J. D. Wirth, pp. 419–458. New York: Academic Press.

———. 1982b. Catachillay: The role of the Pleiades and of the Southern Cross and δ and β Centauri in the calendar of the Incas. In *Ethnoastronomy and archaeoastronomy in the American Tropics*. Edited by A. F. Aveni and G. Urton, pp. 203–229. New York: Annals of the New York Academy of Sciences, vol. 385.

———. 1982c. The sidereal lunar calendar of the Incas. In *Archaeoastronomy in the New World*. Edited by Anthony F. Aveni, pp. 59–107. Cambridge: Cambridge University Press.

———. 1983a. Hierarchy and space in Incaic social organization. *Ethnohistory* 30 (2): 49–75.

———. 1983b. Towards a general Andean star calendar in ancient Peru. In *Calendars in Mesoamerica and Peru: Native American computations of time*. Edited by Anthony F. Aveni and Gordon Brotherston, pp. 235–262. Proceedings of the 46th International Congress of Americanists, BAR International Series 174. Oxford: British Archaeological Reports.

———. 1986a. *La Civilisation Inca au Cuzco*. Paris: Presses Universitaires de France, College de France.

———. 1986b. Inka dynasty and irrigation: Another look at Andean concepts of history. In *Anthropological history of Andean polities*. Edited by J. V. Murra, N. Wachtel, and J. Revel, pp. 177–200. Cambridge: Cambridge University Press.

———. 1988a. A quipu calendar from Ica, Peru, with a comparison to the ceque calendar from Cuzco. In *World archaeoastronomy: Acts of the Second Oxford Conference on Archaeoastronomy*. Edited by Anthony F. Aveni, pp. 341–351. Cambridge: Cambridge University Press.

———. 1988b. The pillars of Cuzco: Which two dates of sunset did they define? In *New directions in American archaeoastronomy*. Edited by Anthony F. Aveni, pp. 143–169. Proceedings of the 46th International Congress of Americanists, BAR International Series 454. Oxford: British Archaeological Reports.

———. 1990. *Inca civilization in Cuzco*. Translated by Jean-Jacques Decoster. Austin: University of Texas Press.

Zuidema, R. Tom, and Gary Urton. 1976. La constelación de la Llama en los Andes peruanos. *Allpanchis Phuturinqa* 9: 59–119.

Index